BECOMING CLARK ROCKEFELLER

MURDER, LOVE, DECEPTION, AND THE CON MAN BEHIND IT ALL

FRANK C. GIRARDOT, JR.

WILDBLUE
PRESS

WildBluePress.com

BECOMING CLARK ROCKEFELLER published by
WILDBLUE PRESS
P.O. Box 102440
Denver, Colorado 80250

WILDBLUE PRESS is registered at the U.S. Patent and Trademark Offices.

ISBN 978-1-960332-56-1 Trade Paperback
ISBN 978-1-960332-55-4 eBook
ISBN 978-1-960332-57-8 Hardback

Cover design © 2023 WildBlue Press. All rights reserved.

Interior Formatting and Cover Design by Elijah Toten, www.totencreative.com

BECOMING CLARK ROCKEFELLER

For Mom and Dad

FOREWORD

Consider this book a time machine. Most of it takes place in the 1980s and '90s. It was a time when people still sent postcards, called each other on the house phone, read newspapers, and moved around without anyone really tracking who was doing what with who and where were they doing it.

So, without a lot of hard documentation, much of what happens here relies on memories of a long-ago time. Fortunately, most of the witnesses are reliable.

At its heart is a crime story unlike any other you might have read—or even thought—could be possible. These pages are filled with the ingredients that make up all great drama: lies, lust, and love. Even before it was officially a murder case, the circumstances were so fantastic that some of the characters found themselves dramatized in a 2010 Hallmark Channel film that contained all the kitschy tropes that were a staple of the Oprah or Phil Donahue shows of the mid-80s.

San Marino, California plays a key role here. It is a truly unique community just a few miles from downtown Los Angeles. Its homes are stately. Some of its residents are powerful titans of commerce, industry, and politics. Others are old-money-nepo-babies. There's an element of Nouveau Riche too, but it is well disguised. The community is built around a great and beautiful park that is mostly inaccessible to nonresidents. However, it is also home to the beautiful and very accessible Huntington Library and its stunningly peaceful grounds.

Great works of art can be found here as can the collected works of scholars who defined the mores and codes of

Western Civilization. It is a decidedly patrician collection, but one that is very democratic too and wonderfully accessible.

Behind its gates and walls, San Marino stands largely apart from its neighboring communities in Eastern Los Angeles County. Murder is not something that happens here often and when it does, someone will be in custody before the evening news airs.

Hallmark stayed away from nearly any mention of murder in their version of this story. Perhaps because here it is gruesome and real, and comes in the form of what one criminalist described as "trisection" possibly done with a borrowed chainsaw.

When discovered, the dead man's body, still clothed, had been cut into three neat sections, the head, torso, and legs were all packaged in plastic, and separated in the grave.

I'll let you visualize that for a second before we go on.

Although much of the entire skeleton was initially examined by officials in the L.A. County Department of Medical Examiner-Coroner in 1994, only bits of the skull remained when the suspected killer was arrested decades later.

There's a bit of whimsy and fantasy buried here too. One of the central characters was deeply into science fiction of the Star Trek variety. He even owned a model communicator in the days before flip phones were anything other than sci-fi. Another leaned toward fantasy. Hobbits, elves, centaurs, and horses were her thing. A proto furry perhaps?

History is so linear and slow that it's hard to imagine time traveling like Marty McFly in *Back to the Future*. What would it be like to suddenly warp into the second decade of the 21st century from 1985? Most of us would be utterly lost. We wouldn't understand the culture, the technology, or the state of our nation, such as it is.

But we can look back. And I think each of us can see some of ourselves in the people and places of that technologically challenged and less fractured time period. But there are moments that we don't completely understand their motivations. I struggled with that.

Some questions raised here may never be answered. Why were certain lies believed? How many people told a story about the case that made them look wiser or more attuned than they might have been. Why did law enforcement take so long to act? Why did some investigators fail to follow leads that may have changed the course of this story in a significant way?

Your guess is as good as mine. Read the book and decide for yourself. If you see me around, you can even let me know what you think, or send me an email at frank.girardot@ gmail.com I'd love to know.

When I first wrote this book, it contained a forward written by my friend, the actor Dean Norris. At that time, he was best known as DEA Agent Hank Schraeder on the AMC Show *Breaking Bad*. Hank was tracking down a drug lord that turned out to be his brother-in-law Walter White, who had a secret identity.

The irony was lost to me at the time. I appreciated Dean's words and think its last paragraph is worthy of repeating here.

"In the end, it is a story of a group of colorful, mostly sad, and desperate characters, who allow themselves to be seduced by a charming man, willing to prey on their desire to perhaps add excitement and meaning to their own lives. It is indeed a morality tale for ourselves."

AUTHOR'S NOTE

Parts of this book were previously published as *Name Dropper.*

There is some language in this book that doesn't conform to the style guidelines as determined by the Chicago Manual of Style. That's because we determined early in the editing of this edition to preserve the words of those sources as they wrote them.

Also, there is language that could be triggering to some. It should go without saying that cultural attitudes have considerably shifted over the course of time that this book attempts to cover.

Finally, there are several primary sources in this book who are quoted by name and a few others who are not—those who chose to remain anonymous did so out of fear of their identity being compromised or for their safety. Although some have since gone on the record, I've chosen to respect their original requests for anonymity.

PART I

CHAPTER 1.

BONES

SAN MARINO—All the Parada family wanted was a new pool. What they got was one huge mystery. Workers digging a 36-foot-long ditch yesterday unearthed broken human bones and found a skull nearby in a dirty plastic bag, all buried four feet in the ground, sheriff's officials said.
—*Pasadena Star-News*, **May 6, 1994**

Joe Perez's bulldozer cut through the soft dirt. Years before there had been vineyards here. The ground was easy to work.

Clay for the first three feet—decomposed granite lay lower.

The bulldozer, a Bobcat, could dig deep and he didn't have to worry about hidden boulders. Alongside his father Jose, Perez had dug nearly 6,000 pools. Both believed this job would be a piece of cake.

Then, the excavating tool hit something that shouldn't have been there. Perez needed to do an inspection before the dig could continue. In his years of putting swimming pools in the backyards of Southern California estates, Perez had encountered everything from large rotten stumps to buried cars. He'd even dug up a horse and a dog or two.

His father jumped into the hole and began to yank at what appeared to be a box. It was probably garbage, they thought. The younger man used the blade of the bulldozer to prod, and then lift the box. One of the teeth at the front end pulled up a plastic bag.

Joe's father, now standing in the hole, began to pull the bag away. He peered into the shadows and saw bones. He grabbed a piece of rebar and hoisted a skull aloft.

"I found the plastic bag," he recalled later that day. "I thought it was dog bones. The head, with some hair, was in the bag."

Upon closer examination, Perez realized the bulldozer had unearthed a human skull. There were other bones in the bag too: A piece of shoulder; bits of spine. Two similar bags lay nearby.

Someone called the cops.

San Marino, with its population of about 13,000 can boast of being one of the wealthiest communities in the United States. The Los Angeles suburb is consistently ranked among the best places to live in the country.

The schools are top notch. Its wide residential streets are lined with old oaks. Its main boulevard, Huntington Drive, features tall palms that sway in the breeze and a wide grassy median covering what used to be streetcar tracks.

Preservation of historic estates has largely kept the community looking as it did when homeowners first started settling there in the 1920s.

***

WWII hero General George Patton grew up here and is memorialized in nearby San Gabriel with both a life-sized bronze statue and unique stained-glass windows at a local church depicting the general slaying a dragon tattooed with Nazi swastikas.

As Jann Elinor, who has been a hairdresser and barber in the community for several decades, would say later, San Marino—unlike many of the municipalities of the sprawling

San Gabriel Valley in the eastern shadow of downtown Los Angeles—isn't a town where murder is commonplace.

Gang violence, fueled by the crack epidemic that swept Los Angeles County in the late 1980s and early 1990s, devastated neighboring communities like Pasadena, home of the annual Tournament of Roses Parade and New Year's football game, but left San Marino unscathed. Members of the San Marino police department, which prides itself as being a no-nonsense but professional force, know most residents by first name. Its officers are experts at keeping driving speeds down and domestic violence cases out of the news and off social media.

A body buried in a backyard? Maybe out farther east in Pico Rivera or Baldwin Park such a find would be understandable. But here, such crudeness didn't make sense.

Rookie Kelvin Wong was first to arrive on the scene. He took one look at the broken pieces of skull, ran back to his patrol car, got some crime scene tape, and waited.

As detectives, coroner's investigators, and more officers began arriving to assess the scene, neighbors gathered outside the crime scene on Lorain Road.

More than a few remembered the former owner, Didi Sohus, an alcoholic chain smoker who moved out after her son Johnny and his new bride Linda disappeared in 1985.

A San Marino detective inspected the scene. There was no mistaking these pieces of skull, jaw bones, and spine. They were human.

She called the Los Angeles County Sheriff's Department and asked them to roll homicide. When the roll-out team arrived, Lt. Ray Peavy, a self-assured and affable homicide veteran, assessed the situation.

The air was heavy with an eerie sense of déjà vu. Mary Ann Kent, who lived nearby, recalled John and Linda's disappearance for the investigators. Cops at the crime scene refreshed their memories by reviewing reports that were nearly a decade old.

The narratives told quite a tale about winter and spring in '85. And the disappearance of the young couple.

It was Kathy Jacoby, Linda's sister, who first called San Marino PD. That was in early February, soon after Linda vanished.

"I had to keep, you know, phoning them and saying, 'Okay what did you—what do you know now?'" she said.

Another report that February, written by a young San Marino officer named Tom LeVeque, described how he took an assignment no one wanted and rolled his patrol car out to Lorain Road for a chat with then-homeowner Didi Sohus.

Didi wasn't really talking. What she did say sounded crazy, like something only a delusional alcoholic would say. Here's what LeVeque gathered: In a nutshell, John and Linda were on a secret mission. Revealing any more to the police at this point might endanger their lives.

"How do you know this?" LeVeque asked.

"I have a secret source," Didi replied.

An older BMW was parked in the driveway. LeVeque made note of the license plate, returned to the station, and ran the car and John and Linda through a background check. The car was registered to Bob and Bette Brown, who lived over on Canterbury Road about a mile away. The Browns were a pillar of San Marino society, especially through their involvement in the Church of Our Savior. It was unclear why their car was parked in the driveway.

Nothing added up. Nonetheless, there was other work to do and LeVeque's report was complete within an hour. The consensus within the department was that John and Linda would eventually reappear.

Weeks passed.

Then, Linda's boss, Lydia Marano, received a postcard from Neuilly-sur Seine, a wealthy suburb of Paris.

"Hi Lydia –
Not quite New York, but not bad –

See you later –
Linda + John."

The postcard arrived at Marano's Dangerous Visions bookstore in Sherman Oaks. Within a day or two, Didi was on the phone with police again. Her secret source was no longer providing updates on John and Linda, and she was worried.

As Didi became more and more anxious, San Marino Police Officer Lili Hadsell took to popping in from time to time for updates, finally writing a supplemental report on the missing couple in July. By then, Didi was beside herself with worry. A heavy smoker and an alcoholic, Didi was half in the bag for many of their conversations on the case, Hadsell recalled.

There was something sinister in the air that summer. In South Central Los Angeles, two serial killers, known as South Side Slayer and the Grim Sleeper, seemingly killed with impunity. The sprees went largely unnoticed. The newspapers and televisions were full of reports about a man identified alternately as the Valley Intruder or the Night Stalker. A Satan-worshiping rapist and serial killer, the Night Stalker, crept through quiet neighborhoods in the San Gabriel Valley, slaying 13 before the summer was over.

San Marino was in the heart of the Night Stalker's killing zone. Cops were on alert and not so focused on missing adults. While many of her neighbors took to locking their doors in fear of the serial predator and cops prowled the streets in hopes of catching him, Didi seemed oblivious.

Instinctively, she knew being out of contact with Johnny and Linda for so long could only mean something horrible had happened.

"Something had changed," Hadsell would say. "(Didi) believed that John and Linda had gone to work with a company. The work was confidential. And, as time went on, she became confused whether or not that was true."

Reviewing the reports from 1985 brought it all back to the cops who assembled in the large backyard of a home that looked nothing like it did when Didi, John, and Linda lived there.

Back then, weeds had overtaken the backyard. The paint was peeling from the single-story ranch home. Inside the walls were stained from years of tobacco smoke. Its tiny rooms were dank, unkempt, and in dire need of repair.

Robert Parada, a general contractor, bought the home from Didi in late '85 and immediately began to remodel. The one-story became a two-story. The guest house out back, which had housed a series of unkempt borders, was transformed into an office. Parada cut the weeds, trimmed the bushes, and turned the place into a showcase on Lorain Road within 18 months.

In retrospect, the extreme home make-over happened fast. By the time he was ready to install a swimming pool in the backyard, Parada and his workers had nearly erased all traces of the 1930s ranch house that once occupied the lot at 1920 Lorain Road.

Now, as cops examined the home where John, Linda, and Didi once lived, they began a task more substantial than babysitting a delusional alcoholic or writing reports on a couple of adults who decided to take off and not call home.

Under Peavy's command, deputies expanded the crime scene. They called the Los Angeles County Department of Coroner and asked for a team of forensic anthropologists. There was the remote possibility that the remains were those of a Gabrielino Indian or had somehow been mishandled by the historic Church of Our Savior cemetery, where Gen. Patton is honored, less than a block away.

Veteran detectives knew those scenarios were implausible—but if they put the story out, it would be a ruse to lure any suspect into complacency. Detectives and cops on the scene knew full well that a large fiberglass container, two plastic bags, and a telephone cord in the makeshift crypt, wouldn't be the tools of the Tongva Indians or a cemetery. These were the implements of a killer who hoped to conceal his crime. Whatever happened here had been hidden for several years.

"It's definitely a whodunnit," Peavy announced to the reporters who had now gathered on the street, after being tipped to the discovery by the City News wire service.

Two months passed before police named a person of interest. By then—and in what had become a pattern with news about the case—the nation's attention was riveted on another Los Angeles mystery involving privileged residents: the double murder of Nicole Brown Simpson and Ronald Goldman.

In that case, the suspected murderer was a USC legend. A Heisman trophy winner and member of the NFL Hall of Fame, O.J. Simpson as a murder suspect sold more newspapers and cable TV advertising than anything involving a decade-old missing persons case.

Besides, detectives thought they knew who they were looking for and figured they'd quickly wrap up. There were just a couple of loose ends.

CHAPTER 2.

TRISECTED

"Someone once told me that time was a predator that stalked us all our lives. I rather believe that time is a companion who goes with us on the journey and reminds us to cherish every moment, because it will never come again. What we leave behind is not as important as how we've lived."
—Enterprise Captain Jean-Luc Picard,
Star Trek Generations, released 1994

Clouds hung low in the chilly spring air of May 5, 1994. A chance of showers coupled with high winds meant investigators had to work the crime scene at 1920 Lorain Road fast. Not only did they need to figure out how a body got sliced into three pieces and buried three feet below ground. They needed to know who it was and—just as importantly—whodunnit.

Forensic anthropologist Judith Daye, a consultant for the Los Angeles Department of Coroner, arrived on scene and began to assess the situation.

Typically it is the job of a forensic anthropologist to collect and analyze human remains. A good anthropologist can determine a lot from bones. An investigator can figure out the age of the deceased individual, how tall the person might have been, as well as the race and gender of the body.

An average forensic anthropologist can get most of the facts right. It takes tools, background, and training.

Some would later argue that Daye—who came off as somewhat disorganized—had none of the above, but she was there for the coroner, and it was her job to get the bones and figure out the characteristics of the dead person whose body appeared to have been sliced into three fairly even pieces. The head, torso, and waist-to-feet had been neatly separated by the killer.

"When I got there, I saw that it was an excavation by Bobcat," Daye said. "I wouldn't have called it undisturbed, but everything I was able to see was pretty much untouched."

Daye said she was able to fix on three separate locations in the backyard. First was the skull. A little further away was an item she described as a "Fiberglass object with some things sticking out of it." To the right of the fiberglass box, a third object was apparent.

She focused on the skull. It was definitely crushed. In burial, the head had been placed inside two plastic bags—double-bagged. The bags were tied with a telephone cord, Daye noted. One bag still bore unmistakable markings from the bookstore of the University of Wisconsin at Milwaukee. The other plastic bag had deteriorated.

As for the skull? Now it was just pieces. Some hair, the mandible (or lower jawbone); the left maxilla (or upper jawbone); fragments of vertebrae (neck bones); and a piece of shoulder blade, Daye said.

At the fiberglass box, a pair of jeans with leg bone. Disconnected from the pant leg and imbedded in the dirt was a sock with "little lumpy bits that felt like a foot bone," Daye said. The pieces had apparently separated when Joe Perez's Bobcat moved the makeshift fiberglass coffin.

Daye soon set to work excavating the sock and removed the bones piece by piece. Stuffed into the top of the container was what remained of a "headless body." The corpse wore a flannel shirt, belt, and jeans. The entire body had been wrapped in plastic. A pelvis stuck out of the top of the pair of jeans.

This had been a gruesome killing. But the burial had been methodical. Both hands had been covered with plastic bags. Inside the shirt were the bones one would expect to find in a human burial including cervical bones, pieces of the lower spine, ribs, and arm bones.

"Everything but the head was in the shirt," Daye said. "The hands were in plastic bags." Someone had taken "great effort to wrap" the extremities. "There didn't seem to be any exceptions."

Following the removal of the remains, the skeleton was taken to the Coroner's laboratory for examination. A forensic examination of skeletal remains requires some reconstruction. So, the bones were laid out on an examination table in their correct anatomical position. Despite the hours of excavation, a few bones appeared to be missing.

Daye performed an examination and wrote up a report. Daye described the process as more art than science. She thought the body was that of an Asian man.

It was an odd finding and Daye's assessment created a rift between her and Judy Suchey, a Cal State Fullerton forensic anthropologist renowned for her work identifying human remains.

If you dug up bones somewhere in Southern California in the 1970s, 1980s, or 1990s, there was a damn good chance that Suchey would be nearby to make an identification. Suchey, who came to California in the late 1960s to study bones, had made a career for herself doing just that. Suchey's expertise helped detectives close cases and families close old wounds.

Among Suchey's triumphs was her identification of the remains of Donald (Shorty) Shea. Years after members of the Manson family committed the Tate-LaBianca killings, Suchey examined a decapitated body buried on the Manson family's Chatsworth property and determined it was in fact Shea.

Then there was her pioneering work in the Hillside Strangler case. Suchey's method of using dental records helped detectives identify the bodies of nine women sexually tortured and killed by Angelo Buono and his cousin, Kenneth Bianchi, in 1977 and 1978.

Suchey's work with dental records allowed scientists to ID some of the 82 victims of an airline crash involving a flight from Mexico City to Los Angeles—it was a horrible mid-air collision over Cerritos in suburban Los Angeles between a passenger jet and a private plane. Bodies and debris rained down on the community and for weeks afterward investigators like Suchey were tasked with picking up the pieces and identifying remains.

Detectives once benefited from her work in the case of Long Beach serial killer, Randy Steven Kraft, who was sentenced to death for the mutilation murders of 16 men in Orange County in the 1980s. Suchey also helped put down the case of the Sunset Strip Killer, a man identified as Douglas Daniel Clark. Authorities said Clark was behind the 1980 sex slayings of six women in Hollywood.

Suchey knew from experience that the San Marino dig supervised by Daye could have gone sideways. She thought back to July 1989, when workers doing construction at Union Station in Los Angeles uncovered human remains buried at the site and removed them before calling the cops or the coroner. They didn't want an old body or two to slow down construction.

That scene had been a disaster. In their haste to get rid of the bones at Union Station, all kinds of havoc were wreaked on the crime scene.

"Further destruction of the remains occurred by the improper action of the AMTRAK police," Suchey noted in a memo to Los Angeles County officials.

"Amtrak police Sergeants Breeden and Sanchez and Officer Johnson … immediately began their own investigation. Sgt. Sanchez identified the bones as being those of an ape and believed they were not important. He began photographing the remains from various angles as well as the trench, during which, he carelessly stepped into the middle of the bones, crushing one of the large cranium fragments. Sgt. Sanchez was asked to leave the site after he almost stepped on the bones on two more occasions while taking photos."

When the coroner finally was called and Suchey rolled out to the scene, she immediately determined that a homicide had not occurred, and the bones were "of antiquity."

Ultimately the problem for investigators at the Union Station scene came down to identification. Were the bones Native American or Chinese. The distinction would be important. It required precise measurements of facial bones—crushed by Sanchez—determination of the height and assessment of the remaining teeth.

Why Chinese? Union Station sits in the heart of what was once Los Angeles' Chinatown. At the turn of the 19th and 20th centuries, the original residents were moved out and north of the location when the railroad came in and decided the land was theirs.

Several Chinese artifacts were found near the body suggesting it was possibly Asian, but an examination of the teeth didn't show typical wear patterns associated with "the habitual use of opium pipes" that might have characterized a Chinese skeleton. Ultimately, the identification was made using radiocarbon dating techniques, which are typically outlawed in California when it comes to identifying Native American remains.

Suchey was a legend in forensic circles. Her presence and expertise were instrumental in developing crucial facts about crime scenes that puzzled investigators and helped answer questions that were harder than a Sunday crossword.

For example, she once helped unravel a Griffith Park homicide that remained unsolved for years. Her work helped determine that the intertwined bodies of an embracing couple, with guns pointed at their backs, did not represent a double homicide, which police originally had thought, but rather the man shooting the woman and vice versa, in virtually the same split-second.

Out in the desert town of Needles, about 300 miles east of L.A., Suchey helped excavate a handful of bones and identify the bodies of a grandfather, his son, and grandson years after their small plane had disappeared.

Steve Dowell, a coroner's tool mark expert who would play a role in the Sohus case, simply called Suchey's work "impressive."

"She's made some remarkable discoveries over the years," Dowell told the *Los Angeles Times*. "I've seen her out in the bush, for instance, literally up to her neck in poison oak, looking for things that look like twigs but aren't twigs—they're bones."

Suchey's hard work at her craft resulted in the Suchey-Brooks standard, a method for determining the age and race of male human remains through a thorough examination of the pelvis. The method—really a simplification of earlier identification systems—was born from an extensive study of bones obtained through the Los Angeles County Department of Coroner, according to a University of Tennessee-Chattanooga article published in 2001.

Although Daye and other officials struggled with the identification of the San Marino remains, Suchey described her own motivations as simple:

"It's such a great feeling, feeling useful and needed, especially if my work helps get to the bottom of an unsolved homicide," she said. "Like most people, if I solve a problem or really help someone, it makes me feel good, as though, 'Hey, here's something I do that really matters.'"

There was no way Suchey was going to stand by and let Daye screw up the ID, especially since it was clear that the remains were probably those of someone who had lived in that house in 1985.

The dead man whose head was wrapped up in a plastic book bag? This was no Asian man, and it wasn't a dead Native American either, Suchey concluded.

Neither the detectives nor the coroner went public with their discord. And it wouldn't have mattered. Just five weeks after the discovery of bones in the backyard of a San Marino mansion, the attention of the media turned to another case involving murder, millionaires, and mystery. It was the Sunday, June 12, 1994 knife slayings of Nicole Brown Simpson and her friend, Ronald Goldman.

What made the case immense and uncontrollable from a media perspective was the suspect—Orenthal James Simpson. A revered and iconic figure in Los Angeles, Simpson, a USC Heisman Trophy winner, was the NFL's first 2,000-yard running back, and an actor known for self-deprecating roles in commercials and films including the popular *Naked Gun* series.

O.J. Simpson sold newspapers, filled a void on all-news cable television stations, and became topic No.1 on talk radio around the United States. Rightfully so. The week following the discovery of Ron and Nicole's bodies outside her Bundy Avenue condominium was one of the most bizarre ever in the annals of LA crime.

First of all, there was the sheer horror of the attack. Unlike some dried bones of a nerdy computer geek who went missing nearly a decade ago, the first reporters at the scene of Nicole's condo could clearly see the aftermath of the carnage. Blood still stained the walkway outside, and it was clear to anyone who looked at the crime scene that Monday morning that something truly evil had gone down.

As that day wore on, the media attention only grew. At first, a few reporters gathered outside O.J.'s place on North Rockingham, but by day's end, the beat-up cars of print reporters competed for space with TV trucks, radio rigs, and mobile studios complete with satellite linkups. By Wednesday of that week, helicopters hoping for a glimpse of O.J. hovered overhead, cable and local TV crews set up dozens of cameras on a neighbor's lawn across the street, still photos from *People*, *Time*, and the *National Enquirer* jostled one another for the best shot, while reporters began interviewing one another. Just outside the gate KFI's John Kobylt and Ken Chiampou took to talking to anyone and everyone—including a guy in a van who claimed the CIA murdered John Lennon.

The only apt description for such a scene was circus. To make matters worse, detectives hadn't acted. They didn't arrest O.J. and he didn't turn himself in. The scene continued through Thursday. By Friday morning, LAPD officials promised reporters they would have an announcement to make at their Parker Center headquarters.

Media from around the globe gathered waiting for the news. Sometime around noon, LAPD commander David Gascon took to the Parker Center podium and made an announcement I will never forget. Not because of Gascon's words, but because reporters in the room gasped when Gascon announced that O.J. was supposed to turn himself in and hadn't.

At that moment, Orenthal James Simpson became a hunted fugitive. Even though it occurred before any newspaper in Los Angeles had a website, reporters raced to a bank of phones or used the brick-sized Motorola cell phones to call an editor. The press conference was carried on live television so it wasn't like editors in newsrooms across the country didn't know what was going on, it was just that reporters like me needed guidance.

"What now?"

"Well you can either go find O.J. or sit on your ass at Parker Center and wait for the cops to give you an update."

The cops and D.A. Gil Garcetti suspected O.J. was hiding out with sympathetic black gang members somewhere in South Central. In reality, he and his best buddy, Al Cowlings, were driving around Orange County in the now infamous white Bronco. A couple on the 405 spotted the pair and the most bizarre chase in the then-young history of L.A. chases on live TV had begun.

It wasn't just O.J. that kept the focus off John and Linda Sohus.

That summer, San Marino's neighboring town of Pasadena hosted the World Cup, a quadrennial tournament featuring the world's top soccer teams. Hotels were full and the amount of space in newspapers or on television was limited. It meant hosting parties in San Marino and Pasadena for visiting foreign dignitaries. It meant John and Linda Sohus quickly faded from memory.

The last time something this huge came to Los Angeles was the 1984 Olympic Games.

CHAPTER 3.

1984

Rollin' down the Imperial Highway
With a big nasty redhead at my side
Santa Ana winds blowin' hot from the north
And we was born to ride
—Randy Newman, *I Love L.A.*

Los Angeles woke up one morning in 1984 decked out in swatches of pastels. Purples, pinks, and faded greens took over, a sky blue fluttered in the wind here and there.

Olympic fever was in the air. Civic pride hit an incredible apex. Close to downtown there was no escaping the pastel fever (or fervor) except maybe on the normally concrete grey freeways, which were suddenly festooned with public art—murals celebrating all that was good about L.A., sports, and citizenship.

Graffiti was suddenly nonexistent. Crime wasn't even talked about.

Contrasting with the pastel flavor and wild public art of the new era, on the grittier east side and in the suburban San Fernando Valley, liquor stores, contractors selling room additions and aluminum siding, mom and pop dairies, and car dealers all got in on the act. Most went bold—red, white, and blue. The Stars and Stripes hung proudly among the pastels.

L.A.—its City Council and Mayor Tom Bradley worked tirelessly for more than a decade to bring the Olympic Games to Los Angeles. They, and thousands of civic boosters from throughout the county, saw the two-week event as a way to lift L.A. and Southern California out of the doldrums of a stifling recession, restore a sense of civic pride, and maybe revitalize long-ignored South Los Angeles neighborhoods lining the Harbor Freeway from south of downtown all the way south to Wilmington and the ports.

Los Angeles hosted the games once before; that was in 1932. Back then, L.A. was so excited to have an international event, the city fathers renamed 10th Street as Olympic Boulevard in honor of the Games of the X Olympiad. By 1978, the stadium built for those games was still in good shape and Bradley promised doubters and fiscal conservatives on the City Council that L.A. would have to spend very little of its own capital on infrastructure to get the Olympics back.

For many of the years between 1932 and 1984, Olympic Stadium, later renamed the Los Angeles Memorial Coliseum, was put to good use, hosting a variety of sporting events. USC has played all its home football games there since the early 1920s. UCLA's Bruins football team called the stadium home from 1928 until 1981. The Los Angeles Rams played there from 1946 until 1980. Upon their move to L.A., the Dodgers turned the Coliseum into a baseball stadium from 1958 to 1962.

It was never a great venue. Parking sucked. In 1984, the seats were mostly wooden benches. The tunnels were narrow and usually crowded. And parking? Forget it. Even in the 80s it cost $15 or $20 to park in the lot on MLK Boulevard. If you didn't want to spring for that, you took your chances on a dude's front lawn up on Exposition and when that didn't work you parked your tin can on the other side of the Harbor Freeway and prayed it was still there when the game was over—if you made it that far without being mugged.

Despite all that baggage—or maybe because of it—the Coliseum landed the Oakland/Los Angeles Raiders. Their stint in the Coliseum is remembered for riots in the stands, vicious stabbings, near fatal—and fatal—beatings, drunken rampages, heightened police presence, and generally out-of-control freaks ruining more than one family outing.

But it should be noted that Los Angeles' last professional football championship before the Rams won the Super Bowl in 2021 was earned by the Raiders in a 38-9 beat-down of the heavily favored Washington Redskins on Jan. 22, 1984, at Tampa Stadium.

I cashed a ticket on that one at Harrah's in Reno. $100 for $110. Not bad for someone betting completely from the heart and willing to take a five-point dog in the Super Bowl during an era when blowouts were common and teams like the Raiders were usually on the wrong end of the final score. It would take another 35 years before I cashed a ticket in Reno, but it was nowhere near as exciting.

I bet the Raiders that year because I sensed they were special in the way L.A. was special that year. I was one of 90,000 Angelenos at the Coliseum who, two weeks earlier, saw the Raiders dismantle the Pittsburgh Steelers by the nearly identical score of 38-10. There was undeniable electricity in the air and a sense of civic pride that's been hard to come by since.

We sat in the peristyle end of the Coliseum—that's the end with the columns that you see on TV all the time. The cauldron for the Olympic flame had yet to be lit, but even then, you could feel a sense of something different, something larger than life would be taking place right there in that crappy old stadium in the shittiest part of Los Angeles that for a moment didn't feel that shitty.

L.A. was anything but hung-over from the Raiders' dominance of the National Football League. No. On the contrary, the town was positively giddy; the party had just begun.

Just weeks before the Games exploded into a national celebration of patriotism and spectacle, Jenelle Hemming of San Marino joined 16,000 people jammed together in a vacant lot on 4th Street near the Harbor Freeway to listen to speeches and hang out with celebrities in the heat of a mid-July afternoon.

"It's like the beginning of it," she told a reporter.

"What a sight you are," Los Angeles Mayor Tom Bradley told the crowd sweating through a 90-degree, smog-alert L.A. summer afternoon. "We're here to tell the world that downtown L.A. is an exciting place."

The hype built to a crescendo that coincided with the opening ceremony in July, and kind of pushed aside all that was happening just blocks away from center stage.

In 1984, downtown L.A. was a poster child of urban blight in Southern California. The crack epidemic was already sweeping through the city from Olympic Boulevard south to Century Boulevard and Imperial Highway.

Exciting place? Sure, downtown was great if you didn't mind the occasional stray bullet, fret about the crazy-eyed zombies clutching a glass pipe and stumbling from dime piece to dime piece or worry about whether your car window would be smashed, the radio ripped out of the dashboard and swiped along with any spare change you had saved for parking.

There weren't any Olympians chasing dreams in that part of L.A.

Dragons maybe. But not dreams.

But there was change in the air. And some took that as a sign of hope.

Ronald Wilson Reagan was in office and America was "back." This was not the long-haired, sniveling, traumatized post-Vietnam America. We're talking the America of land of the free, home of the brave; "Go ahead make my day;" America of *Rambo* and "Dirty Harry Callahan."

What was it about President Ronald Reagan? Well for one thing, he wasn't backing down in the Cold War. He was the symbol of what many believed was a welcome resurgence, a rebound. It was Ronnie who welcomed the world to Los Angeles at the Games' opening ceremony on July 28.

Reagan and the American team—loaded with superstars like Carl Lewis, Edwin Moses, Mary Lou Retton, and a young Michael Jordan—were greeted with flag waving, chants of "U-S-A," "U-S-A" amid a swell of patriotic pride.

Gasoline was no longer scarce, prices were steady. Interest rates were beginning to fall. Americans were returning to work. It was a fist-pumping, mullet-wearing, truck-driving, stump-pulling, corn-husking U.S.A. team that was going to take the field, the track, and swimming pools of Los Angeles. It was time to cut loose and kick some serious Third World ass on the field of play.

In fact, in 1984, Los Angeles—L-freakin-A —was at the heart of a cultural revolution taking the country back from the malaise of the Carter years and the acid fueled 1960s with the intent of turning back the clock on American values, mores, and institutions to the simpler 1950s of Marty McFly in *Back to the Future.*

That 1985 classic was preceded by a whole host of iconic movies released in 1984. It's a range of films that remained well-known almost 30 years later. Among them: *Terminator, Ghostbusters, Gremlins, Red Dawn, The Killing Fields, Karate Kid, This is Spinal Tap, Ghostbusters, Police Academy, Sixteen Candles, Once Upon a Time in America, Die Unendliche Geschichte* (AKA *"The Never Ending Story"*), *Beverly Hills Cop, Dune,* and *2010.*

Popular music in 1984 experienced a renaissance as well. Bruce Springsteen released *Born in the USA,* and Prince put out *Purple Rain.* The Smiths recorded their debut—and self-titled album—featuring Morrissey. Sade debuted *Smooth Operator,* Madonna entered a new phase of her career with the release of *Like a Virgin.* U2 put out *Unforgettable Fire* and Don Henley showed he could make it without the Eagles by recording *Boys of Summer.*

On the three major TV networks one could choose from a variety of series including: *The Cosby Show, Dynasty, Dallas, Knot's Landing, Falcon's Crest, Cheers, The A-Team, Murder She Wrote, Magnum, P.I.,* or *Simon and Simon.*

At the height of it, townsfolk in San Marino feted the Honorable Domenico "Nick" Bruschi, president of the Olympic Committee for the Republic of San Marino. Joyce and Howard Morrow hosted the party and had 150 guests who stood in a receiving line in hopes of getting a picture with Bruschi.

"Nick was here a year ago to attend a meeting of the International Olympic Committee," said Mo Springer. "I met him at a party given by the sheik of Kuwait and thought it would be fun to get him together with some San Marino people here."

Among the guests, according to a contemporary newspaper article, was a young man identified as Christopher Chichester, "a former member of the British Peerage and grandson of the legendary sailor Sir Francis Chichester, who is now an American citizen and a resident of the Californian San Marino."

"I'm the one who put Howard Morrow together with the fundraisers for the Republic's Olympic team," Chichester told the reporter.

He went on to explain that his "mother owns a construction business in the other San Marino."

Christopher Chichester, the XIII baronet, was among several royals spending that summer in San Marino or Pasadena.

Prince Philip, the Duke of Edinburgh—visited Pasadena where he took part in a tea sponsored by the local chapter of the English Speaking Union, which sponsors a Shakespeare program at San Marino's Huntington Library.

Chris spent plenty of time at the Huntington and Pasadena's Gamble House. It was there he attended a tea with the prince, who was upset that only actual tea was on the menu.

"That's all that's offered," the prince muttered to a reporter. "I've been surviving on iced tea all afternoon."

Making the occasion even more uncomfortable was the presence of too many posers who had crashed the tea party. It made it hard for the prince and other royals to catch a breath.

"His presence was met with such a mad rush of attention that he had a difficult time even moving forward much of the time," reads one account of the mad tea party.

The old boys didn't care for the party crashers. The Duke didn't care for any of the unwashed Americans. He wore his disdain like a pair of soiled white gloves happily discarded when the riffraff and hoi polloi were removed from his presence.

"It's terribly rude to stare at him like a fish in a tank," remarked one party attendee who noted that at "similar garden parties in England the guests stay in one place and royal family members stroll about talking to whomever they choose."

A lot was happening in and around L.A. that summer. For some, the spectacle took backstage. By the time the Olympics blew out of town on Aug. 12, John and Linda Sohus and other fans of science fiction were gearing up for an event they had been anticipating just as eagerly as sports fans awaited the Olympics: Worldcon 42 in Anaheim.

The late August event would be the science fiction convention to end all science fiction conventions, with a bonus for Linda—she would get to showcase her paintings in the main exhibit hall. John hoped he could expand his knowledge about computers and their role in filmmaking.

John and Linda were huge sci-fi nerds. Before collecting became fashionable, John had a good number of souvenirs from Star Trek, like a life-sized communicator and even a costume. Linda, who liked fantasy as much as anything, worked in the sci-fi business.

She was an employee at the Dangerous Visions bookstore in Sherman Oaks. The store was famous among fans for its devotion to the genre that included readings, book clubs, and camaraderie among those who shared their love of all things from Tolkien to Asimov.

Together John and Linda were an unforgettable couple. She was a big redhead who was boisterous and full of life. He was shy and guarded. More into computers than people. But they were happy and obviously in love.

Science fiction fandom stretches back to the late 1920s and early 1930s, when clubs like the Los Angeles Science Fantasy Society were formed. Early members often discussed Communism, whether to adopt Esperanto as a language and put together conventions—the first being held at the New York World's Fair in 1939.

For a country emerging from the throes of the Great Depression, the 1939 World's Fair celebrated an imaginary future, creating a vision of what folks believed the world would be like in 1960. The fair showed off new technologies including television, milking machines, and giant robots like Elektro, that both talked and smoked cigarettes. The centerpiece was a General Motors exhibit called "Futurama." It came with its own science fiction movie of sorts.

"The world of tomorrow is a world of beauty," the *Futurama* film narrator intones on screen. "A greater world, a better world. A world which always will grow forward."

The future, as General Motors saw it anyway, promised productive and disease-free farms, cheap and abundant electricity, clean water, and highways where safety was the norm at 100 miles per hour.

"This is where we are going to spend the rest of our lives in a future that can be whatever we propose to make it."

As we know now it was just that—science fiction—at its best.

In 1954, writer Stanley Moskowitz wrote a detailed history of the origins of sci-fi fandom titled *The Immortal Storm*. The book, which covers a period from about 1929 to 1939 was republished in the mid-1980s. It's considered a legendary chronicle of fandom if only because its drama is overblown to the point that one contemporary critic said it made WWII seem like an afterthought.

The outgrowth of that first science fiction fans convention in 1939—the 42nd World Con—was held at the Anaheim Convention Center between Aug. 30 and Sept. 3, 1984. Linda and John were geared up.

The convention featured book dealers, a masquerade ball, film exhibits, Japanese animation videos, a blood drive, and several panels including "Tourist Spots for the Time Traveler," "Fantasy Dinosaurs in the Movies," "What If?", "Does History Repeat Itself?", and "Making science fiction Movies—Special Effects."

The "What If?" panel, for example, posed questions like "What if political parties were based on scientific theories instead of socio-economic ones?" or "What if humans had a mating season?" In a humorous twist, The "Does History Repeat Itself?" panel was a nearly exact duplicate of the "Tourist Spots for the Time Traveler." Showing, I guess, that even sci-fi fans have a sense of humor.

"L.A.con II was a landmark," blogger Greg Thokar wrote on the fancylopedia website. "It was, far and away, the largest Worldcon ever. The *Star Wars* trilogy was shown together (at midnight!) for the first time ever. The 300-table 'Hucksters' Room' was a vast expanse of books, fanzines, movie memorabilia, and related material. The Art Show took several passes to view all of the 400-plus panels and tables containing a remarkably high overall quality of art. The Showcase area was especially memorable, where each artist represented chose their best piece of the year to display. (Even the Art Show sales set a record of almost $100,000.)"

As for the exhibits? Sort of what one would expect at a gathering of fans in the mid-80s. Among them, were large still photos and a slide show from the soon-to-be released movie *Dune*, models of two ships, and a hologram sticker from *2010*, also in pre-release, stills and press release materials abut *Ladyhawke* due out in 1985, props from George Lucas' *Star Wars* and *Indiana Jones* films, the flying saucer from the movie *The Day the Earth Stood Still*, the robot from *Lost in Space*, and a car from the 1960s television show, *Man from U.N.C.L.E.*

On the floor, Frank Herbert, author of the *Dune* series signed books. Folks dressed as centaurs, Klingon warriors, mermaids, robots, Elvira, werewolves, Egyptian princesses, girls in skimpy bikinis, creatures from Mars, and members of the *Ghostbusters* team roamed the Convention Center and the lobby of the Anaheim Hilton.

Outside the hall was the art sale. Evelyn C. Leeper, who also wrote up a complete report on the show, later reprinted on the "Fan's History Project's" website, "The art show at LaCon II continues the trend toward a larger standard deviation in art shows that I've noticed lately. The good stuff is very good (and very expensive), and the amateur stuff is generally pretty bad."

"There were some exceptions to this trend, but not many. I'm really sick of unicorns, media art (how many pictures of Spock can one look at?), and cutesy-funny artwork," Leeper concluded.

Among those who attended was a Northern California man who, despite Leeper's criticism of the proliferation of unicorns, minotaurs, and centaurs, found himself taken with Linda's Sohus' art and artistry.

"Worldcon was like the biggest thing as far as science fiction fantasy," the man would later recall. "There were actual people from the industry there. People who went still pretty much talk about it to this day. People came from around the world to go to this one. I still have the program guide from it. The theme was 1984 and basically it was right across the street from Disneyland so there was this whole theme of Disneyland as a police state."

The theme involved a creature known as Reynolds Rat.

"Certainly, the most unique event of L.A.con II was the discount day they arranged for fans at Disneyland the Wednesday before the convention," Thokar wrote. "The con had incorporated its mascot's picture into many of its publications, and convention souvenirs, including baseball caps and T-shirts. It must have startled many at Disneyland as thousands of fans descended on the unsuspecting park wearing, not Mickey Mouse, but Reynolds Rat."

Sci-fi is full of terminology that is unique to the genre. For example, Thokar used "fen" instead of fans as a grammar convention he compared to using "men" as the plural for "man" (instead of "mans").

When it was over a week later, Linda sold some paintings. Most importantly, Linda and John believed their lives were about to change for the better.

The money helped the young couple buy a new Nissan pickup truck to haul Linda's artwork. And they were about to get married and move in with John's mother in San Marino. It would be enough room for Linda to set up a painting studio. Besides, even though John's mom, Didi, rented out a guest house on the property to a man named Christopher Chichester, she could still use a little extra income. And maybe if they were lucky enough, he'd move out and they could take over the guest house.

CHAPTER 4.

GIPSY MOTH

On the night when the lazy wind is a-wailing
Around the Cutty Sark
Yeah the single-handed sailor goes sailing
Sailing away in the dark.
—Dire Straits, *Single-Handed Sailor*

If Sir Francis Chichester didn't exist, then perhaps the name Christopher Chichester wouldn't have had as much resonance among some privileged and wealthy residents of San Marino.

First of all, the young man bore some physical resemblance to Sir Francis. Secondly, his affected—albeit slight—British accent gave the ruse some plausibility.

Then there was his business card which read, "Christopher Chichester, XIII bt. San Marino, California; San Rafael, California." Above the type, the calling card carried the Chichester coat of arms and the Latin phrase "Firm en Foi"—Firm in Faith. Of course, there was also his bearing and mannerisms.

Some would describe them as nearly royal; Chris could be polite, subservient, dismissive, and rude all at once. Slight with longish blond hair, he fancied himself an auteur. And, with his wardrobe always one cut above, he gave off the vibe of being different, special, and weird all at once.

The title of baronet is an interesting one as it is among those uniquely British creations designed to place one in one's proper class. In the peerage, baronets rank below earls, viscounts, and barons, but above knights. According to rules of etiquette, a baronet should be addressed as "Sir", his wife as "Lady."

There were those in San Marino society who called the young foreigner "odd", "strange," "weird," "suspicious," or "queer". No one ever called Chris "sir."

"When someone tried, he would wave them off and say, 'please call me Chris," recalled one longtime resident who had her share of dealings with the young man.

William Stewart, a San Marino attorney who would later become a Los Angeles Superior Court judge, recalled striking up a conversation with young Christopher after the two met at a church service. As Stewart tells it, Christopher bragged about his impressive resume.

"He said he was an instructor at the USC Film School," Stewart said. "When I first heard his name, I asked if he was related to Sir Francis Chichester, who had some notoriety for accomplishing the first solo circumnavigation of the globe aboard the Gipsy Moth IV.

"He said that was another branch of the family— remotely related. It wasn't a real close relationship."

Stewart, a pilot, had to know the amazing tale of Sir Francis Chichester. Born in 1901, Sir Francis' father, Charles Chichester, an Anglican reverend, was the seventh son of the VIII Baronet of Chichester, Sir Arthur Chichester.

Sir Francis wasn't born with a title. He had to earn it.

At the age of 66, Sir Francis sailed around the world from west to east following the "clipper route." The route follows the preferred path of clipper ships during their heyday in the 18th and 19th centuries. Sir Francis made just one stop and completed the journey alone aboard the Gipsy Moth in only nine months—a record that stood for almost 30 years.

Sir Francis once told the *New York Times* that, "the only way to live life to the full is to do something that depends on both the brain and on physical sense and action."

For sailors, the key to making a quick journey around the world depends on reaching southern latitudes between

40 degrees and 49 degrees south of the equator. There, for all sorts of scientific reasons, wind speeds are some of the fastest on earth. Thus, it has been named "Roaring Forties."

Sir Francis took full advantage of the "Roaring Forties" to seal his record jaunt in the Gipsy Moth. It earned him a knighthood from Queen Elizabeth II and international notoriety.

Sailing wasn't the only adventure tackled by Sir Francis. As a younger man, he was an aviator and the second man to fly from London to Sydney, Australia. He was the first to take a plane across the Tasman Sea, which separates Australia and New Zealand. Not one to shy away from adventure, Chichester survived crash landings in Libya, and later in Japan, on a mission to fly around the world.

The crash in Japan was serious. It nearly took Chichester's life. The Victorian spirit in his nature turned the near disaster into an adventure. In his memoir, *Ride on the Wind*, published in 1979, seven years after his death, Sir Francis recalled hoping to write a book about his travels to pay for a boat that would take him back to England. It wasn't that he was afraid of flying. He just knew there would be no way to repair his De Havilland Gipsy Moth airplane—or for that matter get another one in Japan.

"I feel my nerve is as it never was before, cold and hard it feels like, and able to take me through any flying difficulty," he wrote at the time.

During WWII, Sir Francis took to teaching British pilots navigation. His method was based on the techniques he learned while flying. When the war ended, Sir Francis bought several thousand surplus maps, pasted them to cardboard, cut them up, and sold them as jigsaw puzzles. Eventually his company became one of the world's leading map makers.

It was only after his solo jaunt around the world in Gipsy Moth IV that Sir Francis, the single-handed sailor, became a knight. In a sweeping gesture, ripe with symbolism, Queen

Elizabeth II knighted Sir Francis with the same sword used to knight Sir Francis Drake, the first Brit to sail around the world with his crew aboard the Golden Hind.

Sir Francis Chichester died in 1972, but his name continued to ring a bell in Southern California a decade later when Chris, the distant relative, arrived on the scene.

Rev. Harold Knowles of St. James Episcopal Church in South Pasadena first laid eyes on Christopher Chichester in September 1981. He asked about the Chichester connection and got little more than a blank stare from the earnest young man.

A modest neighbor of Pasadena and San Marino, South Pasadena prides itself on its small-town atmosphere. In fact, the town is often likened to fictional Mayberry from the Andy Griffith show. The city is home to artists and writers and vigorously fought all of Los Angeles County for decades to keep a freeway—that most Southern California of landmarks—out.

Huntington Drive, one of South Pasadena's' two main drags, runs from San Marino through South Pasadena into Los Angeles, where it becomes Mission Road in Los Angeles and terminates just a few miles south of the Los Angeles County Coroner's office and that TV landmark General Hospital—better known as the Los Angeles County-USC Regional Medical Center.

"The first time I met the guy he told me he wanted to join St. Johns," Knowles recalled. "It was the summer of 1981 and I had just returned from a trip abroad."

What immediately struck Knowles was Chris' apparent lie about his connection to the Episcopal Church. He couldn't name the parish where he was confirmed. As a matter of ritual most Episcopalians are confirmed in their teens. Here was a boy barely out of his teens who couldn't remember where the ritual took place.

"He answered, 'St. James or St. Johns.' That's not usual. But he pretended as if suddenly he couldn't remember even what town," Knowles said.

When pressed, Chris blamed his memory lapse on parents who moved quite a bit.

"What do you do? I took his word on faith. There was no reason to suspect nefarious reasons. But I suspected something amiss. I knew he was not truthful."

As he settled in Southern California on the South Pasadena/San Marino border, Chris took an apartment on Huntington Drive at Maple.

"A lovely older gentleman, Buford Lewis, whom we called 'Mr. St. James' took him in," Knowles said.

"Mr. St. James" introduced Chris to people in the parish. Soon the two were ushering services side-by-side. Chris, who described himself as an aspiring film student at USC, was able to play on people's sympathies, and they looked out for him in close-knit South Pasadena.

"Chichester said his family back in Connecticut was well-to-do. They didn't approve of his being in film school," Knowles said. "He always had an excuse for being hard-up. Sometimes he would claim they sent the money late. Sometimes he would say they didn't send any money at all."

Lewis rented the apartment to Chichester at below market and was soon shocked to find Chris cavorting with a group of young women when he came by to collect the rent, Knowles said.

Burford came to Knowles and expressed his outrage that a young man like Chris could show an interest in groups of young ladies.

"He said, 'Father, I'm disillusioned by this young man.' Chris had illegally sublet the place for quite a profit. He signed a contract promising not to, but he couldn't keep his word."

Soon Chris was living with another family in Pasadena. The family—an elderly psychiatrist and his younger wife—

had three or four small children at the time. They also attended St. James.

Chris befriended the young wife and the children. In turn, she paid him to be a nanny.

"He and she appeared almost as if they were a couple," the reverend recalled. "We'd see them every Sunday coming across the parking lot with those small children."

Chris' arrangement with the Pasadena couple and their children didn't last much longer than his turn in Lewis' apartment, Knowles said. When the wife found several valuable antiques missing, she got angry. Chris was asked to move.

From there, he took up with an elderly doctor and his wife in the San Pasqual neighborhood between Pasadena and San Marino near Caltech. That too came to an abrupt end, Knowles said. Within days of asking the young student to move in, the woman of the house believed Chris had been stealing from her and her husband. She told him to pack up and leave.

"It was then I heard that Chris had moved to San Marino," Knowles said.

The introduction to San Marino society came from Ted Colliau, a Chevy dealer on South Fair Oaks in South Pasadena who had cut a deal to provide cable television to the communities of South Pasadena and San Marino. The deal required Colliau to provide local programming.

To do that, Colliau latched on to the only young film student he knew—Chris. At the time, Chris was already making the rounds in San Marino and had recently joined the Episcopal Church of Our Savior in San Gabriel.

Muffy and Tasha Whitmore, sisters who met Chris there, introduced him to Didi Sohus, who lived on Lorain Road, just a few blocks from their church. Sometime in early April 1984, Chris became an official resident of San Marino.

Who knows what crossed Chris' mind when he ran his Plymouth Arrow along its winding tree-lined roads? When he got a look at its stately mansions and a whiff of the power that flowed from behind the closed doors of the town's picturesque architecture? This place was powerful since the day of its founding by Gen. George Patton's grandfather Benjamin "Don Benito" Wilson. By the 1980s, it was a place with a deep connection to that most American of institutions, the annual Tournament of Roses Parade and the Rose Bowl football game known as the "Granddaddy of 'em all."

The connection can't be overstated. Talk to almost anyone in San Marino and there is a very personal link to the annual Rose Parade. For some, it's through volunteering, for others the connection comes through participation. Of course, there are San Marino's queens and princesses.

A Dec. 30, 1982, *Associated Press* story by Hal Bock summed up the importance of the Rose Queen/San Marino connection in an interview with 17-year-old San Marino resident Suzanne Kay Gillaspie, the 1983 Rose Queen.

"Most of my friends and both of my sisters had entered when they were in high school and they encouraged me," Gillaspie, now a realtor in Laguna Beach, told Bock. "I did it for the experience and for the fun of it."

Many girls tried out because that's what their parents wanted, and it's what the community expected, especially as San Marino reached the pinnacle of its White Anglo Saxon Protestant influence in the late 1970s and early 1980s.

It was a tradition that city fathers vigorously protected and one that their daughters strived to take part in. Preparations for the 1984 parade were no different.

"Word was out that they were going to choose a girl from San Marino," recalled one former participant. "There were three of us. I sat next to (one), and she was so mean to me before the final interview. I had known her in class, and she was always dressed up and perfect. I liked her. But the day of the interview she freaked me out so badly that when I walked in my face must have looked chalk white. She got the court."

The loss led to scorn and shame, the almost Rose princess said as she recalled the moment she wasn't chosen, while standing on the steps of the Wrigley Mansion—known as Tournament House—in nearby Pasadena.

"The day they announced the court we were all up on the hallowed steps of Tournament House. The San Marino High School principal, vice principal, and parents were on the sidewalk. When I wasn't named, no one would talk to me. I went back to high school and ate lunch alone on the lawn. My mother, who was a socialite somewhat, wouldn't talk to me for three days. When I approached her, I said, 'Mom? I do think it's good I got that far.' She just looked at me and turned around and went back to her bedroom. I'm still not over it.

"In fact, several years later I came back home and looked at the framed finalist thing they gave. I threw it on the floor and stomped on it, obliterating it," she added.

San Marino was also the enclave of many of California's wealthiest conservatives and home of the state's chapter of the John Birch Society. The town's other wealthy residents were the Chandlers—publishers of the *Los Angeles Times*—and their company's high-powered executives and former executives.

Among those whom Colliau introduced to young Chris was Ken Veronda, headmaster at Southwest Academy, a boarding school for wealthy and privileged children built on a former ranch and set among towering old oak trees on a winding road in the heart of the community. The school styles itself as a military academy and some in the community describe it as the last stop for children of the wealthy who were unable to get into another private school.

Even then, late 1983 or early 1984, Chris looked older than his 22 or 23 years. He always dressed in a suit and tie and was ever the engaging conversationalist.

"From the beginning he was interested in the town," Veronda recalled.

Chris expressed that interest in the form of questions about some of San Marino's minutiae.

"He wanted to know, 'Was there industry here? Did San Marino have a financial base?"

Veronda gave Chris some of San Marino's history. He pointed out its three "zones": "I mentioned the usual, Sub Marino, San Marino, and Super Marino."

"Each had its own culture," Veronda explained to the young man. Sub Marino was for the less-well-off; San Marino proper was civic-minded. Super Marino to the north, and on the hill, was mostly old money.

"This was just before the main influx of Asian families. I told him many of the hill people were major executives, corporate executives, attorneys, and such. He asked me some names."

Who was among the names? C.F. Braun, founder of an engineering firm that would go on to become part of military contractor Halliburton; The Strub family, whose patriarch founded the Los Angeles Turf Club, brought Seabiscuit to Southern California and developed thoroughbred racing at Santa Anita Park; and, of course, Chris would want to know about John McCone.

At the height of the Cold War in the 1960s, McCone, co-founder of the Bechtel Steel Corporation, headed the Central Intelligence Agency. Later in the decade, he chaired a commission charged with identifying the cause of the 1965 Watts Riots and recommended policy changes that resonate in the Los Angeles Police Department nearly 50 years later. In hindsight that report was loaded with coded racism and other tropes that have caused it to be largely consigned to the dumpster, but it is interesting to note that all these years later a key recommendation, to provide emergency literacy training and pre-schooling from the age of three to "disadvantaged" children in an area occupied by more than 1.2 million Angelenos, might still be a recommendation of a commission studying the area today.

Nonetheless, San Marino has built a virtual wall around itself to prevent the hoi polloi and riffraff from taking over in any sense.

All that political power, wealth, and connection that existed in the 1980s played itself out among the town's young people in their cliques at school and their social activities afterward. The stratification of differences was obvious.

"The interaction of the girls at San Marino was hurtful," one longtime resident recalled. "In fact, I've run into a lot of them, and they hated it too. So much pressure to be the smartest, most popular, the richest; I didn't feel the smartest and I was not the richest or most popular. I never got to ski. I never got family Hawaiian vacations. My dad was working his ass off. My friend's dads were freaky wealthy, lawyers, judges, doctors, entrepreneurs.

"Our high school was loaded with huge successful families: Mike Chandler, *L.A. Times* heir who drove a Porsche; Lorrie Warren whose father founded eHarmony and whose daughter married Greg Forgatch who ran the original company. There was Wayne Hughes whose father began Public Storage. There are so many more."

Chris learned right away how to play on the insecurities of the young women, even as he sought the patronage of their wealthy parents. Soon after Chris' arrival in San Marino the list of young ladies who crossed paths with the would-be continental playboy/aspiring filmmaker continued to grow.

Some parents even hoped their daughters would hook up with Chris.

Carol Campbell recalled how her father met Chichester at Rotary and was impressed enough to send her date with him. He made that sort of an impression on the men of the town.

But, for Campbell, an afternoon driving around on errands with the supposed scion of European royalty was anything but impressive.

"I went out with him, and he was going on and on with these tales where he was from and you know he was the second duke of such and such," Campbell said. "He was driving this cheap little (car), you know, compact ... and he had all these little sticky notes all over his windshield. He was just so mysterious all the time."

Others would later note that the car was so beat up that anyone else driving it in San Marino would be immediately pulled over by the city's ever-vigilant police force.

Ensconced in their European-styled paradise, San Marino's Rose queens, its wealthy conservatives, Los Angeles' high-powered media executives and their families had access to California's top public schools, its most exclusive private academies, world-renowned museums, and a top-notch public library. They were truly a gentrified class of Americans Chris hadn't yet encountered on his American journey.

In San Marino of the late 1970s and early 1980s, parents still taught their kids manners: when to say please and thank-you, how to properly set a table, and make small talk with a smile.

"If I hadn't had that upbringing, I wouldn't be who I am now," the aspiring Rose Parade princess said. "I am very appreciative of San Marino."

At the same time, San Marino retained its hometown U.S.A. flair. Take this entry titled "OLD GLORY WAVES ON DESPITE A HOT SUMMER" from a historical society newsletter published in the early 1980s:

> After one of the hottest summers in history, the floral flag at Huntington Drive and San Marino Avenue valiantly wages on— just barely. The executive board has voted unanimously to put on a full-time gardener to nurture it through the winter to a new spring planting...

We must also express the gratitude of the citizenry to Ed Forde, treasurer of the society, who, each morning on his way to his offices at San Marino Savings and Loan takes time to turn on the flag's sprinkler.

Forde and his brother Stephen and their San Marino Savings and Loan got caught up in the mid-1980s savings and loan scandal. Both did federal prison time.

When Chris arrived on the scene, the key to success in the middle rung of San Marino society was volunteerism. And he volunteered for everything.

"It is a game. San Marino is a huge volunteer type city," the almost Rose princess said. "If you don't volunteer, they don't pay attention to you."

Veronda introduced Chris to that aspect of San Marino society too. Chris joined Rotary, attended Chamber of Commerce mixers, and made friends. When a group of women associated with San Marino organized a volunteer effort to repaint San Marino High School, Chris was front and center.

"Chris was all enthused and offered to help pay for the paint job," Veronda recalled. "He really liked ingratiating himself with most anybody."

In 1984, the San Marino Unified School District was in the throes of a severe budget crunch. Officials were short of money to pay teachers, considered closing schools, and leasing facilities. Some parents also struggled with an influx of Asian residents and pulled their children from classrooms that were rapidly shrinking thanks to a decrease in post-baby boom students.

There was an effort to maintain the façade and the memories of the past.

Painting the high school over the course of several weeks fit in with a variety of activities undertaken by boosters hoping to save San Marino's quality of life and the educational opportunities it afforded its residents. It also served the purpose of getting residents to know one another.

At least once, Veronda picked up Chris at the school and gave him a ride down to Lorain Road. It wasn't what he expected. After all, not a lot of royalty called Sub Marino home.

"Where can I drop you off?" Veronda remembered asking the young man.

"Just leave me here at the corner," he replied, urging Veronda to stop a few doors down from Didi Sohus' rundown ranch house. Chris wasn't living in the house so much as renting a detached garage that had been converted by Didi Sohus.

"He got into Didi's house through my mom. He was part of my mom's little crowd," Tasha Whitmore would later recall, remembering that Chris was part of her mom's Bible study group.

The Whitmores' grandmother had rented the converted garage on Didi's property that had previously been occupied by Didi's mom. Now that the grandmother was gone, Didi needed a new renter. She got Chris.

"When we knew him, he must have been barely out of his 20s, but you'd think he was going on 41. He tried to act a certain way," Tasha Whitmore said. He certainly didn't want to get dirty or do actual physical labor.

Once when Chris' broken-down car needed brakes, the Whitmore sisters did the replacement job as he sat and watched.

"He bought the pads," Tasha said. "But he was happy as a clam to watch the work get done."

At about the same time, Chris promised the girls to show them his estate in Glendale. He said they couldn't stop in, though, as he was renting the place out.

"So, we drove up to the Glendale Hills and after about half an hour he points to a place and says that's his house."

Didi, an alcoholic, who lived with her son in a run-down ranch house that once belonged to her parents, needed the sort of extra income that could only be provided by a renter. Chris needed a place to stay. The house on Lorain Road was just around the corner from the Church of Our Savior and a couple of blocks away from where Rotary meetings took place.

"I let him out of the car. I paid no particular attention to where he was going. I was never invited in by him, nor did I particularly wish to be invited in."

CHAPTER 5.

JOHN SOHUS

"Science fiction has always had strong appeal to a certain portion of the adolescent audience. Most life-long science fiction fans are made in their teen or pre-teen years. But in the past, this coterie was small and clannish, as most ghetto populations are. In the past ten years, however, science fiction has shared many aspects of the so-called youth revolution."
—Ben Bova, "The Many Worlds of Science Fiction." *Elementary English* **47, no. 6 (1970): 799–804**

John Sohus was a little guy. A loner. An underdog. The quiet guy in the corner who could talk about computers and science fiction for hours—if you just gave him a chance. But science fiction and computers were oddball pursuits—neither enjoyed the mass appeal each would find in the 21st Century—so John was content hanging out with a few close friends, mostly kids at Caltech or the Jet Propulsion Laboratory who shared his passions.

Like a lot of other Baby Boomers in the late 1960s and early 1970s, he followed the Apollo missions to the moon, talked with his friends about what was next for the United States in the exploration of space, thought about the origins of the universe, and worried about the possibility of nuclear holocaust.

John, like his contemporaries, was a product of the Cold War.

John Sohus was born Phillip Robert Chapman on Dec. 20, 1957. Soon after his birth he was adopted by Robert and Didi Sohus.

John's adoptive father, Robert, grew up in San Marino. He attended South Pasadena High School and graduated in 1943. His father, Morris O. Sohus, was born in Nebraska and ran a gas station. Robert Sohus' grandfather, John Sundstrom, a Swedish immigrant, lived with the family in an estate just off Oak Knoll Drive.

In the late '50s, Bob built—and raced—cars on the Southern California road race circuit. The circuit was a series of tracks in Pomona, Riverside, and Santa Barbara that grew out of Southern California's burgeoning car culture. Between 1958 and 1960, Bob entered 14 races. His first race car—the silver "Sohus-Larkin Special" sporting a 5050 cubic centimeter Mercury engine—finished 9th at Pomona just a few weeks before John's birth.

The road races, which sometimes attracted upwards of 15,000 fans, typically featured top European cars and top racers like Max Balchowsky, a West Virginia-born movie stuntman, who built and raced cars on the side. It was Balchowsky's "Ol' Yaller VI" that became Bob's second racer, the "Reynolds Wrap Special." The car was a mashup of other vehicles that Bob and his racing partner, Jim Larkin, pieced together.

Here's how author Harold Pace described the venture in his 2004 book *Vintage American Road Racing Cars 1950-1969*:

Road race vehicles were often pieced together with what could best be likened to bubblegum, shoestrings, and rubber bands. As Pace described it, Bob's car was the kind of vehicle that had to be cobbled together from week to week. And it was often transformed with various engines, chassis, and transmissions. Sohus bought Old Yaller IV, put his own Pontiac engine into it, and christened the vehicle with the same name he had given all his race cars—Reynolds

Wrap Special, in honor of the brand of aluminum foil. It likely signified that less-than-road-worthy materials were somehow incorporated into the design.

"Bob Sohus was the original buyer of 'Ol' Yaller VI,' which was powered by a Pontiac engine that he removed from the 'Reynolds Wrap Special.' It goes without saying that Sohus and Larkin were men of good humor and never took themselves too seriously. They loved to race, and they loved their race cars no matter what they looked like."

Bob's cars were "distinctive."

"Distinctive body work" is a gentlemanly way of saying the car was unattractive. There's no other good way to describe it. There was nothing aerodynamic about Sohus' creation; nothing sexy. It was just a heap covered with lumpy pieces of metal that appeared to be haphazardly welded together a couple of hours before each actual race.

Vintage auto historian Ron Cummings told Northern California blogger, Tam McPartland, that Bob took to calling the car "Godzilla" after a falling out with Max Balchowsky over money.

"Sohus installed an ugly homemade body along with (a) Pontiac motor from the 'Reynolds Wrap Special'," Cummings told the blogger.

Cummings also recalled watching Sohus race.

"The only time I saw the car was at Santa Barbara in 1965. It took Sohus a long time getting the car ready because of money problems. "Although the car took two years to build and could reach speeds of up to 125 mph, Bob never won a race. He eventually dropped off the circuit. Didi got the car in their divorce. She immediately sold it.

In the back of the Lorain Road house the couple shared, Bob built a carport. There he worked on his creations.

"That's where he had his shop," Tasha Whitmore said. "He repaired old Jags."

Following his divorce from Didi, Bob split from San Marino attempting to get a new start in Arizona.

He left behind a reputation for borrowing, and not always paying back, money from friends.

"He was always in financial trouble," said Bruce Stewart, a friend of Bob's at the time. "He borrowed a lot of money from me and skipped town and we never saw him again."

Another acquaintance, Fred Finocchiaro, a Pasadena accountant, remembered Bob had a brief career as a stockbroker. He was always chasing the next scheme and always borrowing cash.

"Everybody loaned him money," Finocchiaro said.

Finocchiaro recalled loaning Bob "a few grand here and there" right up until the day he moved.

John's mother, Ruth "Didi" Detrick, was the wild child of her family. A USC debutante, Didi married young, had a child, Harry Lee Sherwood III, divorced, dropped him off with her mom Freida, and partied for a few years before settling down back at her mother's house on Lorain Road with her new husband, Bob, and their adopted son, John.

***

For the first few years of young John's life, the family frequently traveled, oftentimes cross-country. Didi and Bob separated on Dec. 26, 1960 after about 10 years of marriage. She and the boy stayed at the ranch house on Lorain Road that had belonged to her parents. Bob took off. First, he went to nearby Altadena and ultimately ended up in Phoenix.

Frieda, "Momma D" to everyone who knew her, moved into the guest house out back.

Like Bob, Didi's early years were filled with adventure. She contributed articles to the local newspaper and held a pilot's license at some point in her young life. Didi's diary, though, and her friends, Don and Linda Wetherbee, describe a woman accustomed to "the good life."

Didi's very personal diary also contained entries describing John's growth from infant to toddler. One entry dealt with John's curiosity while on a vacation with his adoptive parents in 1960.

> Sept. 9, 1960—John is really a clown. We are here in Springfield, Mo. tonight at the Parkview Motel. ($7) He is on the couch with the cord to the Venetian blinds, calling Momma & Papa and Daddy, holding the end to his ear having a great conversation.

A few months later, Didi wrote about her separation and pending divorce from Bob:

> "Dec. 26, 1960: Bob moved out. Had already had an apartment for over two weeks. We had a lovely Christmas. He was in good humor. From then on everything was as nice as pie until he mentioned he had been to see a lawyer."

Bob would later say that Didi slugged him, giving him a fat lip. Didi's friends said the separation and divorce caused her to cling tightly to her adopted son, and to sink deeper into alcoholism.

John became her purpose in life.

"She idolized (John)", longtime friend, Marianne Kent, said of Didi. "She loved him very, very deeply."

Even with—or perhaps because—she had John and her mother to care for, Didi drank and smoked more than she did anything else.

After the separation and divorce, Momma D helped raise John. Momma D was also the unofficial neighborhood grandmother for most of the children growing up on Lorain

Road. When John was in junior high, Momma D died in her sleep.

Didi dreaded the day, but immediately knew something was wrong when her mother didn't come up for breakfast one morning. She called Kent and asked if her friend and neighbor could pay a quick visit to Momma D in the guest house.

"She called one morning and said, 'would you go up and check?" Kent said. "I did. And she had passed."

With her mother dead, Didi turned to renting the guest house to generate a steady income. Tasha Whitmore's grandmother moved in first.

The drinking became more pronounced. No longer the belle of the ball, an overweight and nicotine-wrinkled Didi, carried her highball glass everywhere. She became surly and difficult to get along with. She never even bothered to change out of her pajamas and dirty, well-worn bathrobe. Her nails and teeth turned yellow. When she opened her mouth, it was mostly to bellow at John.

"She was a real old hag," Tasha Whitmore said. "Drunk, mean. Always smoking and always with a drink in her hand. I guess at one time she was lovely in her heyday. But when we knew her, she was an overweight loudmouth. Even my grandmother, who was worldly and fun, thought Didi was out of control."

Eventually Didi stopped coming out of her bedroom. She would stay inside for days subsisting on a steady diet of daytime television, emphysema meds, cigarettes, and booze.

Living in the house with his mother and grandmother, John, who suffered from diabetes and ulcers, grew up in the sort of bubble that only overprotective alcoholic mothers can create for their children.

"She watched him so carefully," Kent said. "If he spent the night at a friend's house there was a whole list of instructions: No sugar, no candy. She would say, 'if he starts looking a certain way, get orange juice into him."

Classmates from Valentine Elementary School remembered John "was a polite, quiet kid who never hurt anyone or anything." A photo of John with his fifth-grade class shows a well-groomed child wearing Keds sneakers and a button-down shirt tucked into a pair of plaid Bermuda shorts.

John wasn't particularly athletic, but he wasn't a couch potato either. He was heavily involved in an Explorer Post attached to the Jet Propulsion Lab in nearby Pasadena, becoming an officer in the unit and recruiting other kids.

Like many kids of the era, he loved *Star Trek* and the exploits of Kirk, Spock, and McCoy.

"John was a small guy—a Trekkie kind of kid," Tasha Whitmore said. "He wanted to work at JPL. He was a sweet, quiet kid and sort of introverted. You could never tell if he was really smart or not. He was a nerd really. I always felt sorry for him because of his mother being the way she was. He was really a badgered boy."

Friends would try to best him in a trivia contest about the television show, but John would often come out on top. John found himself drawn to other forms of science fiction and fantasy literature. He loved Frank Herbert's *Dune*, the *Lord of the Rings* trilogy, the *Hobbit*, and *Dungeons and Dragons*. He was fond of large belt buckles and blue jeans. John usually wore collared shirts, and he always tucked them into jeans.

At JPL, John would experiment with balloons. He and his friends created a balloon craft that ascended to an altitude of 60,000 feet, then broke apart dropping a High-Altitude Experimental Payload or HAEP back to earth.

"We would have a little transmitter on it—a little directional thing," John's friend, Patrick Rayermann, said. "Sometimes we found them. Sometimes we didn't. In those days we were pretty much doing temperature and pressure experiments and trying to refine our skills at finding the craft."

It was *Star Trek's* adventurous look at the future and futuristic societies that appealed most to John and what led to his participation in role playing games like *Dungeons and Dragons.*

The episodes that appealed most to John were the ones where the crew of the Enterprise took on alien life forms like the Romulans and the Klingons, Rayermann said. And John and his friends could discuss the finer points of the show for hours.

Carol Campbell attended San Marino High with John and remembered him as a quiet kid who always wore a green, hooded sweatshirt.

"He was the guy who was always in the same green hoody every single day and always had a smile but was a loner," she said. "He was always in a hurry to be on time and do what he was supposed to do.

"He was in the class before me," Campbell continued. "He had energy and a smile with yellowish teeth. He kept to himself. I thought it odd that he wore that same evergreen hoody every single day. It made me wonder if he just didn't care what the other guys were wearing. We all had backpacks and so did he. I always thought something was up with him.

"He did not fit in with the sociables and didn't want to."

As his friend Rayermann would recall, Didi's overbearing nature and protectiveness of her adopted son combined with her bizarre behavior as a result of her alcoholism ultimately left John disconnected and alone. But John had a heart of gold and dreams of doing something big.

Rayermann met John in the winter of 1970. Both boys were in the sixth grade, about 11 years old. Rayermann and John soon became close childhood friends and confidants.

The two attended junior high together at Huntington Middle School, joined the Boy Scouts, and belonged to the JPL explorer post. John was into computers and owned an Apple II, which he bought in May 1977.

The purchase came just after his graduation from San Marino High. John was headed to Pasadena City College to study computers and programming because he loved it and he was good at it, Rayermann said.

"In the spring of 1977, John and another member of the explorer post went in together on the purchase," Rayermann said. "The computer would spend part of the time at John's house and part of the time at the other young man's house."

With the computer to practice on, John quickly developed an affinity for programming and the Apple II, which included Applesoft BASIC, a stripped-down programming language, and later the world's first spreadsheet program—VisiCalc. It became the perfect platform for John. He loved showing off his system, which included a crude CPU, a couple of floppy disk drives, and a printer. Most times he'd hook the device up to his mother's television set and work for hours.

"He'd write some programs and get it to do things," Rayermann said. "And from then on he couldn't get enough."

In September 1981, John joined the Los Angeles Science Fantasy Society. As the organization notes on its website, LASFS was founded in 1934 and claims to be the world's oldest continuously active club of its kind.

The group meets Thursday nights in Van Nuys to discuss their shared hobby, swap stories, listen to authors, tell jokes, and sometimes deride one another.

A popular legend on the internet is that John's love of computers and science fiction collided in a serendipitous way when he was chosen to maintain a computerized address database for science fiction author and editor, Harlan Ellison. Best known among sci-fi fans for his collections of stories titled *Dangerous Visions*, Ellison lived in the Los Angeles suburb of Sherman Oaks in the 1980s, about a 25-minute drive from Pasadena and San Marino.

I called Ellison to ask him about the rumor. When he answered the phone, I explained that I wanted to know more about John and Linda Sohus and their boarder, Christopher Chichester.

"Is that the kid that got buried in the backyard?" he asked. "This is about the guy who was posing as a Rockefeller right? You are probably the 99th guy to call asking about that rumor. I don't know how it got started. And the kid never did any such thing for me."

Ellison said he occasionally threw computer work to "kids down on their luck" but he never hired John, at least as far as he could remember.

The Sherman Oaks bookstore where John's future wife, Linda Mayfield, worked as a clerk, paid homage to Ellison. Owner Lydia Marano, Linda's boss, got the author's permission to call the store Dangerous Visions and almost immediately after it opened it became a hub for science fiction/fantasy fans from throughout the Los Angeles area.

There were other outlets too. For much of the 80s, Ellison appeared regularly on *Hour 25*, a show broadcast on KPFK, a member-supported Los Angeles radio station and part of the Pacifica network. The broadcast, which ran Friday nights from 10 to midnight, featured discussions of science fiction books, films, and related topics.

In the pre-internet era, *Hour 25* was one of the few mass media outlets distributing news and information to sci-fi fans. One can imagine young John as a fan of the program, if only for that reason.

Several websites maintain archives of *Hour 25*. Among the most interesting of its broadcasts was a 75-minute interview conducted by host Mike Hodel with author Phillip K. Dick. In the piece, Dick, best known for stories like "Do Androids Dream of Electric Sheep," which later became the movie *Blade Runner* and "We Can Remember It For You Wholesale", which was turned into the Arnold Schwarzenegger classic *Total Recall*, takes on his publisher, reads from a manuscript, discusses current events, and lays out the perils of drug addiction.

Science fiction fans in Los Angeles County also had TV's KTLA, Channel 5, in their corner in the late '70s and early 1980s. For several years, the station played *Star Trek* episodes at 11 p.m. followed by back-to-back *Twilight Zones* at midnight.

Rayermann, who joined the United States Army in September 1981, said he and Sohus often tested and compared one another's knowledge of the genre—even long after Rayermann entered the service.

John's love of computers also brought him into the fold at JPL. Managed by Caltech for NASA since 1958, the lab has been the primary planetary research center for the federal space agency, putting devices on the Moon and Mars as well as into deep space. By the mid-80s, John had gone from Explorer to employee at the lab.

Rayermann said his friend fit right in. "His love of math and science are some of the reasons he wound up at JPL.

"He was shy, (but) generally very upbeat. John usually had a smile. He had no complaints, and he was always seeing the positive in people. John was reliable, faultlessly reliable. If he said it, he did it. If he could help you, he would."

While John stayed close to home after graduation from high school, Rayermann attended UCLA, where he joined the Army ROTC. From UCLA, Rayermann moved east, but kept in touch with his friend.

I don't have a recollection about John saying he had a special someone in his life until the summer of 84," Rayermann said.

That someone was Linda Mayfield, a free-spirited redhead, who liked to be called "Cody." She and John were madly in love.

CHAPTER 6.

CODY

"There is a saying that the Seventh Sister ran off with a horse trader… but, that seventh lass is still encountered here and there around the world."
—"Land of the Great Horses," R.A. Lafferty, *Dangerous Visions*, 1967

When it came to science fiction, Linda Mayfield was a fan's fan. And, in her late 20s, she was becoming a hell of an artist. She loved to draw unicorns, mythical creatures, and horses. Especially horses. She was good enough at it that her work got noticed. Linda took on a pseudonym, and when she painted, she became Cody.

She said she liked the name after reading about the small town of Cody, Wyoming.

"She tended to draw Hallmark-like critters," her boss at the science fiction store, Lydia Marano, said, describing some of Linda's early art. "Really nice unicorns and horses."

Linda's art was colorful, without being cartoonish, and detailed enough to get noticed by collectors.

At 15 and just a sophomore in high school, Linda moved out of her mother's house in Los Angeles and moved in with her grandmother, Faye Simpson, in the San Fernando Valley.

"My mother would give her anything she wanted," Linda's mother, Susan Mayfield, said. "She didn't like the rules of the house. She didn't want to stay there, and she moved in with my mother because my mother let her do whatever she wanted."

As far as Susan Mayfield knew, her daughter wasn't into drugs or alcohol, she was simply a free spirit. Linda did bounce from boyfriend to boyfriend. At one point in her late teens, she got pregnant and sought and obtained an abortion. It bothered her ever after.

Susan Mayfield knew Linda didn't like her, but it never bothered Susan. Linda, for her part, would float from relationship to relationship in hopes of finding something that she lacked at home.

Like her future husband, John Sohus, Linda acquired life-long hobbies as a pre-teen. While John and his friends were sending balloons into the stratosphere, Linda and her friends were buying and showing model horses.

Linda's affinity for horses and art stretched back to her junior high school days. At least, that's how Susan Coffman remembered it.

As young women, Linda and Sue did model horse shows together. It was a hobby the two shared and obsessed over. Basically, model horses are a lot like model cars. The secret to success at either hobby is an exacting attention to detail.

In the '50s, '60s, and '70s, the Breyer Company cornered the market on the models associated with the hobby.

It is a unique hobby in that collectors rely on the manufacturer to come up with the perfect show horse. The models, with names like "Proud Arabian Mare" or "Man O' War," named for the famous thoroughbred, are sold painted, which means it's up to the buyer to determine what makes a good model and what doesn't.

In the 1970s, shows typically took place with a group of enthusiasts exchanging photos of their horses. Many of the hobbyists would create stables, tack, and gear to give their model horses a better appeal. By the late '70s, collectors like Linda and Sue were taking their horses to shows instead of exhibiting by photograph. It gave their friendship a consistency.

"It was consistent," Coffman said. "We were doing the model horse showing together once or twice a month."

Eventually, the two held their own show, "The Model Horse Spectacular," Coffman said.

"I think she did much better on her modeling. She was very, very good at detailing what a horse looked like," Coffman said. "She was fun, she was silly, we just had a really great relationship based on the horse love," Coffman said. "We were buddies experiencing life together as we got older."

Linda was maid of honor at Sue's first wedding.

"We were going to be friends for the rest of our lives."

If Linda and Sue went somewhere, Linda would drive. She was always the driver.

But, Coffman added, "She didn't rule a group, she would assimilate herself into the group. When it was the two of us, we were having a good time laughing and joking."

Linda shared everything with Sue. When Linda met John, a diminutive guy of 5' 5" or 5' 6" and all of 140 pounds, he became part of Sue's life too. And Sue was happy for the friend who had a "series of unfortunate events with the men in her life."

They were The Three Musketeers.

"Once John was in her life it was the three of us," Coffman said. "It was great. It was the first time I'd seen her with someone where she was happy. I called them 'Mutt and Jeff.' Her demeanor around John was content. Her artwork was finally taking off and he was very supportive of that."

John and Linda met through a mutual friend, a man who was engaged to Linda and lived in San Marino. The friend asked John to keep an eye on Linda when he was at work.

John took it from there, Coffman recalled. Linda called him her bodyguard.

Linda loved animals. She had cats and even owned a horse that she doted on. If Linda had one flaw—it was her lateness. She couldn't be on time for anything, Coffman recalled. John, on the other hand, was known for his punctuality. Mutt and Jeff though they appeared, the young couple loved and adored each other and seemed a perfect fit to all who knew them.

Sometime after Christmas 1982, Linda moved into Didi's house on Lorain Road.

John and Linda married on Halloween night 1983. Linda wore a pink dress and white veil. John, attired in his ever-present thick glasses, wore a charcoal grey suit with twin white carnations pinned to his left breast as a boutonniere. Pictures from the event show the couple smiling and happy—John barely reaching Linda's shoulder.

Following John and Linda's wedding at Sue's house in Orange County, Coffman saw her friend just a handful of times.

In January 1985, they got together for an invitation-only showing of Linda's art at a gallery in San Gabriel, a small community bordering San Marino.

Among the paintings were works like "Adrienne" described as a fairy seated on a bed of flowers, wearing only translucent wings. "Dreaming" was described as an elaborately decorated carousel unicorn, come to life. The painting titled "Ladies of the Lake" depicted black swans floating on a moonlit waterway.

Most of the work was done in colored pencil. An art critic described Linda as a "down-to-earth" redhead who was about to have her work published in a book titled *The Joys of Horsing Around.*

Linda told the critic that she had shown her work at over 500 science and fantasy conventions around the U.S. And she was winning awards. At the Worldcon sci-fi event in Anaheim, a piece titled "Children of the Lyn" was one of 50 works honored on a showcase wall at the Convention Center. At the CopperCon Convention in Scottsdale, during September 1984, she showed her art in the Flagstaff Room in the Sunburst Hotel and won the award for best work of fantasy for the "Ladies of the Lake."

John spent most of his time in the computer room at CopperCon which featured a lecture on the difference between the Apple IIe and Commodore 64. Gary Grigsby, "the founding father of strategy games for the PC" was among those scheduled to speak.

It was the perfect weekend for the couple.

Speaking to the art critic, Linda said her work reflected the themes of her own life, which had its ups and downs.

"Most are happy pieces—they're not hard-core science fiction with guns and rockets. They're more fantasy with a touch of whimsy and magic," she said. "With fantasy you can get away with a lot more—you don't have to do a blue sky; you can do a red sky or a green sky. Fantasy is everyone being a kid again."

At this point in her nascent career, Linda was earning anywhere from $250 - $275 for each work. That money supported her and John. And allowed them to afford a small pickup truck to travel from show to show.

"You really got to be dedicated—a lot of artists don't have the hunger. It can involve eight to 10 hours a day at the drafting table on top of a full-time job."

She hoped the money would get John and her away from the house they shared with John's mother.

Despite outward appearances, Linda wasn't too happy, and she definitely wasn't in charge of the house. In fact, she did not like her mother-in-law's domineering and controlling nature and frequently complained about Didi to anyone who would listen.

[Didi was] "Not an easy person to live with," Linda's friend, Sue Coffman, said. Coffman didn't care too much for Didi either, primarily because she was an obnoxious alcoholic who slurred her words and was never pleasant.

Lydia Marano also knew her employee had mother-in-law troubles. Following Linda and John's wedding at Coffman's house on Halloween night 1983, Didi was a frequent topic of conversation. What emerged from the complaints was a sense that Linda "did not like (Didi) Sohus."

"I don't blame her," Marano said.

So, she was determined to succeed in what she saw as a man's world. She told the critic that her goal was to continue winning awards, including a Hugo Award for her art.

"I just want to have a stable living from the artwork I enjoy doing. It makes me happy; it makes other people happy," she said. "Artwork seems to be in the blood; it's one of those things where you gotta do it. When artwork stops being fun and being a challenge, that's the time to start looking for another profession."

Sue said the San Gabriel show really boosted Linda's confidence.

"She was very proud and very happy, and kind of nervous that she was out there," Coffman said. But "(Linda) sold some pieces that day and she was so excited. John was just kind of puffed up and was like 'Whoo hoo!' He helped her set it up."

It wasn't just a marketing or PR campaign; collectors began to take notice of Cody's work as well.

"Basically, I had seen her stuff in an art show," one collector recalled. He was struck by her painting of a centaur on a green background.

"It looked like a woman facing sort of away, stretching her arm in front of her face," he said. "The rest of it is a horse body matching that sort of pose."

The art collector described Linda's work as "interesting."

She had two styles," he said. "One was a very high contrast. The other was standard fantasy art. There was also some non-fantasy stuff that wasn't like her other pieces."

As Linda/Cody packed up her paintings and easels as the Worldcon 42 show came to an end, the two began to talk. The collector bought a shapely and topless female centaur and commissioned a second piece, which Linda/Cody promised to deliver.

"I was thinking—you know from what I saw—he would have been a very, very prominent fantasy artist," the collector said.

The sale netted her $110 when she got around to shipping it to the collector in Campbell, California on Sept. 5, 1984.

Although the art collector thought Linda was strong-willed and determined, Marano said her former employee had a touch of naivety about her.

Linda was also a large woman—she was about 6 feet tall, weighed 200 pounds, and stood more than six inches taller than John. Marano said she was muscular from tending to horses.

And she appeared to be very much in charge of her household—at least when speaking on the telephone to the art collector.

"Every time I called down there to talk to Linda, she was always the one that answered the phone," he said. "She was really nice all the times I interacted with her—high energy, a little on the bubbly side. She was kind of a horsy person, really into horses, very excited talking about horses. She falls into that category. She wasn't a flake either. When she said she was going to send something, that was a real big positive. Linda seemed very reasonable."

In late December, she wrote the man describing some of her works in progress.

> Enclosed are 3 centaurs that I'm sending to Don—if interested in any let me know ASAP—
>
> The one with the feather whip is the one I told you about—she is an 'exotic dancer' geisha type—though she can be a bit on the dominating side—she is a dark mahogany

bay with golden dapples—blk hair, green eyes—named 'Toi' (I really want to do more with this one she drew herself...)

On the other 2, the one with the clouds will look much better in color (depth, etc.) Thou I don't know what color yet, she has no name yet either—and the other is probably going to be a red/gold chestnut (red/blonde hair + tail) she should be a looker too—Kinda young like Ambra—her name is 'Heather.'

Hope you like them—more to follow soon—

"Happy New Year!"

Cody

CHAPTER 7.

1985

"It is rather difficult being rich. If it wasn't
for the money, I'd rather be poor."
—**Thurston Howell III,** *Giligan's Island,*
CBS Television, November 1964

When they were alone, Linda described her plans to John.
She wanted to either get away from Didi, or at the very
least move into the guest house where Didi's renter, Chris
Chichester, lived.

The problem was, in early 1985, Chris didn't seem to be
going anywhere.

Along with regular church and Bible study, Chris was
active in social circles and joined dozens of clubs including
the San Marino Rotary.

Rotary plays an important role in the civic life of many
in the community and Chris fit right in, Ken Veronda,
headmaster of Southwestern Academy recalled.

"Those men and now women as well work very hard on
their endeavors and raise a lot of money," said a resident who
has had a several-decade affiliation with the club. "Their ties
are tied to a 'T' and not a hair out of place. But that's what
we like about San Marino. We expect people who reside
here to follow their former leaders in that they will not stray
from what our founders envisioned."

Rotary opened other doors for Chris.

"When I met Chichester, he was in a circle of Rotary men
at the church in the courtyard," one woman recalled. "Chris

just immediately offered a handshake from the opposite side of the circle and introduced himself as "Chris Chichester."

At that moment, "The circle of maybe seven men just stopped because he was obviously ceasing whatever conversation was going on."

Resident Mary Payne still remembers a three-minute conversation at Rotary with the man who briefly swept her off her feet.

"He had a fabulous accent," she said. "And, he was so interesting, so well spoken. He was not good looking by any means; he had a very small frame. But the personality was very engaging. I was very charmed by the British accent and whatever it was that we were talking about was so much more interesting."

Payne said she believed that charisma and charm paved Chris' way into normally reserved San Marino society.

"Here in San Marino, people wanted to be around a Chichester. The influential and educated people he was around (and trying to be like) were naturally attracted to him. I can understand why, after just three minutes."

Chris could carry on a conversation about anything. He was always knowledgeable and when he wasn't, no one was the wiser.

Chris quickly swept the matrons off their feet, impressed the old boys, cadged meals where he could, and told stories about his near-royal upbringing. But he never paid his dues and was eventually persona non grata, former members would later recall.

Even so, to many San Marino residents, Chris was fun and approachable.

To others like Dan Banks, he was a menace and danger— especially to young girls.

Banks said he first encountered Chris at Church of Our Savior.

Don Benito Wilson himself—the great-grandfather of WWII American General George S. Patton—arranged in

1872 to have the church built in San Gabriel. It would be paid for by philanthropist Marie Vinton who, according to Nat Read in his book *Don Benito Wilson: From Mountain Man to Mayor*, had paid for two other churches of Our Savior. The first in Providence, Rhode Island; and the second in Clermont, Iowa; San Gabriel would be the third.

With a $4,000 investment, Vinton completed her life-long dream of building churches from the Atlantic to the Pacific. The dirt comprising the deep brown bricks of the church was taken from Don Benito's vineyard and fired in a kiln on the spot.

When he died in 1878, Don Benito was buried in the newly consecrated cemetery adjacent to the church.

When Chris left St. James, he immediately joined Don Benito's Church of Our Savior. Doubtless he gazed upon the stained-glass windows that honor Don Benito, his wife, and their descendants, including General George S. Patton. The general's memorial is contained in stunning stained-glass window just inside the church's entrance.

The window—about 4 feet high—is an intricate masterpiece of excellent craftsmanship. At first glance, one sees the figure of St. George slaying the dragon from atop his white steed. Upon closer inspection, the window gives up its secrets.

First the inscription, from 2 Timothy, Chapter 4, verse 7:

> I have fought a good fight.
> I have kept the faith.
> I have finished my course.

The dragon comes next. The beast is covered in scales shaped like Nazi swastikas. St. George's shield carries the "A" insignia of Patton's Third Army, which crushed its German opposition in the winter of 1944 in western Europe.

Surrounding St. George are the patches and insignia of groups Patton commanded. In the lower right corner, Patton himself rides atop a heavily armored WWI-vintage tank. At the bottom, a simple reminder: "In loving memory, General George S. Patton 1885-1945."

The general's grandfather, Benjamin Davis "Don Benito" Wilson, made his way to California in 1841 as part of a group of men seeking passage to China. Ultimately, he settled on a ranch that encompassed much of present-day South Pasadena, Pasadena, San Marino, Altadena, and San Gabriel.

In his day, Don Benito chased rogue outlaws, killed grizzly bears, was a justice of the peace in Riverside County, and served as Los Angeles' second mayor.

Don Benito's home at Lake Vineyard—now San Marino's Lacy Park—wasn't too far from Church of Our Savior and he was a devoted parishioner and demanded the same of his family and friends as entrance into Los Angeles' early society scene.

Despite the impressive and historic surroundings, Chis had an air of being better than anyone around. He seemed to look down his nose on the majestic church, its history, and its parishioners. There was nothing to back it up.

"For being royalty, he never had money," Banks said. "He was always hitting us up for money."

It was also through his budding affiliation with the Church of Our Savior that Chris first met Bob and Bette Brown who lived on Canterbury Road. Chris treated Bob and Bette as though he were their adopted son—even if they didn't need or want such a relationship.

"He often came by our house and just dropped in," Bob said. "Several times it was for a religious study group with my wife and some other friends. I think we probably (shared meals) though not regularly. If we'd go to eat somewhere together, somehow, he never seemed to have cash. He couldn't find his credit card or some silly thing."

Chris gave the Browns the impression that he was from New England.

"He was talking about where he had lived or where his parents had lived, but it was never a pinned-down location."

Once, Chris told the Browns that "his family owned a tea plantation somewhere in the Middle East." He showed up at their home with a single bag of tea that he claimed was grown at the site. Another time he showed up announcing he had tickets to the Academy Awards and "wanted to know if one of us would go with him." Chris explained the tickets were a perk that came with teaching at the USC film school.

"What?" they asked. "You're teaching at USC?"

"Why yes. Didn't you know?"

Chichester would often casually mention his role in the film school at USC. In a region that thrives on the economy of motion pictures and television, involvement with the USC school of Cinema and Television is nothing short of prestigious.

Sometimes Chris would claim he was a mere student. Other times he was a teacher's aide. More than one person believed Chris said he was a professor at the influential school.

Established in 1929 as a joint venture with the Academy of Motion Picture Arts and Sciences, the original faculty included a who's who of early Hollywood. Early professors included actor Douglas Fairbanks, director D.W. Griffith, producer Irving Thalberg, and studio exec Darryl Zanuck.

By the 1980s, the list of alums would have included producer Brian Grazer, director Robert Zemekis, and *Star Wars* creator, George Lucas.

For Chris, one can imagine that a claimed attendance at USC alone would have imparted some credibility to his claims of wealth. In the early and mid-1980s, it wasn't called the "University of Spoiled Children" for nothing. The fact that he was one of the chosen 500 or so in the USC film school made his resume even more impeccable.

And in the San Marino crowd, no one batted an eye or questioned the credential, even when Chris wasn't giving straight answers.

"He was somewhat elusive," Brown said when describing his fellow parishioner. "He gave the impression that he was somewhat involved with USC and their film school, and he was teaching and advising there."

Tickets to Oscar night only made the boasts more credible.

"He was enough of a mystery person that I thought it possible," Brown said.

Even as he played out the film school ruse, Chris also worked his pretend connection to Sir Francis and the Gipsy Moth.

He also desired to build his network of contacts beyond Rotary and Church of Our Savior. And, as an inveterate gossip, Chris soon learned he could get a solid bead on San Marino's ins and outs, its players and pretenders, by hanging around Jann Eldnor's barbershop.

In San Marino, the main drag, Huntington Drive, is lined with rows of small stores that cater to the residents' needs and whims. Jann Eldnor's barber shop, "Jann of Sweden," sits in the heart of San Marino proper on the south side of Huntington, just about a mile north of Lorain Road, where Chris had now taken up residence.

Although his birth name is spelled with one "N," Jan, which he pronounces *"Yaahn,"* uses two "Ns" for professional purposes to become "Jann." And to those who know him best, no last name is necessary.

"I was born Jann Eldnor," he tells all who want to hear. "But here in America I am Jann of Sweden."

He is the town barber and its keeper of secrets.

Unless you've visited Jann, you've never been in a barber shop quite like his. Cutting away in a loft atop a mission-style building on the east end of town, Eldnor's spent the better part of 40 years in San Marino. He's devoted a good chunk of that time collecting interesting stories to while away the hours and impressive knick-knacks to line the walls, clutter the floor, and surround his well-worn leather barber's chair.

The knick-knacks are uniquely Jann's: leather saddles with sterling silver inlay; pictures of Jann with Ronald Reagan and Jann with Jay Leno. The theme is decidedly western—Old western, to be exact. A bleached cattle skull perches above the worn leather chair. A poster of John Wayne hangs prominently displaying all his feature film glory. The furniture is nearly all antiques—wooden—like something from an Ethan Allen catalog.

Growing up, a young Jann Eldnor thought he might be an auto mechanic. His father and grandfather encouraged him to attend school, and his father thought that if Jann was going to attend a vocational school he might as well learn how to be a hairdresser like a distant relative.

Other than various hair tonics, barbering tools, photos, diplomas, and Jann's barbering license, anything in the shop that's not wood, leather, or bone is sterling silver. On one wall is the diploma Jann Eldnor received after graduation from a Stockholm trade school in 1962. It certifies him as a trained barber. The only resemblance the picture of a clean-cut young man has to Jann of Sweden now is the broad, gap-toothed smile. Jann proudly tells visitors his diploma was signed by the King of Sweden, "The grandfather of the king we have now."

As a young man, Jann Eldnor didn't care much for Sweden. Jann likes to tell everyone he was the star of a 2008 Swedish language film titled *Jann of Sweden: Best in the West*.

The 13-minute movie, described as a documentary, dramatic comedy short, tells the story of Jann's journey to America.

"My wife had lived in America."

"Her father was an engineer and worked in America for seven or eight years. I was always complaining about Sweden. I complained about the bad weather, the high taxes, everything was bad," he recalled. "We got the idea to get a green card and the American Dream."

So Jann set up shop in San Marino. His customer base began to grow, primarily because folks thought they were coming to a barber shop run by a Swedish girl named "Jan." Not wanting to be thought of as anything other than a manly man, Jann fixed that by adding the extra N to his first name.

Sometime in the late 1970s, Jann began to let his hair, mustache, and beard grow. He also learned to play the mandolin and his take on *Ghost Riders in the Sky* adorns the documentary's soundtrack.

"You know I have been a cowboy all my life, but you know it took me so long before I came out of the closet, and one day I come out of the closet and my wife said, 'Oh how long have you been a cowboy?'"

Being a cowboy goes alongside with Jann's love of horses, particularly his prized walking horse, Rochelle. Jann said his love of horses began at an early age, when he received three toy horses for Christmas.

His ability as a horseman earned Jann of Sweden 19 straight entries in Pasadena's annual New Year's Day Rose Parade. His skill even took him on a trip to the ranch of Ronald Reagan to visit and ride with the then-president at Santa Ynez in 1988. For the occasion, Jann donned a red, white, and blue shirt patterned after the flag of the United States, his adopted home.

A photo of the trip hangs on the wall near one of Jann on the set of *The Tonight Show with Jay Leno*. The pair of photos hangs on the wall with awards from Jann's time marching in the Rose Parade, old cowboy hats, and a plastic six-shooter. There are also the paintings folks have dropped off.

Chris was a regular.

As Jann remembers it, Chris arrived in town sometime in 1981 and had been immediately recommended by another customer. After that first meeting, the young man hovered in Jann's shop. Often, he came by in the morning to scheme and figure out ways to have breakfast with one of the other customers. Often, Chris didn't pay for those meals.

Jann remembers Chris had a knack for working his way into a conversation. For example, if the man in the barber chair was an anesthesiologist, Chris would discuss the latest techniques of the trade. Inevitably the customer would be done with his haircut and ask the young man if he had eaten breakfast. Chris would reply no—or something of that sort—and eventually wind up with a meal—Spanish Omelet, Potatoes O'Brien—usually served at the Colonial Kitchen, a family-owned greasy spoon a couple miles west of the barbershop.

Usually, the meal would end with the young man profusely apologizing for forgetting his wallet. To which his new friend would say, "Don't worry about it. You can get it next time."

Inevitably in San Marino, as in any other town, rumors would get back to Jann's barbershop. When they involved Christopher Chichester, it was either something about an elderly woman he was taking advantage of, or one of many prominent townsfolk who were gay, but in the closet.

"Oh yeah, he was a double dunker," Jann said as he related a story from the early 1980s about a naked Chichester cavorting poolside in the backyard of a well-known San Marino politician. A couple of neighbors caught a glimpse of the couple before gossiping about it later in Jann's shop.

In the 1980s, gay and bisexual men were not generally out in the open. The fear of ostracization or other repercussions kept many in the closet. That naturally led to gossip, suspicion, and fear.

Bob Brown thought Chris might be gay and questioned his reasons for working so hard to ingratiate himself in the everyday lives of San Marinans.

Veronda also wondered about Chris' sexuality.

"Before being introduced, I had heard of him in South Pas either living with, or friendly with, another priest in a male-male interest," Veronda said.

When they first met, Jann knew the young man didn't live in San Marino, but where he was staying was anyone's guess.

"I don't know where he was living at first, but he would say different places in San Marino, Alhambra, or San Gabriel," Jann recalled. "Later on, he was recommended by some girls that he might have a chance to live in San Marino."

After hooking up with San Marino society through Colliau, the car dealer and fellow parishioner, Chris met Peggy Ebright, a bubbly and personable actress who volunteered alongside him at San Marino High School. Their first meeting took place during the elaborate planning for a city-wide talent showcase called "Father's Night."

A community fund-raiser for the PTA, "Father's Night" is an annual event at the high school starring San Marino's dads. Chris wormed his way into an invitation to take part in the 1984 performance. Within days he went from volunteer to organizer, promising to hasten the show along using computers in some way.

More than one participant remembers Chris getting overwhelmed early, only to reappear at the end of the process seeking a role on stage.

He was recommended to be a helper for what we were doing," recalled Winnie Reitnouer, the wife of San Marino mayor Lynn Reitnouer. "I was the stage manager, but during the production period, everybody did everything they could."

A grainy VHS tape of the show clearly focuses in on a young Chris. Like the actual fathers on stage, he is wearing a white gown and singing. He's the only one there wearing sunglasses. No doubt he had a reason for them.

The show was played in March, with rehearsals through January and February. Chris was the new kid on the block. He told Reitnouer and others that he possessed "great expertise with computers teaching at USC and wanted to help."

Essentially, Chris promised to build a database. His computer would hold the names of the actors and their planned roles. The database would make it easier for organizers—and Reitnouer—to access information.

Chris came to five or six weekly meetings with Reitnouer and her friends. He would walk in with a briefcase and an accordion file loaded with paperwork. Winnie thought the energetic young man had a wonderful idea, but he couldn't make it work.

"He was more or less out of my sphere," she recalled. "I would see him here or there. He liked my cookies. He seemed to be hungry."

When asked to explain how he got to San Marino, Chris said his mother had a house on Lorain Road. It was part of a vast number of holdings, and Chris was here doing his part to help. Chris also told Winnie and her friends that he was a direct descendant of Sir Francis.

"He wanted to be in that show," Winnie said. "And he was in that show."

The event was a "great way to meet all the people in town," Peggy said.

For meeting people, San Marino was the perfect spot. Not only did L.A.'s wealthiest call it home, but San Marino boasts some of the country's greatest minds in the form of professors and administrators from the nearby California Institute of Technology.

Known as Caltech, the school was founded in the early part of the 20th Century as an engineering trade school.

In the 1930s, Albert Einstein toured the campus for three separate stints as a "visiting scientist."

In the 1940s and 50s, Caltech was the center of jet propulsion studies in the United States. By 1983, Caltech professors and administrators had won 23 Nobel Prizes for work ranging from Carl David Anderson's discovery of a sub-atomic particle known as the positron to Linus Pauling's Nobel Peace Prize. The institution sponsors NASA's Jet Propulsion Laboratory in nearby La Cañada Flintridge.

San Marino can also lay claim to a great trove of art works housed on the grounds of the Huntington Library in the center of town. Among the works on display are 18th Century portraits like Thomas Gainsborough's "Blue Boy" and Thomas Lawrence's "Pinkie."

The Huntington also holds the papers that would make up Abraham Lincoln's de facto presidential library as well as a Gutenberg Bible and early editions of Shakespeare's Hamlet. Researchers from around the world frequently visit the library, which opens its collections to scholars.

Among the wealthy, smart, and connected, Chris spotted Peggy's star potential. Several months later when the opportunity to produce *Inside San Marino* arose, he picked Peggy to host.

Another person he met about that time was attorney William Stewart. In the fall of 1982, the two flew in Stewart's private plane to spend a weekend in Santa Barbara.

It's what people did. These—after all—were the early days of the "Go-Go 80s," as Ken Veronda would later describe them.

Saturday Nov. 6, 1982, might have marked the turning point between the malaise of the Carter years and Veronda's 1980s. It was an auspicious day for Chris and the attorney Stewart, who (several years later) was asked to recall the trip to Santa Barbara.

College football season was in full swing. USC would host the University of California, Berkeley at the Coliseum.

UCLA, which made its home in Pasadena's Rose Bowl, had traveled to Washington to play the Huskies in another Pac-10 match up. Although the morning was overcast, by 8 a.m. the clouds had burned off. In Santa Barbara, the temperature would reach nearly 70 degrees by 1 p.m.

The United States was in a deep economic slump. Just two years earlier—nearly to the day—Ronald Reagan had been elected the nation's 40th president. On Nov. 2, 1982, his party had lost 26 seats in the House of Representatives. But as had become his tradition, he took to the nation's airwaves to give his weekly Saturday address from the Oval Office at the White House.

"How deeply I wish that we could relieve our current situation with some immediate magic method," Reagan told the country in the final weeks of the early 1980s recession. "But there is a new spirit building—of optimism and hope for America's future. The severe problems which have been neglected for years and which caused unemployment to trend steadily higher—problems of runaway spending, taxing, double-digit inflation, and sky-high interest rates— are now being attacked at their roots. Inflation is down to 4.8 percent. Interest rates have dropped by nearly 50 percent, and taxes on the people are being cut."

It's likely Stewart and his young companion talked about the elections, Reagan, and the economy. When Disney stock began to rise between late 1982 and 1984, Stewart recalled the young man "almost implied he was riding that wave. He asked me if I had some and I said I didn't."

For certain, Stewart and Chichester discussed the young man's involvement in the USC Film school as an instructor. Chichester would later hint to Stewart that he played a role in the production of Paul Newman's film, *The Verdict*, which was released in December 1982.

Privately Stewart thought Chris was too full of himself and a bit of a phony.

Despite the young man's characteristic braggadocio, if anything, Chris' connection to the USC film school was as a bit player. As such, he had a role in a silent student film by Tom Dugan titled *Suspension*.

The film opens with what appears to be a woman on an operating table in the morgue. About 1 minute 59 seconds into the roughly six-minute piece, Chris appears. He's holding a large syringe. There are several close ups of his face. In the film, Chris wears medical garb. At one point, he fondles a scalpel.

Eventually the woman on the operating table wakes up and begins to run. Dugan appears to have shot much of the action sequence with a hand-held camera. By the end of the film, the young woman, who is wearing heavy mascara, sits against a wall. The viewer is left to assume that her pursuer has caught up with her.

There is no other footage of Chris, although it appears in the film that the actor killed the young woman and stuffed her in a morgue refrigerator, just before the screen fades to black.

Admitted to the California State Bar in 1968, Stewart would later become a Los Angeles County Superior Court judge in Burbank handling a nondescript civil calendar. But just like practically every other jurist in Los Angeles, Stewart has had his brushes with celebrity. In January of 2012, Stewart issued a three-year restraining order against alleged stalker, Thomas Brodnicki, who threatened to kill Disney Channel star, Selena Gomez.

Following the weekend getaway to Santa Barbara, Stewart frequently encountered Chichester at church. The more he encountered Chris, the more Stewart thought the young man was a bit of a conniver, a mooch, and a cheapskate who spoke with what Stewart believed was a decidedly Germanic accent.

"I wouldn't say he was always looking for a free meal, but if it was there, he'd take it," Stewart said. When Chris spoke, Stewart said he heard a "sound I've only heard in German speakers. It threw me off."

It was in late 1983 that Colliau, of South Pasadena, turned to Chris, the young, aspiring USC film student for help producing the cable access TV show that was required as part of his contract with South Pasadena and San Marino.

The show, titled *Inside San Marino* filmed its first episode on Jan. 10, 1984. In anticipation of that year's Olympics, which were to be held in Los Angeles, Chris had Peggy interview Lynn Reitnouer, the mayor, as well as civic leaders and visitors from the country of San Marino who were preparing for the Olympic Games.

"We started small, but grew quickly," Peggy Ebright said of the 13 shows she and Chris videotaped between January and late March of 1984. When they ran out of local guests, Chris began booking political figures. His biggest get was a one-on-one with Los Angeles Police Chief Darryl Gates. Soon the show changed its name from *Inside San Marino* to just *Inside* Ebright recalled.

When questioned by anyone about why he was producing such a lowly TV show, Chris would explain that although he was nearly royalty, the weekly show was a great career move for someone fresh out of USC Film School and setting up a household in San Marino.

Ebright said she was constantly amazed by Chris' ability to book interesting guests for their insignificant cable access show. Chris' explanations of who he was and where he came from constantly changed, Ebright recalled.

"We said he was a remittance man, a black sheep—you know, sent here to mostly get out of town. We thought he was one of those kids a rich family would want to be rid of," Ebright said. "Of course, while he was here, he seemed very, very harmless."

Gustavo Perea, who lived next door to Didi Sohus and her renter Chris Chichester in the early 1980s, recalled the young man as an energetic film student who bought him beer and once invited Gus to visit him in the guest house. The visit ended with Chris offering Gus a table that apparently belonged to Didi.

As Gus recalled, Chris lived there long before John and Linda and Linda's cats moved into the main house with Didi.

"I believe he mentioned that he did film. He did tell me he had a cable program," Perea said. "I do believe he mentioned being from England, but I'm not certain."

In late 1984, now well known around town, Chris spoke to the San Marino City Council about their planned purchase of a "Wordplex" word processor. A newspaper article at the time described Chris as a San Marino resident who "teaches computer science at USC."

The article noted that Chris urged the City Council to buy an IBM product instead.

"Don't take my word for it," he implored. "Just ask anyone who follows the industry, and they will tell you that IBM, compatibility, is essential."

He was persuasive. As the article notes, city staff members agreed to scrap their plans for a $7,300 Wordplex device and try out an IBM instead. I think history would side with the decision too.

Given his vantage point from the second floor of his home in early 1985, Perea, who socialized often with Didi, saw only a happy—if full—household at 1920 Lorain Road.

Some, looking from farther away, wondered about John and Linda's future. Others questioned Chris' origin story and his growing presence in San Marino. There were people who knew some of the answers. Elmer and Jean Kelln, an older couple in Riverside County, 70 miles due east of San Marino, knew a lot about Chris. Only they knew him by a different name. Christian Gerhartsreiter.

CHAPTER 8.

ORIGIN STORY

"What is identity?" he asked himself. 'Where
does the act end? Nobody knows."
—**Philip K. Dick,** *Through a Scanner Darkly*, 1977

The town of Bergen in the district of Traunstein in Bavaria,
Germany rates all of a sentence in Wikipedia. It lies on the
northern edge of the Alps and is a mid-point on the highway
between Munich, Germany and Salzburg, Austria.

Not too far away is the hometown of Joseph Ratzinger,
Pope Benedict XVI. Rightly so, I guess, as the region has
long been a stronghold of German Catholicism. But there's
also a dark side to the beautiful and remote region. In the
early 1920s, Bavaria was favored by the fledgling Nazi Party,
and one of the final massacres perpetrated by Adolf Hitler's
feared SS took place just outside the village of Traunstein,
very near Bergen.

Christian Karl Gerhartsreiter was born in a hospital
in neighboring Siegsdorf on February 21, 1961, to Simon
and Irmengard Gerhartsreiter of 19 Banhofstrasse, Bergen.
His father was a housepainter, a struggling artist, and a
bon vivant. His mother, a seamstress, was beautiful, but a
recluse.

Susanne Mittermaier, who lives and works in the
Chiemgau region in which Traunstein, Bergen, and Siegsdorf
lie, says daily life there is an extension of traditions that
stretch back hundreds of years. There are expected behaviors,
expected roles, and rigid castes.

Irmgard, whose maiden name was Huber, grew up in Bergen; so did Simon. Huber's family owned a store that sold household goods. Old timers remember the store—now a café—as "blue shutter-Huber."

"Is it an accident that the [house Christian grew up in] now does also have blue shutters?" Mittermaier said. "It is not a common color for shutters in Bavaria. The custom is to have brown or green shutters."

Before WWII, much of Bavarian society was stratified, with rigid castes. There were landholders, shopkeepers, servants, and peasants and very little mixing. The divisions were apparent everywhere—beer halls and cafes were no exception. A thing as simple as the color of shutters could offset the balance and harmony of consistency and conformity that is so much a part of Bavarian culture.

"Even in church one could see the difference. The places in the benches had signs with the names of the families. And the well-off families had their places in the first rows going backwards by wealth," Mittlemaier related.

"Some of the families have been living in Bergen or at least in the region as long as you can go back in church records. In former times, a man could not move because he was bound (by tradition)."

Like most Bavarian villages, Bergen had its farms. But it was also the site of an important iron mine, Maxhütte, which was in continuous operation from 1562 until it closed in 1881.

"In some of the buildings you can see this history because they are made from iron slag, as for example the railway station of Bergen," Mittlemaier said. "Houses do have special meanings. It is not usual to move very often and…houses are passed from one generation to the next."

Since the closing of Maxhütte, Bergen has relied on tourism. It annually hosts mountain climbers, skiers, and hikers by the thousands.

"Bergen is no high-society village, it is a village more for older people or families, more small guest houses than big hotels," Mittlemaier said.

The entire Chiemgau region is steeped in history. In the 19th Century, King Ludwig II—Ludwig Otto Friedrich Wilhelm, "Mad King Ludwig" had a palace built on the islands of Lake Chiemsee, about 25 miles from Bergen. The Mad King, as he was known, intended to make it a contemporary rival of the palace at Versailles. German historians say he built the 20-room Herrenchiemsee as a symbol of the absolute power of his monarchy. A huge fan of composer Richard Wagner, the king likely inspired Richard Wagner to compose the opera *Tristan and Isolde.*

Wagner described King Ludwig, who ascended the throne at 18, as "so handsome and wise, soulful and lovely, that I fear that his life must melt away in this vulgar world like a fleeting dream of the gods."

Others saw the king as lazy and irresponsible. He squandered his family fortune and is often recalled in modern times as a daydreaming eccentric.

Ultimately Ludwig's craziness wore thin. He was deposed and possibly murdered. Summing up his place in the world the king once said, "I wish to remain an eternal enigma to myself and to others."

The king's palace became the place where Germany was reborn after WWII and it's where its constitution—the Grundgesetz or "ground rules"—was created as well.

The region is also the final resting place of a well-known imposter. Polish-born Franziska Schanzkowska, known to Germans as "Miss Unknown," lived near Bergen in 1927 as a guest of the Duke of Leuchtenberg. Throughout her life, Schanzkowska posed as Anastasia Romanov—last survivor of the Russian ruling family. She left Germany in 1968 and married an American history professor in West Virginia. Upon her death in 1984, Schanzkowska's ashes were scattered on the grounds of a 10th century monastery about 10 miles north of Bergen.

Needless to say, families with homes—like the Gerhartsreiters and the Hubers—have lived in the region for centuries. In the late 1960s and early 1970s, life in Bergen and other Bavarian towns began to change. Suddenly, these places were no longer remote, and the traditions began to evolve and, in some cases, disappear outright.

"A lot of people were able to build their own houses, the farmers had no more servants and had even had to seek outside work," Mittermaier said. "But there were also farmers who got very rich when they were able to sell ground as building places for new houses or streets."

Campaign posters from the 1960s and 1970s show nationalist political candidates were careful to distance themselves from the West German capital in Bonn, while at the same time stressing their Bavarian heritage. At celebrations, the men still wore lederhosen and drank their Lowenbrau from ceramic mugs. But the region was also emerging from the shadow of tradition and the lingering effects of World War II. To celebrate it coming out, West Germany hosted the 1972 Olympics in Munich. It helped erase some of the nativism, and by the late 1970s, politicians in the region largely supported the nation's efforts to form the European Union.

"Unfortunately, we are known for things like Hofbräuhaus, Oktoberfest, beer and *Bretzel*, but the Bavarian culture is an interesting mixture of influences," Mittermaier said.

And a sense of tradition in Christian Gerhartsreiter's home remained strong.

A Christmas card Irmgard sent to friends in 1981 with the printed message "frohe most—Weihnachten und ein gluckliches Neues Jahr"—Merry Christmas and a Happy New Year—features an image of Bergen, covered in snow and nestled against the imposing Alps with the caption.

"Bergen mit Hochfelln" showing off Hochfelln, a 5,400-foot peak with a famous ski resort.

Neighbors remember Irmgard and her sister as different than most—even at a young age.

The Huber sisters were "somewhat weird—overblown in speech and behavior."

Irmgard was a seamstress, known around town for her ability to craft bridal gowns and other formal attire. The art of customer relations was never a strong suit.

"She was a tailor and made my bridal dress as well as the bridal dress of my sister," a longtime resident told Mittermaier. "One day, about 25 years ago, I met her and she told me: Next time you want me to tailor something for you, you can't just come and ask for it, but you have to ask for an appointment."

The behavior wasn't all that out-of-character though.

"She was very full of herself," the neighbor continued, speaking to Mittermaier in a dialect unique to the region. "We got baby-boys about the same time and when the children were about nine months old one day she came and asked me: 'Can your son already walk?' When I said no, she answered: 'Well, there you can see how intelligent my Christian is."

On the other hand, Simon, usually called by his nickname "Simmerl," was much beloved.

"He was a nice man, down to earth, quiet," the friend recalled.

Simon served in the German Army, but upon returning home it was discovered he contracted some sort of lung disease, perhaps tuberculosis. Over time, his condition deteriorated.

He attended the Academy of Arts in Munich. The oldest and most respected art school in Germany, the academy has been influential throughout Europe and the United States for several centuries. He likely passed on his love and knowledge of art to young Christian.

Smitten with the artist and bon vivant, Irmgard told her friends she intended to snag him. When he went to Munich, "Irmgard was running after him and asked (her friends to) pray 'that Simmerl will marry me" Mittermaier said.

Christian was born soon after.

At an early age, Christian's peers thought of him as a weird loner. He once received a toy airplane as a gift and rather than play with it, he placed it on a shelf and forbade other toddlers to so much as touch it.

Very few children who grew up in Bergen wanted to play or talk with Christian.

"He has never been normal," one neighbor told Mittermaier. "They name him as 'Eigenbrötler."

Mittermaier noted that when translated into English, "Eigenbrotler" roughly means Chris was "baking his own bread, a queer fish;" a lone wolf.

"Christian went to elementary school in Bergen for five years and two or three more years in the so-called 'Hauptschule' which is the lowest school form in Bavaria," Mittermaier said.

For the most part, Hauptschule prepares young students for careers—really apprentices—as masons, butchers, salesmen, or hairdressers.

In Germany, the states determine a student's qualifications for secondary education. Students of the highest caliber qualify for "Gymnasium"—or college prep. Ranking between Hauptschule and Gymnasium is Realschule, which emphasizes office and banking and technical careers.

"In Realschule the focus is on subjects as mathematics, accounting, stenography, and typewriting," Mittermaier said, "I'm sure his mother would have liked if he went to Gymnasium."

About that time Christian's school acquaintances noticed that he took an interest in reading "paragraphs" or law texts, Mittermaier said. He also took to riding a moped around town.

"When he was a teenage-boy, about 13 or 14, the other children believed Christian to be weird as he was always reading 'paragraphs', obviously books with juristic topics."

While Christian had his mind set on bigger and better, his younger brother, Alexander, born in 1973, has never left town and refuses to talk about Christian.

In 2008, Alexander worked in Siegsdorf for the Adelholzener, a spring water company not unlike Arrowhead or Sparkletts. The shop where he is employed lies less than a mile east of his family home.

Depending on whom you ask, Christian was either the poster boy for the ill effects of bullying, or a devious troublemaker. I've heard him called everything from a "simple-minded Bavarian peasant" to a "typical German prick/asshole."

Take your pick.

Dateline summed up in about 20 seconds what reporter Mike Taibbi and producer Liz Brown learned from locals who knew Gerhartsreiter as a child.

The script from a 2010 broadcast went like this:

> Eighty-nine-year-old Luise Huber owns a little store in Siegsdorf, the town where Christian Karl Gerhartsreiter was born in 1961 to a seamstress and a painter. It's a friendly, comfortable place… but apparently, he didn't think so.

> Huber remembers Gerhartsreiter as a child always thinking he was better than everyone else. He picked fights with his friends, she said, berating one friend in her own store.

> Huber: (In German) All of a sudden Christian shouted at him, "Stay out, you dog!"

An elderly woman told one writer that she thought young Christian had "discipline issues" growing up in the small village. She said that, as a teen, Gerhartsreiter "had to be different" from other village youngsters in clothes, hairstyle, and attitude.

Alternatively, Christian was described as "weird", "clever", "well-read", well-spoken mama's boy who once came to school in a business suit and spent countless hours watching American films while dreaming of his escape and practicing the art of fakery.

He spent time in a garage—or shop—attached to the back of the family house. There he repaired radios and listened to the Voice of America, and practiced his English.

Childhood friend, Thomas Schweiger said that, as a youngster, Christian loved to adopt different identities, once posing as a millionaire from Holland in a prank call to a government office.

"Although the clerk was skeptical, Christian persuaded him, his friend said. "He really played this role perfect," Schweiger said.

Other friends recalled the young man coming up with extreme excuses for tardiness at school or being downright mean to teachers—even blowing pepper in one's face when he got angry.

The Bavarian dialect favored in Bergen can pose its problems for translators, Mittermaier noted. She believes that a quote attributed to Christian's father—about his wandering son—is an example.

"The father used to say 'Christian ist ein verrückter Hund,' which some say means his son is a mad dog," she said. "It doesn't mean that. It's actually a compliment and an expression of appreciation for a person who does crazy, not common things, or has new ideas, running against the mainstream, expressing his own character, daring to do something, but always in a positive way."

Christian's goal was to get the hell out.

The opportunity presented itself on a rainy Bavarian road in the form of a tourist couple from the similarly tiny, but less isolated, town of Loma Linda in Riverside County, California.

During the late summer of 1978, Elmer and Jean Kelln traveled through Europe en route to Africa where their daughter lived and was about to give birth to their first grandchild. Elmer, Canadian by birth, German by heritage, loved all things Deutsch and recalled the trip as an opportunity to connect with his heritage.

One afternoon as the couple drove along the autobahn connecting Munich to Berchtesgaden and Salzberg they were caught in a massive downpour and sometime around 4 p.m. decided to pull off the road and find a place to eat and spend the night.

"We saw this kid hitchhiking at the off ramp," Elmer recalled as he sat across the kitchen table from me on a warm summer morning. The couple invited me over to discuss the wild tale of the kid they met along the side of the road all those years ago. Back then he was known simply as Christian Gerhartsreiter. He was 17 when they first met.

Among the mementoes of a life lived full and well, Jean keeps a plastic container full of Christian Gerhartsreiter memorabilia. The box is stacked with news articles, documents, old photographs, and even a Christmas card from Chris' mom.

In conversation, Elmer—a short and solid man with a fringe of snow-white hair ringing his head from ear to ear and a perpetual twinkle in his eye—and Jean—a happy redhead who looks much younger than her years, —nearly always complete the other's sentence. Elmer had been a practicing dentist in Canada. After 10 years of cracking open patients' mouths, applying the drill, or dispensing advice about hygiene, Elmer realized he needed something more.

"I couldn't imagine the thought of spending the rest of my life in the same office, staring out the same window and seeing the same people day after day," he said.

Eventually the couple and their children found their way to Loma Linda. Elmer began teaching. Eventually, he became the dean of dentistry at Loma Linda University. Elmer and Jean spent their summers traveling. In another box in another part of the house, Elmer keeps his perfectly typed curriculum vitae, which lists his educational background and summarizes a list of lectures he gave at various dental get-togethers. The Kellns live by the Midwest Canadian values with which they were raised. Folks are welcome in their home and treated like family.

"Do you plan to stay for lunch?" he asked me as we settled in to talk about Chris. "I hope you are not a vegetarian. We're having stew."

"Thanks, I'd love it," I replied. "Back to Chris; what do you remember most about him when you first met?"

"He was soaking wet by the time he got over to us," Jean said.

The trade-off was this. The Kellns needed a place to eat and a place to stay for the night. Chris needed a ride. He said he had spent the day as a tour guide in the larger Bavarian town of Rosenheim and was now headed home. His English, which Elmer said was spoken with an almost Oxford accent, was flawless.

"Every syllable just right," Elmer said, faint traces of his Canadian accent still noticeable—even after decades in Southern California.

As for a place to get a bite and settle in for the night?

"He simply insisted we come and meet his parents and stay at their house there in Bergen. At the time we didn't know why, but I suppose he was beginning to think in term of setting himself for leaving Germany and wanting to make connections."

When Chris found out the Kellns were from California, he got nosy asking questions as the trio made their way to the Gerhartsreiter home at 19 Banhofstrasse.

Nestled in the foothills of the Alps, The Kellns saw Bergen in Southern Germany through the eyes of tourists. Families grew colorful flowers on their second story balconies. Windows were typically framed with thick wooden shutters.

They saw the roofs built with steep slopes to keep winter snow from piling too deep. The Gerhartsreiter home, built in 1926, is no different. A two-story Bavarian classic, the Kellns noticed that the exterior windows were framed by unusual blue shutters.

Follow Banhofstrasse south from A8 through Bergen, past the Gerhartsreiter home, and in a matter of minutes you will stumble upon the 16th century iron foundry, Maxhütte.

Today Maxhütte has been transformed into the Blauer Anger historical museum which promises tourists visiting its website, "Here you can see the past of our village and the way of living of our ancestors. The name derives from the ancient name for Bergen "Am Blauen Anger" (On the blue meadow)."

Perhaps it explained the blue shutters, but it represented something Christian wanted to get away from.

As Elmer Kelln saw it, young Christian was an Anglophile and wanted nothing to do with Germany, past or present.

The rainstorm subsided about the time the Kellns and their teenaged passenger pulled up to the Gerhartsreiter house. Chris's father was on a ladder fixing rain gutters. He didn't come down and didn't say much. Inside the house, Chris' mother, Irmgard, described by Jean as a blonde "beautiful lady" and Chris' brother Alexander, described by Elmer as a typical little boy, were happy to receive their American guests.

"We hadn't eaten yet and we wanted to go to a restaurant, and I invited them to go with us. They turned us down, but Chris went with us. They insisted we come back and stay overnight."

Jean pointed to her photos of that night. A nice-looking young blond man, Chris wore a white pull-over sweater over an open-collared white shirt. His hair fell nearly to his collar. Chris didn't smile as he bent his right elbow, made a fist, and bent his head sideways. Peering out from behind an oversized pair of wire-framed glasses, Chris' blue eyes appear intently focused.

Another photo shows a couple of lederhosen-clad man playing accordions in a corner of the town hofbrauhaus. As Elmer later recalled, it seemed to him a typical Bavarian scene on a typical Bavarian summer night.

"I ate it all in because my mother was Bavarian," he said.

Elmer said he learned that night that Chris never allowed himself to be candidly photographed and he never smiled. Instead, he insisted on setting a pose. It took just about a minute to set up the shot. He also discovered Chris had a pretty bad temper.

I was sitting on the outside of our booth, and I had on western boots, Elmer said. "Some total stranger comes over and asks if I'm a cowboy.

Chris got steamed at the affront.

"He really raked that guy over the coals," Elmer said. "I saw at that moment that Chris could get really angry. I saw that he had a temper that could switch from nice guy to bad guy."

When dinner was over, Gerhartsreiter and the Kellns headed back to the Gerhartsreiter family home on Banhofstrasse for the night. Chris continued to ask questions. He was downright persistent.

What was the exact address of the Kelln's home? How many children did they have? What about the other family?

What sort of cars did they drive? What was their phone number? What did Elmer do for a living?

Once they settled into their room in the rear of the Gerhartsreiter house, they realized it was Chris' father Simon's studio—he was a painter. The room was littered with tools and other implements of Simon's trade. Although Elmer got comfortable right away, Jean felt uneasy.

"All night I was up," she said. "It was something inside, call it woman's intuition. I did not feel comfortable around him—around Chris. It was just a feeling I had."

Elmer: "He was very persistent in getting information from us."

Jean: "Maybe that's why I was uncomfortable. They had our telephone, address, everything."

As the couple retired for the evening, Chris paid them a visit. To let them know there would be a continental breakfast of rolls and coffee in the morning.

In the morning, dressed and ready to continue to Bertchesgarden, Elmer and Jean met with Chris, Irmagard, and little Alexander one last time. They ate, exchanged pleasantries, and wished each other good luck.

"She said, "Maybe you'll get a Christmas card. And later on, we did."

"That was it and we were on our way," Jean said. "We never gave it a thought that we would ever see him again.

CHAPTER 9.

COMING TO AMERICA

You may not be lookin' for the promised land
But you might find it anyway
Under one of those old familiar names...
—Living in America, Performed by James Brown,
written by Dan Hartman and Charlie Midnight

After saying goodbye to Elmer and Jean, it didn't take long for Chris to get the paperwork he needed to get from Bergen to the United States. According to immigration documents, he arrived in December 1978.

His brother remembered the moment vividly.

"I think Germany was too small for him," Alexander said. "He wanted to live in the big country and maybe get famous."

Elmer remembered getting a phone call from the young man almost as soon as Kelln got back to California from that 1978 European adventure.

"All of a sudden the phone rang," Elmer recalled. "A voice said, 'This is Chris. I'm in the United States...I'm in Connecticut and I'm working as a ski instructor. We thought nothing of it. One thing we did not ask him, which we should have, was how did you get the paperwork to come here?"

In spite of the enthusiasm, Chris was mysterious about his situation.

"He made hay getting over here that's for sure," Jean recalled. "We said, 'It's good to hear from you. No doubt if you ever come out this way give us a call.' He would call us but never leave a phone number. He never said where he was staying or anything about his goings on."

Over the years since his arrival, Chris' travels can be well pieced together. With a tourist visa in hand, Chris arrived in Meriden, Connecticut in the fall of 1978.

He hooked up with a Connecticut teen who had been backpacking in Germany that summer. Peter Roccopriore graduated Middlesex High School in 1977, he was a musician, a motorcyclist, and loved adventure.

Gerhartsreiter showed up on his doorstep one morning and for a few weeks, complaining about the length of time U.S. students spent in the classroom: As far as the German visitor was concerned, it wasn't enough.

Eventually, Gerhartsreiter placed a want ad in local newspapers identifying himself as a German exchange student in search of living arrangements. Soon Chris was living with Gwen Savio and her children in Berlin, Connecticut.

Chris obtained a social security number about the same time. Even though he had graduated the German equivalent of high school, in January 1979, Chris enrolled at Berlin High School as an exchange student senior.

His hosts, the Savios, were charmed at first, but soon Chris wore thin. He told them he was the son of a wealthy German industrialist. He implied he was of royal heritage. He questioned their taste, spoke disdainfully about what he insinuated was their poverty, and laughed at what he called their lack of manners.

"We hung out a lot together," Ed Savio would later recall. "I liked Chris. I was a sophomore; he was a senior. I had dreams of getting out of my small town.

"Chris and I would stay up late at night and talking about making it big. He told me he came from a family that was well off. His father was a parts supplier for Mercedes Benz. And he said his mother was a housewife."

Ed said Chris was "really great to me. He and I got along really well, but he wasn't very nice to my mom; he was kind of rude to my mom and to the rest of my siblings."

There was nothing about Chris that said he was an American kid. He and Ed practiced Americanisms together, so that Chris' accent wouldn't be so pronounced. In so many words, Chris would tell Ed that he wanted to be an American. Chris took to wearing tight jeans that were in style because he wanted to make it big and be assimilated into the American lifestyle.

Ed remembered that Chris would also gauge his impact on others. And he would adjust the tone or words to fit the audience.

"If the listener didn't respond well, he would notice it and he would stop," Ed said.

"He would also say something to one person in a certain way and to another person a different way. He liked or gravitated toward what he thought was the finer society in our small town. In terms of when he would tell stories, there were people he just dismissed that he didn't feel were worthy of his time. He would be very short with them. If he was trying to impress somebody, he would start to tell them a story. The more they bought into it, he would feed on it."

***

Chris also had weird mood swings and disdainful reactions to things and people he didn't think were on his level. One minute he could be extremely fawning and kind to someone and in the next minute immediately dismissive of another person who didn't meet his expectations.

Some of the small-town folk loved to hear stories about the outside world and how big it was. Chris would embellish his stories so that the audience got exactly what it wanted to hear—even if it wasn't wholly true.

The Savios were decidedly middle class. Not up to snuff as far as Chris was concerned. As a result, he was especially mean to Ed's mother and one of his sisters, a young woman the family had nicknamed "Snooks."

As part of his English immersion program, Chris sat around watching a lot of television—especially *Gilligan's Island*—and would spend hours mimicking the upper crust accent of the millionaire character, Thurston Howell III. Eventually he wouldn't eat Gwen's food, implying it was beneath him.

Ed Savio said that once he was comfortable, Chris began to act out.

"I recall him thinking he's better than the rest of us," Savio said. "I recall him telling stories about having servants growing up and like that."

"He just thought he was better than anybody else and he could do anything, and there was no way to stop him," Ed's mother, Gwen, added.

Gwen recalled Chris as someone who thought he could do anything and get away with it. To her, he was nothing more than a jerk or a crumb.

Chris' run as a guest of the Savios ended abruptly in the winter of 1981.

The last straw was a fight over the television between Chris and Snooks on a snowy, cold day. Chris tricked her into going out of the house. Then, he locked the doors, leaving the young girl shivering on the doorstep for hours.

It was the last straw. When Gwen arrived home from work, she threw Chris out.

Chris bounced from place to place after that, but eventually graduated with his classmates in late spring of 1979.

Next stop for the young German who desperately wanted to be American was the most German place imaginable in

America, Eastern Wisconsin. Ethnographers who study such things note that the shoreline of Lake Michigan from Kenosha, Wisconsin north to Green Bay has the highest concentration of Germans anywhere in the United States.

Elaine Jersild met Chris at the University of Wisconsin, Milwaukee in 1981. By then, he had changed his last name from Gerhartsreiter to simply Gerhart.

"I thought he was attending the University. He was on campus whenever I saw him and I thought he was in the theater or film department," she said. "He came up to a friend and myself and asked if we would want to see a theater production for free."

Chris didn't star, direct, or produce. He was an usher.

He told Jersild that someone named Chichester was a distant ancestor. Did he say he was from Germany or England? She couldn't remember.

"He had a string of about eight names that were part of the family tree. He flashed them in front of my face and crumpled up the paper. I really didn't see him interact with anybody else," Elaine said.

The couple dated that fall through spring of 1981. Chris said he was going to go to California to pursue an internship at USC with George Lucas, the director. Before leaving, Chris asked Elaine to marry him. He wanted a green card. He didn't offer any compensation, but Elaine didn't want to get involved in that way. So, she suggested that Chris marry her sister, Amy.

They married in May.

Chris' best man was classmate Todd Lassa, now an editor with *MotorTrend* magazine in Detroit. Lassa told an Associated Press reporter that he and Chris hung out during the few months Chris was in Milwaukee. "Nothing special."

"Then at one point he asked me to be a witness in his wedding in Madison, Wisconsin," Lassa said. "I don't remember him very well, but I do remember that I found him a little bit strange. First, strange that he would ask someone like me—who he barely knew—to be the witness in his wedding. He was just kind of an odd person."

The nuptials put Chris solidly in line for a green card.

"We didn't remain friends for very long, probably weeks," Lassa recalled. "I remember I didn't trust everything he was saying."

Green card eligibility in hand, Chris split for California.

The sisters never saw Chris again, although Elaine did receive a postcard from Cornwall, England that had been signed by the young man. The front of the postcard depicted Queen Elizabeth and her husband, Prince Philip, alongside some beefeaters outside Windsor Castle.

The card said something like, "England is great. It's sad we can't see each other." Chris also mentioned he was doing some writing and had gotten involved in the Church of England, and he was asking the Queen to change some law or another. He told the woman he was teaching Sunday school and would soon be in Africa teaching children.

"He said his family had lived in Africa and that the exchange was such that you could live quite well and have servants quite easily," she recalled.

Although the card was postmarked Cornwall, there was no way to respond to it.

Periodically, during his adventures, Chris would call the Kellns. As always, he was full of stories. Each time they talked, he explained how he now held some important position or another as he moved up the employment ladder.

"He would call us, but he would never leave a phone number." Jean said. "He never gave us a number. He never said where he was staying or too much about his goings on."

Shortly after arriving in Milwaukee, Chris telephoned the Kellns and spoke to Elmer.

"Isn't that a coincidence," Elmer recalled telling his young friend. "I have to go to a meeting at Marquette University. I must have told him what month and so forth and he knew that."

When Elmer arrived in town, he checked into his hotel and attended his conference. Midway through the first day, the Loma Linda professor received a page.

"Who in the world would page me?" he thought. "No one knows I'm here." Here it was Chris. He was in Milwaukee. He came to the hotel, and we visited for about half an hour. I went back to the meeting, and he went back his way.

Soon after Chris arrived in California, he was knocking on Elmer and Jean's door. He always gave Jean the "creeps."

On the other hand, Elmer and the couple's children were OK with Chris—even if he was a little eccentric.

"I don't get the creeps, I'm well-seasoned. I'm an old moose hunter," Elmer said.

Chris paid frequent visits to the Kellns home—about 60 miles east of Los Angeles. He ate Sunday dinner with the family and back in LA sometimes babysat their daughter. Always hungry when he arrived, the tiny, bespectacled German spun tales of his new life in the movie business.

On walks with Elmer, Chris would get expansive.

"He talked about having too much, like a brand-new Chrysler that talked to you when you pushed the buttons on the door.

The Chrysler never showed up at those Sunday dinners.

In reality, "Chris had a small Plymouth," Elmer said. "I think he drove the Plymouth all the way from Wisconsin or further.

The little German also bragged incessantly about the magnificent house in which he was now living.

"We'd mostly talk about his side of the field which was film noir—black and white. He'd throw stuff at me, and you'd have to say, "That guy's going fast. He's climbing that ladder too fast. Something's wrong here. Pretty soon he was telling us he lived in this fine house in San Marino."

Chris frequently shared scripts with the Kellns' son, Wayne.

"One time he told us, 'You know I collected all the film fluid and sold all the silver and made $5,000 and that's the point where I knew this guy had a black side," Elmer said.

There was a time when the Kellns believed Chris was floating from house to house. As they understood it, he lived in Pasadena for a while, then in Glendale.

"He'd call and say, 'Can I come out?' He'd come out and spend the day and have dinner with us, our children, and their kids," Jean recalled.

"He was always hungry," Elmer added, finishing Jean's sentence.

During one visit, Chris explained that being a professional in Hollywood meant he had to change his name.

"He sat right here and got the phone book out," Elmer said, pointing at the family dinner table. "It made no difference what name we gave him he said, 'No. It wouldn't work.' Chris said the name we gave him would have to be a sophisticated British name. It had to have a little bit of a tag like he was royalty."

Jean picked up Elmer's story.

***

"His name was Gerhartsreiter, so I said to him why don't you take either one of those names, you know something like Chris Reiter or Chris Gerhard?"

It bothered Jean that Chris wanted to be somebody different. Elmer said, "Don't worry; it's what they all do in Hollywood."

Chris ultimately let the Kellns know he had settled in San Marino, a wealthy suburb just east of Los Angeles known for its high rollers in the finance, publishing, and entertainment industries.

"When he was living in San Marino, he finally did give us his phone number," Elmer said. "It so happened that I was invited to speak at the San Gabriel Dental Society one afternoon. I was done early you know and I had about three hours to kill so I phoned him up."

Chris was home. He gave Elmer directions to Didi Sohus' tiny ranch house. When Elmer arrived, Chris took him inside an even smaller house out back.

John, Linda, and Didi were home. Linda was probably working on a painting. When Elmer asked why Chris wouldn't give him a tour of the larger home in front, Chris had an excuse.

"He said, 'They are doing some decorating,' Elmer said. "I began to go, 'Show me your new Chrysler."

Chris couldn't show anything.

"Well, no,' he said, 'that would be very inconvenient," Elmer recalled. "Then and there I realized everything he told me was a lie. This man was living a double life."

Chris also mentioned to Elmer, he had settled on a new name. From now on he would be Christopher Chichester.

CHAPTER 10.

DANGEROUS VISIONS

"Science Fiction was escape literature. We were
escaping. We were turning from such practical
problems as stickball and homework and fist fights
in order to enter a never never land of population
explosions, rocket ships, lunar exploration, atomic
bombs, radiation sickness, and polluted atmosphere.
Wasn't that great?
But now you can colonize the Moon inside the
good, grey pages of the New York Times; and
not as a piece of science fiction at all, but as a
sober analysis of a hardheaded situation."
**—Isaac Asimov, *Dangerous Visions*,
edited by Harlan Ellison, 1967**

Like the owner of any small business, when Lydia Marano
left town, she wanted to make sure her livelihood was in
capable hands. In Marano's case, that meant entrusting
Dangerous Visions, her Sherman Oaks bookstore, to Linda
Sohus, who had been working there for nearly three years.

Not quite a newlywed, Linda took on the task, agreeing
to mind the store for a long Lincoln's birthday weekend in
early February 1985.

That Sunday, Feb. 10, 1985, Lydia needed to cash a
check. She stopped by her store and discovered it hadn't
been opened. In fact, there was no sign that Linda had been
around the day before either. Sure, Linda had a habit of being
late to everything. But not this late. And not for this long.

Marano was ticked off. Just when she thought she could take a breather from the day-to-day grind of running a popular bookstore; she had to confront the fact that her best employee, a woman whom she considered a friend, couldn't pull her own weight.

"She was the most trustworthy person I had working for me," Marano said.

Marano, a tiny dynamo whose very demeanor dares anyone to speak ill of her long-lost friend, is at heart an entrepreneur who seems expert at catering to some narrow niche markets. She has several blogs and is an artist in her own right.

In 1981, Marano and science fiction author, Arthur Byron Cover, founded Dangerous Visions in Sherman Oaks, a community in the San Fernando Valley directly north of downtown Los Angeles and about 20 miles west of San Marino. Together, they specialized in stocking and selling new, used, and rare science fiction, fantasy, and horror.

Website "Broad Universe" noted in a March 2003 post that: "Along the way, (Marano and Cover) hosted hundreds of autograph parties, got married, and raised several fine dogs. The current cat count is five. Art had a number of novels published, hosted a radio show on Pacifica's KPFK, and taught writing. Lydia's written animation for a number of studios including Disney, had two young adult books published, and taught herself html. At the end of 1999, Art and Lydia began Babbage Press and have published 11 science fiction, fantasy, and horror books to date."

Lydia and Cover also did some acting. Each secured bit parts in a 1989 Z-grade horror flick titled *The Laughing Dead.*

The movie follows the exploits of a defrocked priest on a tour of ancient Mexican ruins. Scenes include ritual Aztec human sacrifice, decapitation, zombies, and a weird mix of sex and gore. By the movie's end, 12 have died in the most awful of manners. The flick has a cult following among horror fans as it was never released in the United States and is considered the best "lost" horror film ever made.

The *Laughing Dead* episode was well after Linda started at Dangerous Visions in 1982—nearly half a decade after she disappeared. Linda's friends, at least those who knew her since childhood, said Dangerous Visions was the perfect outlet for someone fascinated by science fiction and fantasy. Linda loved both and Lydia's bookstore was the center of the universe for anyone interested in the genres.

Authors like Harlan Ellison, who gave permission to Marano to name the store after his legendary 1967 collection of short stories, often dropped by. So, too, did *X Files* creator Chris Carter. Ellison once wrote a short story titled "Objects in the Mirror of Desire are Closer than they Appear" as he sat by the store's front window.

The idea for the story, which later appeared in a 1999 collection of horror stories, came from Carter who gave Ellison a small piece of paper that said: "The 100-year-old pregnant corpse."

Science fiction writer Jaime Todd Rubin described it.

"Ellison sat in that bookstore window for several hours tapping away at his manual typewriting and taping up pages as they came out. By the time he was finished, he's written a story."

If you think about it long enough, Dangerous Visions is a great name for a science fiction bookstore. The Ellison-edited collection of the same name contains some of the first published stories from science fiction's New Wave. The 300-plus page anthology, which in paperback sold for $1.50 includes stories from Philip K. Dick, Larry Niven, Poul Anderson, and Lester del Rey—some of the leading authors of the genre.

By all accounts, Dangerous Visions was a lively, fun place to be for a science fiction fan. And sometimes the fans got to work there. Among Linda's co-workers was Galen Tripp, who said he was often paid in books.

"I would come in to the DV Bookstore on a Thursday afternoon and do a shift-change with my fellow employee. The woman I took over for each Thursday was none other than Linda Mayfield," Tripp wrote in a blog post. "She was a science fiction fan (and horse enthusiast) who I had met first at the Los Angeles Science Fantasy Society. Linda was an artist who did artwork under the name "Cody." She had some professional success as an artist. She told me once that she sold (at least) one small illustration to *The New Yorker* magazine for $700. Most of her success was in fandom."

While Marano was ticked off by her missing employee, Linda's sister, Katherine Mayfield of Marina Del Rey, was scared. So was her best friend, Sue Coffman. It wasn't like Linda to disappear.

The cops wouldn't take a report from Coffman, so on Feb. 8, Kathy called the San Marino Police Department to report her sister had vanished. Rookie Officer Thomas LeVeque performed a records check on the missing woman.

LeVeque, tall, broad-shouldered, and good natured, got some drivers' license information, ran a couple of other reports on Linda, and met with his sergeant in the San Marino Police Department's lunchroom.

At 9 p.m. LeVeque stepped out of a patrol car and approached the front door of Didi Sohus' home at 1920 Lorain Road. Walking up the driveway, he spotted an older BMW with a blue and yellow California license plate 093XJH.

Didi answered the door. LeVeque couldn't tell if she was drunk, but explained he was there because Linda's sister had filed a missing persons report. Didi wasn't cooperative. She told LeVeque that Linda and her son John were "on a top-secret mission in Paris, France."

She had a source for the information, but there was very little she could say because it could "endanger" the couple." Didi told LeVeque she could get in touch with Linda and Johnny but would not reveal how.

"She said she had written to them, and she could contact them," LeVeque said. "And the unknown source could reach them too." Beyond that Didi wasn't authorized to tell LeVeque—or anyone else for that matter—any other details.

"She basically reiterated for me that she was not going to give me any further information in a nutshell," LeVeque said.

He thanked Didi. Even though the circumstances were unique and unusual, he took what she said seriously. It didn't prevent him from doing a little follow up. LeVeque went back to the San Marino police station. He ran John Sohus and the plate on the BMW.

Sohus came back kind of suspicious. He had a suspended driver's license. Other than that, his birthday was listed as 12/20/57; height 5' 6"; weight 150. Info on the car came back weird too. It was registered to a Robert T. or Bette Brown of Canterbury Road, about a mile east on the edge of San Marino.

An hour later, LeVeque was on his way home. His report wouldn't be complete until April.

Although she didn't say anything to LeVeque, Didi was worried too. She reached out to John's longtime friend, Patrick Rayermann, for answers.

"At first I'm sure she asked me if they had gone to Hawaii," Rayermann said.

He thought back to his last get together with John and Linda during the final weekend of January 1985.

"I can't prove it without a time machine, but I'm fairly confident we went to dinner and after walked over to a bowling alley to play arcade games," he said.

Rayermann said there was tension between John and Linda over Didi, the oddball renter in the back house, and the couple's living arrangement.

"Linda didn't want to remain in that home for a long period. John didn't want to leave his mother in the lurch for a long period of time without someone there to care for her.

I saw in that that Linda was more motivated to establish a new house than John was. He had made a commitment to live with Linda but did not want to leave his mother without some appropriate degree of assistance. I don't have a sense it was a fracture point between them.

"I think both of them really did want to be living outside of her house, I mean, they are a young couple. Do you really want to be intimate with one of your parents in the next room? No. Give me a break."

There was no mention of a secret mission, and they didn't say anything about Chris.

"John and Linda were a young couple; they were in love with each other. They didn't have a reason to talk to me about somebody that was boarding with his mom," Rayermann said. "They were talking about their plans for the future. Other than that, we talked about science fiction and fantasy and some of Linda's aspirations," Rayermann said.

Regardless of the tension stemming from Didi and Linda's inability to get along, the three laughed, talked, and bounced from game to game, playing *Pong*, *Missile Command*, and *Pac-Man* before calling it a night.

"Then we came back to my house, and we said goodnight."

Didi continued to check in with Rayermann, hoping beyond hope that he would have heard from John. By the third phone call, Didi wanted to know if Rayermann thought John may have been recruited by the government for a special job.

"She asked me, 'Do you think John went off on some secret mission?' I knew that John's father had done something for the government that he mostly couldn't talk about. But John had never intimated a desire to do something like that. He never even expressed an interest in it.

"Her question just seemed like it's a little over the top and on the other hand I don't know what's happened to John. And, by this time I'm a little concerned too. All of a sudden, it's not like they went away for a couple of weeks on a honeymoon."

The idea that John had become some sort of government spy didn't sit well with Rayermann, who by late 1985 was on his way toward directing the Army's return to space.

"John never sat and talked to me about going into the CIA or becoming a spy. He talked to me about being a computer programmer and working at JPL. I would think that if he had an aspiration like that—we knew each other well enough over 15 years—that I would have had an awareness. Most people who do go to work for those organizations, do talk about it; they don't talk about what they do. And if you know them before they go, like I knew John, they talk about it. He never did. John liked Star Trek. Sure, he may have seen all the James Bond 007 movies, but he never played spy."

Linda—on the other hand—told a variety of people she planned to leave town for a few days.

The art collector who was so anxious to buy an original Cody painting during Worldcon several months earlier in Anaheim was beginning to have his doubts he would ever see the piece he commissioned. Linda was apparently avoiding his calls. And he was anxious about artwork he paid for, which had not been completed or shipped.

As February approached, the collector suddenly felt as if he was getting the cold shoulder from the aspiring artist.

"There was a period of three or four days, where I couldn't get through to anybody and so it was just like oh great, is she a flake? I called over to Dangerous Visions to see if she had been at work. The person I talked to there said, 'I think she was here yesterday.'

"I waited until I got home, then around 8 p.m. or something like that on January 30 or January 31 or the first or second of February, I called and talked to her."

The collector remembers the conversation in detail.

"I said, 'Hi. Linda?'

"And she said something like, 'yeah.' She basically said, 'I'm sorry I didn't get back to you, things are just kind of crazy here; my husband's gotten a job offer in New York and it looks like I'm going to have to move and I'm just running around like crazy.'

"I said, 'A job in New York?'"

"Yeah, some classified thing for the government."

"Are you able to say?"

"Something about satellites."

"That's cool. So, are you going to be able to do your artwork?"

"It's just, I've got to get to the east coast. Once I get settled in, I'll get you this commission."

"Good luck with everything."

"She sounded like exactly the way people do when they are in the process of moving: anxious; a little excited about it. She sounded frustrated about the fact she was going to have to move all of a sudden. I could hear that she was anxious and frustrated."

Linda also mentioned the possibility of a job to her best friend, Sue Coffman.

Even though they bought a new truck, John and Linda struggled with money troubles; Coffman knew that. She also knew John and Linda's plan was to get out on their own and away from Didi.

"I don't believe he had a steady job at the time. He was into computers and wanted to get into the computer gaming industry so that they could live and get out of that house," Coffman said. After the San Gabriel art show in January, it "seemed like they were finally taking off."

Linda also told Coffman about the exciting possibility of a "government" job for John back east. The best part? There was a job possibly waiting for Linda as well. She said the couple planned to take a trip to New York but would return in time to drive out to Phoenix for a sci-fi convention, the annual Phoenix LepreCon in March.

"We'll be back in time for that," Linda told Sue.

Linda's mom, who felt San Marino officials "blew off" her concerns about Linda, really wished someone would listen to her.

She, too, heard about a possible job in Connecticut.

"She came to the house to ask if she could leave the truck for two weeks," Susan said. "I didn't allow her to leave the truck there. At the time it wasn't convenient to move it back and forth for street cleaning.

"They were going to Connecticut," she continued. "John supposedly had a job offer there and they were going." Linda promised when she got back, she would take her mom to see *Cats* at the Shubert Theater.

Linda's mom noted her daughter never traveled too far from California, never owned a passport, and together her income from the bookstore and John's from a part-time clerk's gig at JPL didn't amount to much.

Sometime after that, Linda took her six cats to a local kennel and paid for two weeks' board.

And then John and Linda were gone.

Soon after LeVeque completed his report on the case in early April, San Marino officer Lili Hadsell paid the first of several visits to Didi's house. Mostly to reassure the woman, who was becoming increasingly distraught.

Two weeks later Linda's mom and sister received a post card—from Paris.

So did Lydia Marano.

Sue Coffman got one too. All three were postmarked April 29, 1985. All three were written in a loopy but precise cursive style that appears feminine.

"Hi Sue —
Kinda missed New York (oops) —
But this can be lived with —
John + Linda"

"Hi Lydia —
Not quite New
York, but not bad —
Linda + John"

Lydia's had an oddly dark rendering of a steel engraving titled "Palais De Justice et Ste Chapelle, Au XIVème Siècle"

Sue Coffman and the Mayfields received images of the Eiffel Tower.

Linda's mother and sister thought the card was an odd gesture and both were puzzled by the postscript "Guess I need a map."

"I wasn't sure it came from her," Linda's mother said. "I looked at it and looked at it and thought, 'it doesn't say anything.' I was puzzled. It was just a comment on the card."

Hadsell said she looked at the cards and thought after a comparison that the cursive looked nothing like Linda's handwriting.

Didi called the cops. She called her neighbors. She called Rayermann. She probably spoke to her "secret source" but as the spring of 1985 drew to a close, she was no nearer to an answer.

Now, Didi and Chris were the only residents of 1920 Lorain Road. Signs of John and Linda were everywhere, but they were nowhere.

Chris, for the most part, abandoned the BMW he bought from Bob Brown and took to driving John and Linda's Nissan pickup.

He even hosted a couple of parties in the main house.

Didi, meanwhile, sank deeper into alcohol, cigarettes, and a deep funk that kept her in a bathrobe and confined to her bedroom most days waiting for word from Johnny and Linda.

CHAPTER 11.

CHURCH CONNECTIONS

"We live in a small town in Southern California called
San Marino. I love this town, and not just because
it's the kind of place where people still smile at each
other but because it hasn't changed much in the past
twenty-five years. And since I'm not a guy who's
big on change, this town fits me like a glove."
—Steve Martin as George Banks in *Father*
***of the Bride*, Touchstone Pictures, 1991**

As the months wore on, the whole Chris experience was
beginning to wear as thin as knockoff designer wear on
the rack in a Pasadena thrift store. He continued to attend
weekly Bible study and was a regular on Saturdays at the
Church of Our Savior Men's Club. But, as parishioner Dan
Banks would later point out, Chris was always borrowing
money and never paying it back.

Plus, Chris couldn't keep away from the young girls,
Banks recalled. He practically stalked Dan's teenaged
daughter and got a little peevish when Dan told him to back
off. Not that it stopped the strangeness; Chris would find
other ways to push the buttons.

Dan also noticed that Chris had a bit of a temper.

One Sunday after services, Dan arrived home and was
pulling his lawn mower out, when he noticed Chris, in a suit
and tie, walking to Didi's home on Lorain Road.

"Here comes Chris in his 'Rockefeller suit.' That's what I
called it anyway," Banks said. "It was a suit he always wore.

Anyway, as he was coming home from church a neighbor's dog ran out and bit him on the back of the leg."

Banks said the dog never bit anyone and was a mostly docile creature.

"Chris was very angry. He was livid. The dog tore his pants," Banks recalled. "He yelled at the owner, 'Don't you know who I am? I will sue you."

The neighbor was fairly concerned when Chris got done berating her and her beastly mutt. Chris' threats were as empty as his wallet, Banks said.

"There was no way he was going to sue anyone."

Once or twice, Banks, who lived around the coroner from Didi's place, saw Chris and John Sohus together. He remembered John as "kind of chubby and very shy."

In fact, the last time Banks saw Sohus and Chichester, it appeared as if the young sci-fi fan was giving Chris a lift in his new Nissan pick-up.

Follow the San Bernardino Freeway east for 60 miles out of L.A. and eventually you will reach the edge of the desert. Just before you get there, you'll pass through the old citrus community of Redlands and its neighbor, Loma Linda.

It's an enclave of Seventh Day Adventists and home of the internationally renowned Loma Linda University Medical Center. Elmer Kelln, who died in 2020 at the age of 93, taught dentistry there for several years before retiring.

On Oct. 26, 1984, doctors at the university did the first—and only—baboon-to-human heart transplant. The surgical procedure involved an infant born with a defective heart. "Baby Fae" was given the heart of a young baboon and hung on for several days before her kidneys failed.

"Baby Fae's experience of a brief month or so has been a uniquely human one," Dr. Leonard Bailey told L.A. reporters who had camped out in Loma Linda for the duration of Stephanie Fae Beauclair's short life. "The courageous decisions made for her by her family and all of us who have loved her, have forced us to confront and examine our human existence."

About the same time Baby Fae was making headlines in late October, Chris and two women Elmer had never seen before appeared on the Kellns' doorstep. Chris had several boxes he wanted Elmer to store for safekeeping.

"He pulls up with a small pickup," Elmer recalled later. "By the time I saw him, he had already unloaded two big cardboard boxes. One of them would be three feet high, one maybe about two feet, and another about a foot square."

The packages were addressed to somewhere in Hawaii.

"He said, 'Can I store these? I'm in a big hurry. I'll pick them up later.

'Oh, and would you mail this one to Hawaii? Keep the receipts. We'll send you the money that it costs to mail it."

"And then he took off. I never got to see the girls face to face. I mailed the box to Hawaii and left the other cardboard boxes in the garage.

Although two of the packages were taped up, the third was open.

Curious about what might be inside, Elmer took a peek.

"It was like he just put the box next to his writing desk and just went like this," Elmer said making a sweeping motion with his right arm across a long, and imaginary, plane. "It was full of disconnected telephones, intercom— electronic equipment. All of the stuff you would expect to see on somebody's work bench or desk. He was probably stealing stuff."

Sometime in December of 1984 or January 1985, Chris tracked down his lawyer friend, William Stewart, and hit him up with an unusual request.

He asked to borrow an electric chainsaw, Stewart recalled. Knowing Didi Sohus' property was overgrown with weeds and generally unkempt, Stewart obliged, with reservations.

"He had a problem with a branch on a tree. The branch was scraping or scratching his window (in the Lorain Road guest house)," Stewart said.

Chris never really struck Stewart as the handyman type, and he fretted about the decision to lend the slight young man the dangerous tool.

"I was concerned he might get hurt," said Stewart.

In late January or early February, Chris went back to Loma Linda to collect his stuff. This time he had a large redhead in the passenger seat.

Elmer and Jean's son, Wayne, told his parents he saw her there and "it looked like she filled the whole car."

The big girl's eyes were red. It was as if she had been crying, Wayne said.

Once again, Chris was rushed. He grabbed the remaining boxes and left.

"He was in a hurry when he brought it and, in a hurry, when he came to pick it up," Elmer said.

Sometime in April, this time without the redhead in tow, Chris paid a similar visit to Bob and Bette Brown, the couple on Canterbury Road who hosted Bible study and sold him their BMW.

"I think it was on a Saturday and he had some things he was disposing of. I think he said he was going on a trip," Brown would later recall.

Chris was driving a Nissan pickup. He had some electronics, some clothes, and an oddly shaped Oriental throw rug.

Among the electronics was an HP calculator, which interested Bob, an engineer for Southern California Edison.

Hewlett-Packard had been building pocket calculators since the early 1970s. While early calculators like the HP-35 ran about $400 and relied on LED technology for its display, by the early 80s, retail prices had dropped considerably and for the most part even the most expensive "scientific" models, with the more modern LCD screens ran less than $150. Even as late as 1985, HP owned the market on calculators.

***

Bob knew that Chris had an interest in electronics. He'd visited Bob at his office and once brought a Compaq computer over to the house so that they could play around with it.

Chris's calculator—"one of the fancier ones"—made enough of an impression on Bob that he decided to buy it.

Standing there in the driveway, Chris also had a question for Bob.

He said he had some chemicals from his work at the USC film lab. Chris explained that the chemicals were toxic and even though he didn't want to flush them down the drain, he needed a place to dump them. What did Bob suggest?

"I told him if I had something I wanted to illegally dispose of I would take them up to the mountain and find a secluded spot," Bob said.

Bette, who had been looking through things in the bed of the pickup, decided she liked the rug Chris was selling—until she inspected it up close.

"She looked at it and said, 'Chris, this had blood on it," Bob recalled. "He quickly rolled it up and left with it. We didn't have any further discussion of it. It seemed rather silly at the time that these were the things he was getting rid of."

As Chris hopped in the cab of the pickup, Bette suggested he get the rug dry cleaned.

For the most part, the Browns' contact with Chris after the driveway sales pitch, "just dissolved."

"I was not surprised, he was sort of a phantom anyhow," Bob said. "He was just different—unusual—and he was very believable up to a point. And you could never pin him down in great detail—at least I couldn't. It was always loose and feathery."

Mary Cologne, who lived next door to the Sohus family since 1974, never really interacted much with Didi or John, but she did know Chris, the USC film student who rented Didi's guest house. Yes, Didi's house was run down; yes, a succession of renters took over that back house, but she never thought she would have to call police—until after John and Linda disappeared and a cloud of thick, acrid black smoke belched out of the guest house chimney.

"There was something in the back house that smelled terrible," Cologne said. "It wasn't cold enough to be burning anything in the fireplace."

Cologne described the smell as something akin to burning rubber. She immediately called Chris.

"What are you burning in that fireplace? It smells terrible."

Chris answered, "Carpet."

"You don't burn carpet in the fireplace. You throw it out. Are you going to stop?"

Chris avoided answering the question.

"Do I need to call someone?" Cologne demanded. "You are stinking up the neighborhood."

Within twenty minutes, the smoke stopped and the smell went away.

Jann of Sweden doesn't recall John Sohus' last visit to his cluttered second floor barbershop, but he remembers well the last time he saw the young man who had spent so much time in his barber shop.

"He come up one evening, it must have been about 6 or 7 o'clock. He told me it was his last haircut," Jann said. "I asked why? He told me he had a call that a relative had died and he had to go to England the next morning to take care of a big estate."

"He said, 'I might never come back. This is a big estate, and I might never come back from England." Jann said he thought Chris was driving John Sohus' truck—a little pick-up.

"I had seen him driving it before, it was a Datsun or a Toyota, one of the Japanese smaller trucks. I think Didi Sohus let him drive the truck."

Chris left Jann and visited Stewart one last time. He returned the chainsaw.

"I didn't inspect it," Stewart said. "But nothing drew my attention to it. In fact, the chainsaw appeared to be in the exact condition as when I gave it to him. When he returned it, he said he hadn't used it and I was really relieved because I didn't want him to hurt himself," Stewart said.

In that last conversation with the young man, he had met several years earlier while serving coffee at the Church of our Savior, Stewart recalled Chris talking about a move across the country. He was headed to Greenwich, Connecticut.

Stewart told Chris how coincidental that was, since he and his family were planning a visit to Greenwich that summer. He hoped they could get together and asked for a phone number.

"Well, he said he didn't want to do it that way. He wanted to make a definite appointment to meet at a certain place and a definite time. I couldn't do it because I didn't know when I was going to be there. It seemed out of the ordinary."

No one asked Stewart if he looked up Christopher in the phone book when he arrived in Greenwich that summer. If he had, he wouldn't have found him. When Christopher arrived, he had changed his name and his story.

Chris was now Christopher Mountbatten Chichester Crowe, television producer, computer expert, and budding financial analyst.

His friends simply knew him as Chris.

CHAPTER 12.

GREENWICH TIME

"The guilty, he reflected as he drove amid the
heavy late-afternoon traffic as carefully as
possible, may flee when no one pursues ..."
—**Philip K. Dick, *Through a Scanner Darkly*, 1977**

It was the summer of 1985 when Chris, behind the wheel of a Nissan pickup truck, arrived in Greenwich, Connecticut. The town of 60,000 or so lies on the southern edge of the state. By train, it's about 30 minutes from Manhattan.

As he had done in South Pasadena and San Marino, Chris first sought out the town's most influential Episcopal Church. In Greenwich, that's Christ Church. Just up the road from the Belle Haven neighborhood, Christ Church isn't too unlike Church of Our Savior in San Marino. The congregation predates the American Revolution by 27 years; it was founded in 1749.

The church itself has a very similar construction to All Saints in Pasadena and Our Savior in San Marino. There is the brick-and-mortar façade, the immense stained-glass windows, the off-site Bible study, and a variety of community ministries. Oh, and the wealthy and influential parishioners.

Like he had done at Church of our Savior, the slight, but imperious young German sought to charm those in power. Just after he arrived in Greenwich, he told the rector, Rev. John Bishop, he wanted to be an usher at Christ Church and hopefully meet some new people.

The rector thought his son would make a perfect companion for Chris. Bishop's son, Chris, was in film school at Columbia to learn the art of screenwriting and film making. He was delighted to meet a young man with the breeding and credentials young Mr. Crowe possessed.

Rev. Bishop wondered if Chris could take some time to discuss the film business with his son.

Of course, Chris replied. How soon can I meet him?

Right away.

It wasn't too much later that Christopher Bishop heard the name Christopher Mountbatten Crowe for the first time.

"There's a guy I just met about your age. He's a film producer, you should meet him," Chris Bishop recalled during the 2012 preliminary hearing in the Sohus homicide.

"Sure. Why not," the film student told his dad. "I'm not naive enough to think that just meeting someone will make a difference. It was a great opportunity to meet someone who was a film professional."

The young recent graduate became friends immediately.

"I gave Chris a screenplay I had written; it was the one I had written to get into Columbia grad school," Bishop said. "He was clearly conversant in film writing and stuff like that."

Chris explained he was from Los Angeles, had been affiliated with the USC film school, and had made some short 16 mm silent films there. One involved a ballerina. He also said he was the executive producer of the new Alfred Hitchcock series, which debuted in May 1985. He even carried an advanced copy of one episode of the series and a voucher for his tale.

He said he was finished with film and television and said he was leaving the film industry to become a bond trader.

Pretty soon the stories began to flow. Fresh from California, Chris knew his way around the film industry. He knew the gossip and bragged about having an impressive array of credentials. Chris the traveler, told the Bishop's son, that he was the brother of writer Cameron Crowe—*Fast*

Times at Ridgemont High—and could help Bishop advance his career.

In '85 and into '86, Chris was ensconced in style on Rock Ridge. Chris Bishop described the pad as a "carriage house" on the back of a property in an extremely wealthy neighborhood. Christopher Crowe frequently entertained the young Bishop. On more than one occasion he spun a tale of the travels that brought him to Greenwich.

"He had a very wealthy mother who had married a wealthy man in Greenwich," Bishop said. "He was from California and had gone to film school."

Crowe explained he had come to Greenwich to produce a TV series for NBC.

"He was there to produce the new Alfred Hitchcock series," Bishop said. Chris Crowe explained he was the executive producer.

Had anyone checked out Chris' story, they would have found out quickly that the real Crowe was several years older than the pretend Crowe. He had also been writing for television since 1977, at a time when Christopher Mountbatten Crowe would have been a sophomore in high school.

No one checked. And the Christopher Crowe living in Greenwich really seemed to know his stuff—especially when it came to film. Bishop gave him a screenplay to critique and (if nothing else) Chris' reply showed he was conversant in film. Chris had a framed film poster on his wall—he claimed he was the producer.

One thing for sure, Chris wasn't driving a pickup. He had an old sedan of some sort. Maybe a station wagon. Bishop never saw him driving a pickup truck. It almost seemed as though it would be beneath him.

Greenwich boasts of being home to several financial institutions. It has its own orchestra and art museum. Relatives of the Kennedys live in Greenwich. In fact, a couple of them were accused in the town's own cold case—the murder of Martha Moxley—on the night before Halloween 1975.

Former LAPD detective Mark Fuhrman wrote about the case in his book, *A Murder in Greenwich*. An early paragraph sums up his thoughts on the town that is home to Ron Howard, Mary Tyler Moore, and designer, Tommy Hilfiger.

"The people of Greenwich are living a lie. They think that by moving out to an exclusive suburb and sheltering themselves with money and all the things and people money can buy that they can avoid, or at least ignore, human depravity. They are wrong. Greenwich may be richer, prettier, and safer than most places on earth, but it is not immune to evil. In fact, the massive state of denial in which the town seems to operate is a form of evil itself."

For a variety of reasons, police were unable to immediately solve the crime. Fuhrman's book resulted in a reexamination of the case and the conviction of Kennedy cousin, Michael Skakel. In 2002, he was sentenced to 20 years to life in state prison. The conviction was vacated in 2013 and the case was dismissed in 2020, when the state's supreme court ruled that Skakel had received ineffective assistance of counsel.

In their 1950 book, *USA Confidential*, journalists Jack Lait and Lee Mortimer had their own take on the Nutmeg State. They called it "New York in pink pajamas."

"The rich advertising executives and the dilettantes who moved up from New York think they took it over," the two wrote way back when. That description held up in to the early '90s.

Doubtless, Chris heard the tales and knew some of the history of the "Land of Steady Habits." After his arrival and introduction, Chris settled into a pattern similar to his routine in San Marino, with a notable exception—he got a real job, with S.N. Phelps and Company, a private investment firm.

A friend named Catherine Demarin introduced to Chris to Stanford Phelps at the Indian Point Yacht Club in the fall.

An upscale establishment, the Indian Harbor Yacht Club which sits on the Long Island Sound, is "convenient to Newport and New York." It's the sort of place where members mingle sockless in their Topsiders and attend formals in blue blazers, white pants, and sailing caps.

Christopher Crowe brought Phelps an impressive resume. He was a 1979 graduate of San Marino's finest private school—Pasadena Polytechnical High School, a 1983 graduate of USC, president of Gypsy Moth productions until 1985, and now president of Crowe Productions and the Crowe Company.

Beyond that, Chris listed an address in Greenwich and claimed he grew up on Circle Drive in San Marino, a street lined with multi story mansions, expansive lawns and expensive cars. Crowe also listed a residence in Midtown East on 52nd Street, Manhattan, just blocks from the Rockefeller Center.

He wrote down a bullshit Social Security Number—it belonged to David Berkowitz, New York's infamous "Son of Sam" killer from the 1970s.

Phelps, a grizzled Korean War vet who boasted of his prowess as a forward observer on the front lines against the commies, liked what he saw and put the old boy to work. He hired Chris to troubleshoot a corporate IT system and bring the company's computers in compliance with National Association of Securities Dealers rules.

"He was doing computer work, not working with customers," Phelps said.

Even so, Chris, who wore shirts monogrammed CCC, passed tests required by the Securities and Exchange Commission of anyone involved in the securities business. On the job, Chris bragged about his heritage, his role as an executive producer in Hollywood, and his fabulous wealth.

His co-workers laughed at him behind his back.

Chris lasted about seven months. Phelps fired him in a dispute over computer files that Chris refused to turn over. Ever on the make for a scam, Chris allegedly figured out a way to manipulate sales figures in the firm's computer system so that he got a cut of every dollar.

Phelps recalled their final conversation.

"If you aren't out of here in 10 seconds, I'll call the marshal and have you arrested," Phelps said.

Chris was out the door in a heartbeat, at least that's the way Phelps remembered it. It goes without saying the S.N. Phelps Company changed its hiring practices.

A friend of mine once marveled at how easily some people advanced in corporate America, while others—honest and smart like him—forever languished in the same desk reporting to one asshole after another. He called his principle "Fuck up, move up."

It applied perfectly to Chris. He might have screwed up at Phelps but moved up in the securities world—getting hired in the summer of 1987 by the Japanese firm, Nikko Securities. The company had just opened a branch in New York City. Chris got through the front door by dressing the part and bullshitting on his resume. He headed the company's bond desk with the initial responsibility of hiring heavy hitters to work in the firm's offices.

At Nikko, which took up three floors of the World Trade Center, Chris met Mihoko Manabe, a translator. The pair soon hooked up. Chris told Mihoko he was originally from Pasadena. He said he attended Caltech and studied film at USC. He explained to her that his real name was Christopher Mountbatten Chichester, but for professional reasons was going by Christopher Crowe.

He whispered to her that his grandmother lived in Windsor, England—the Royal Borough. The obvious implication being that his grandmother was somehow related to Queen Elizabeth—if not the queen herself.

As for his parents?

"His father was an anesthesiologist and mother was a child actress. They lived in Pasadena, California."

Chris bragged to Mihoko he was also a TV producer on the side.

"He was involved with the Alfred Hitchcock TV series," she said.

A soft-spoken woman, Manabe, a senior credit officer, took a subservient role in the relationship. What Chris said went. No questions asked. She loved him. He never treated her with anything other than contempt and disdain.

Eventually Chris ran out of steam in the high-rise offices of Nikko. In summer of 1988, he was let go for a variety of performance issues. True to the "fuck up, move up" principle, Chris took what Dan Banks called his "Rockefeller suits" and soon landed on his feet at Kidder Peabody, where Ralph Boynton hired him in October to do Eurobond sales.

Wall Street in the late '80s was the Wild West. According to Boynton, you ate what you killed. And Chris was the perfect fit for the new desk. He wanted to develop trading foreign backed securities to raise capital in non-dollar currencies. It takes a certain sort of presentation to get involved in it and Chris had the look and demeanor of a Eurobond trader.

"It was Oct. 5, 1988," Boynton recalled. "He came to my office at Kidder unannounced, but in those days, in 1988, New York City was a different place. The problems the WTC had experienced had not occurred. There was very little security. Terrorism hadn't happened yet. You could go in and knock on someone's door without looking suspicious."

Boynton said Chris struck him as very eager, even energetic. Chris said he could do the work and was hired on a temporary basis.

Before he could be a fulltime trader, "What I wanted to do was to get to know him better personally," Boynton said. "There was some checking I wanted to do and had not done."

In October 1988, Boynton and Chris traveled to L.A. They stayed near Pasadena and Boynton had a Hertz rental car. Chris gave him a tour of some sort and at one point, he and Boynton ended up on a deserted mountain road in the Angeles National Forest. Boynton thought it was weird but didn't give it too much thought given his companion was kind of a weird dude.

One afternoon before he left town, Chris asked to borrow the car. He didn't say where he was going or why he would need it, but Boynton said sure, and Chris disappeared for a few hours.

Did he go to San Marino? Probably not. Didi was dead. The old house had a new owner.

He did, however, pay a visit to Linda and Don Wetherbee, a family who was living in a trailer park in La Puente, a working-class community about 10 miles southeast of wealthy and powerful San Marino. In 1985, Chris introduced the couple to Didi. They became her housekeepers and ultimately the executors of her estate. In her last months, Didi too had moved to La Puente and the Wetherbees said they were taking care of her.

Boynton and Chris returned to NY on the redeye Friday night. On Monday morning, Chris was a no show at work. Something was up.

CHAPTER 13.

DISINHERITED

"I intentionally and with full knowledge of any consequences, specifically disinherit and omit any provisions for JOHN ROBERT SOHUS."
—The Last Will and Testament of Ruth D. Sohus, 17350 East Temple Avenue, Space 454, La Puente, California 91744

High school student Harry Sherwood IV arrived in Los Angeles from North Carolina sometime around Thanksgiving, 1985. A teenager, Sherwood came to spend some time in San Marino with the grandmother he had never met—Didi Sohus.

He flew into LAX, caught a bus to Pasadena, and was met by Linda Wetherbee, who had moved in with Didi and was taking care of her.

Eight months had passed since John and Linda disappeared. Chris was gone too. A new boarder was living in the back house.

Sherwood's father, Harry Sherwood III, was Didi's son from a previous marriage. Sherwood III had two daughters, Sirena and Juliette, who still lived in Southern California. The younger Harry met the girls for the first time during that 1985 visit.

Didi was a mess. Suffering from emphysema, she stayed in her bedroom watching Dr. Gene Scott, a cigar smoking televangelist who was 1985's version of Glenn Beck—chalkboard and all. Doc's church was headquartered in Glendale—and when he asked viewers for money, he usually got it.

Don and Linda Wetherbee witnessed her rapid decline too. Didi complained about Johnny using her credit cards for purchases in New York, but never phoning to see how she was doing.

John and Linda had to be coming back. Right? She would ask.

"We would go to her house and find her sobbing uncontrollably, saying they could have at least sent a letter saying they weren't coming back," Don told friends at the time.

It was the culmination of a weird time. First John and Linda disappeared, then Chris did too. It left the police recalling their encounters and trying to figure out just what had happened.

San Marino police Sgt. Lili Hadsell paid occasional visits to Didi in the weeks since April, when Officer Leveque filed his written report on the case. She didn't write any reports summarizing her visits, Leveque had done that already. Little by little, though, Lili began to see a change in Didi's outlook.

"Her demeanor had changed," Hadsell said. "And she was really, really worried about (John). Something had changed."

In hopes of delivering the grieving mother some sort of news, Hadsell called Linda's mom and sister. "It was mostly to reassure (Didi)." She learned about the postcards they received.

Nothing, it seemed, placated the distraught and usually inebriated Ruth "Didi" Sohus.

"She believed John and Linda had gone to work for a company," Hadsell recalled. "The work was confidential and as time went on, she became confused whether that was true or not."

Hadsell's partner, San Marino police Officer George Yankovich also made a call to Lorain Road. It was in April, there was a call for service, a disturbance of some sort. Yankovich walked around the side of the house and went to the back, to the guest house where Chris lived. He filled out a Field Investigation or, FI, card, which is a sort of memorandum of encounters police have in the course of an investigation and left.

His encounter with Chris was a weird one. After Yankovich knocked at the door of the guest house, Chris opened it wearing nothing and stood there completely naked. Yankovich didn't know where to look.

"What are you doing?" he asked.

"I'm a nudist," came Chris' reply.

Yankovich couldn't get out of there fast enough. Not too long after, Chris vanished.

Yankovich ran Christopher Chichester, XII, baronet of Chichester through CLETS—the California Law Enforcement Telecommunications System and entered a BOLO—or "be on the lookout" for Chris, John, and Linda. Chris was described as a "person of interest," 5' 8", 140, with a DOB of 2-21-61.

About the same time as San Marino officials attempted to unravel their messy missing persons case, the art collector in Cupertino became intent on tracking down Linda Sohus and contacted Didi via telephone.

> **Art Collector:** I told her we were working on a piece of art together. I asked, 'Have you heard anything from them?' She just started crying. Basically, it was incoherent babbling.

> **Didi:** I haven't heard. I don't know what's going on. They wouldn't just not call.

> **Art Collector:** The rest of what she said was disjointed fragments of stuff. She said

something about France. I said I thought they were moving to New York. Basically, at that point I was big into computers and stuff, and I decided to see if I could use what I had access to see if there was anything out there. I told her I would let her know if anything turned up.

"Even after that she was still kind of shaky," the art collector said. "I did try, and I never did find anything. At that time, a friend had access to an archive of (Associated Press) and (United Press International) raw news feeds. I checked for about two months after I talked to her. There was still no news story at that point."

***

Even though he didn't know all the particulars or nuances of the situation, Harry Sherwood IV figured he walked in on something bigger than he could explain during that first visit to grandma Didi's strange house.

"She was in her bedroom. She just sat in her room and watched TV," Sherwood said. There were lots of medications lying around mostly for emphysema and heart problems."

Didi, in need of cash, rented the guesthouse to a new tenant.

"When I arrived, she took me out back to the guest house to meet the tenant at the time," Sherwood recalled in a 2023 interview. "She was like, 'Here are your eviction papers. It was a bit awkward. But she was selling the property so …'"

Left alone for the most part, Sherwood, as teenagers are wont to do, began to explore.

The room where John and Linda had lived remained undisturbed 10 months after they vanished. He could see the room had been previously occupied. Clothes were strewn about. Linda's art supplies were haphazardly stacked alongside her artwork—a group of fantasy-type drawings that impressed the young Sherwood.

"There was a workstation there," he recalled. "There was no indication that someone had moved on or was planning to move. All the toiletries were still on the counter."

There was also a large box of syringes, a shaving kit, and a toothbrush.

"It just looked like someone was gone for the day," he said. "Not forever."

Harry asked about the needles. Didi, dressed in a house coat, took a drag of her cigarette and explained John used them to treat his diabetes.

At the end of the week, Harry admitted he was happy to have met his half-sisters, but glad to be headed back to Charlotte. Didi had Linda Wetherbee, who "was extremely involved in my grandmother's life at that point."

"When I was there, she barely left the house. I remember walking to a grocery store and buying food. She would sit on her bed and watch TV. Much later after I went back home, she contacted my uncle with whom I lived. She wanted me to move there and live with her."

The Wetherbees didn't want young Harry around. And he wasn't keen on it either.

***

It was around Thanksgiving 1985 that Linda Wetherbee and her husband Don—began to take a more active role in Didi's life. Even though the house was a shambles, Didi still had means. There were her valuable antiques and a wide portfolio of investments in the stock market.

Linda and Don would give Didi rides and help with the groceries. Not only that, but Linda was also a realtor who arranged the sale of the San Marino house and located a mobile home in La Puente for Didi to live out her remaining years.

Before meeting Didi, Don and Linda Wetherbee bounced around the San Gabriel Valley, living in Covina, Walnut, and Azusa. Linda sold mobile homes. The source of Don's income is less clear.

Don, who was living in La Puente, met Chris, in 1984. The young man with the sharp attire and odd accent had been looking for someone to care for Didi.

***

Before Chris split town for good, Don introduced him to his wife Linda. Chris then introduced Linda Wetherbee to Didi in exchange for a $40,000 "finder's fee." Cash in hand made it easier for Chris to skip town. With their connection essentially having disappeared, it was up to Don and Linda to manage the day-to-day affairs of their new and very needy "client."

Didi represented a big opportunity for the couple— inheritance. They borrowed the $40,000 from her to pay off Chris.

There was a back-end payoff too, the Wetherbees promised Chris 50 percent of Didi's estate. Doing some quick math, based on what he knew, Chris figured that would have been at least another $100,000.

Much of the transaction is covered in Didi's will and the wording of the document, signed in 1987, could be interpreted to indicate that she believed John was dead and that perhaps Linda Sohus had something to do with it. She also disinherited Harry Sherwood's half-sisters, who were very much still alive.

"I intentionally and with full knowledge of any consequences, specifically disinherit and omit any provisions for JOHN ROBERT SOHUS, JULIETTE SHERWOOD, and SABRINA SHERWOOD and their issue in this Will. All provisions of this will shall be interpreted as though they had predeceased me."

In all, Didi would leave $50,000 to her grandson, Harry Sherwood IV, and make Linda Wetherbee the trustee of the estate. The balance was divided up in other ways:

- $2,000 went to the Braille Institute of Los Angeles
- $2,000 went to the John Tracy Clinic for the Deaf in Los Angeles
- Didi's mobile home and her remaining possessions went to Don and Linda.

Nothing went to Dr. Gene Scott.

Later on, the will contains a provision forgiving a $40,000 loan to the Wetherbees.

It was the $40,000 they paid Chris.

"If at the time of my death there is any balance owing on a note that I hold executed by Don and Linda Wetherbee in the amount of forty thousand dollars ($40,000.00), I hereby direct that the debt be forgiven, and the Note marked 'paid.'

"The rest, residue and remainder of my estate I give to Linda and Don Wetherbee, or to the survivor of them … Except as otherwise specifically provided herein, I have intentionally omitted to provide for any of my heirs."

It was clear Didi believed John and Linda were gone for good.

"I have intentionally omitted to provide for any of my heirs. In the event that any beneficiary under this Will or any heir or person claiming under any of them shall contest this Will or attack or seek to impair or invalidate any of its provisions or seek to avoid the effect of this Will, or conspire with or voluntarily assist anyone attempting to do any of those things, I specifically disinherit each such person and all gifts or interest given under this Will to or for that person shall be forfeited and my estate shall be administered as if that person had predeceased me without issue."

Slowing down and growing shorter and shorter of breath, Didi lived out her final days in a La Puente doublewide just a few feet inside the entrance of nicely named Covina Hills Mobile Country estates. Her smokes, booze, and oxygen were never out of reach.

But even if the guard at the front gate could keep out unwanted visitors, he couldn't shield Didi from the reality that less than a half mile away was the BKK landfill, a toxic trash dump that filled surrounding streets with heavy waste-hauling trucks and the air with the stench of decaying refuse brought in from nicer places Los Angeles County and dumped just steps from her front door.

It was not the sort of thing to which a San Marino native like Ruth "Didi" Sohus could ever grow accustomed. Although La Puente and San Marino had a common early history, by the mid-1980s they were figuratively miles apart in terms of racial demographics, crime rates, income levels, and politics. That gap would continue to grow.

Other than trash, the glue that holds L.A. County's disparate communities together is L.A. County Sheriff's Homicide. Known as "Bulldogs," the nation's premier murder investigators aren't typically versed in the niceties of tea at the Huntington or weeks abroad in Greece. At any hour of the day, a sheriff's homicide detective could be dispatched to Lancaster in the High Desert or Terminal Island and the Ports. The pages of their Thomas Guide that mapped out the grid of the grittier communities of the San Gabriel Valley, trisected by three major interstates, were doubtless well worn.

Bones – The crime scene image reveals the skull and jawbone of John Sohus. (Courtesy: LASD, Los Angeles County Superior Court)

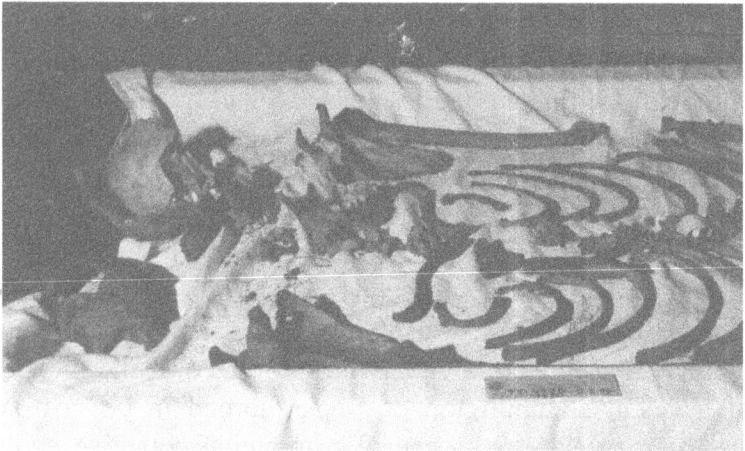

When the coroner laid out the skeleton, they realized the body had been cut into three parts, or trisected.

An early photo of Chris after his arrival in California in the early 1980s. (Photo courtesy: Jean Kelln)

SACRAMENTO CONNECTION. Assemblyman Richard Mountjoy will be the featured guest on the May 29 edition of "Inside of San Marino," scheduled for 7 p.m. on American Cablevision Channel 6. Above, Mountjoy (center) discusses the program's format with producer Christopher Chichester and moderator Peggy Ebright. Mountjoy represents the 42nd District, which includes San Marino, and is one of the state's leading conservatives. On the cablecast, Mrs. Ebright asks him about reapportionment, legislative reform, the school finance bill and his grassroot political beginnings.

Chris and his co-host on 'Inside San Marino' were profiled in the local newspaper just before airing a show featuring a local politician. (Author's collection)

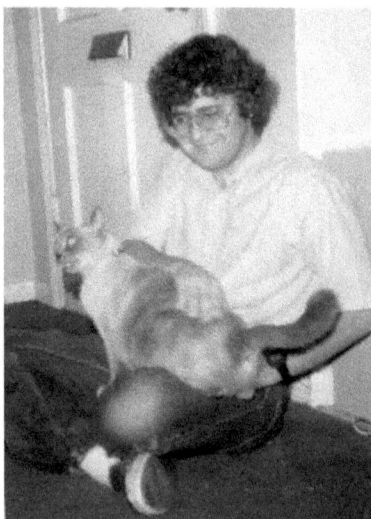

Photo of a young John Sohus in the 1980s. (Author's collection)

Photo of a young Linda Sohus in the 1980s. (Author's collection)

Christian examines a glass of wine during dinner with the Kellns in 1985. (Photo courtesy: Jean Kelln)

The House with the Blue Shutters where Christian Karl Gerhartsreiter grew up. (Courtesy: Susanne Mittermaier)

Irmgard Gerhartsreiter in 1960. (Photo courtesy: Susanne Mittermaier)

Gerhartsreiter's INS Photo. (LA County Superior Court)

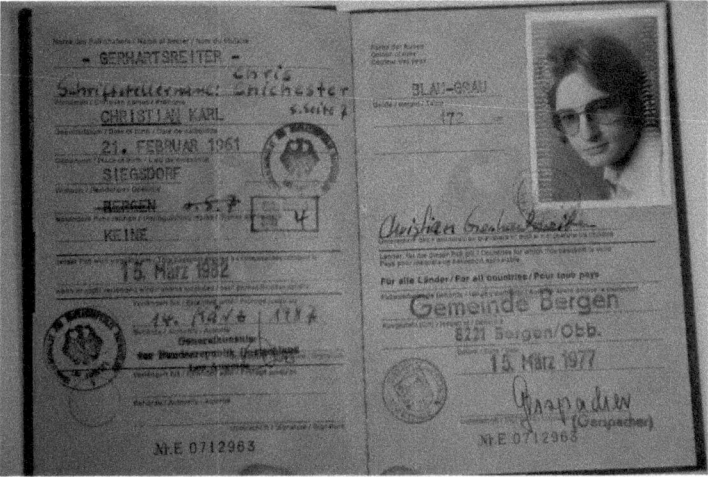

Gerhartsreiter's German Passport, stamped in 1988 when he was on the run. (LA County Superior Court)

One of Linda's paintings titled 'Ambra.' (Author's Collection)

John and Linda goofing around at Dangerous
Visions. (LA County Superior Court)

John and Linda celebrate their wedding on Halloween night.

Years after it had disappeared, John and Linda's pickup truck turned up in Greenwich, Connecticut. (LA County Superior Court)

One-time friend Chris Bishop was among those who testified against Gerhartsreiter at the murder trial. (Pool Photo: Walt Mancini / Pasadena Star-News, LA County Superior Court files)

Chris as Clark Rockefeller. (Author's collection)

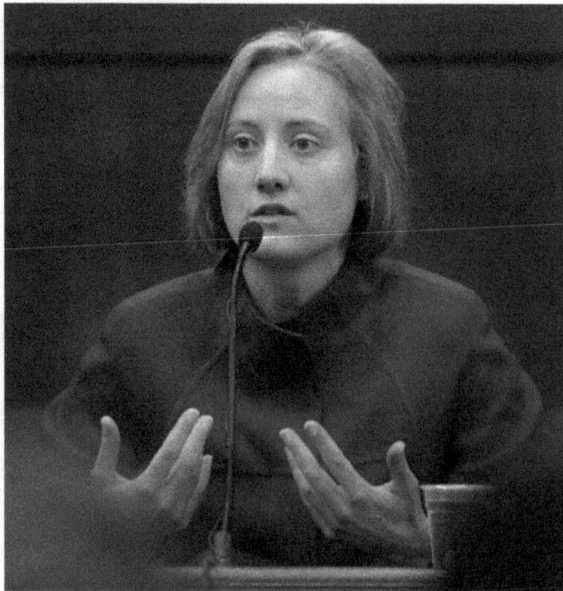

Chris's wife thought he was Clark Rockefeller and testified against him twice. (Pool Photo: Walt Mancini / Pasadena Star-News, LA County Superior Court files)

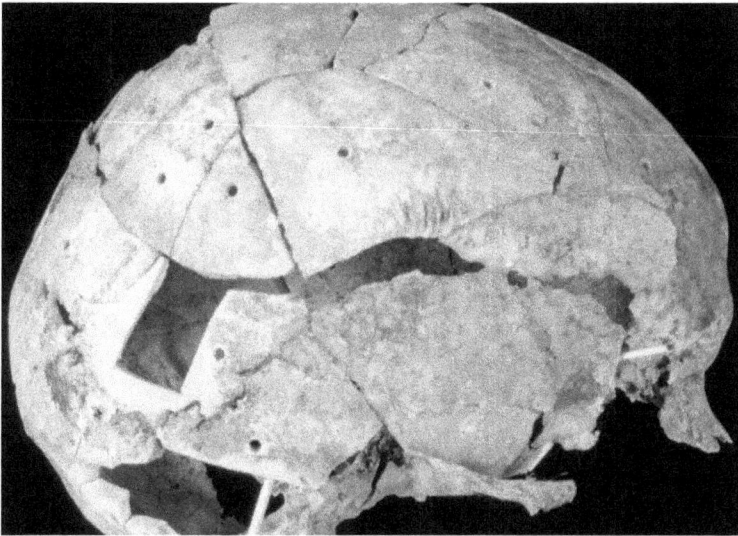

The reconstruction of John's skull shows injuries from the murder and crushing damage from the backhoe that uncovered it nine years later. (LA County Superior Court)

Convicted of the 1985 killing of John Sohus, Christian Karl Gerhartsreiter carries a stack of handwritten papers into court in 2013, which make up a portion of his appeal. (Pool Photo: Walt Mancini / Pasadena Star-News, LA County Superior Court files)

CHAPTER 14.

PEE WEE, MALO, AND YOUNGSTER

Haynes: You ever notice how a 'mother of four' is always catching hell? Murder? Hit-and-run? Burnt up in a row house fire? Swindled by bigamists?
Price: Tough gig, 'mother of four.'
Twigg: 'Innocent bystander' is worse.
He's always getting the short end.
Haynes: Not a lot of them around anymore. Not a lot of innocents anymore, you ask me.
—Conversation between reporters and editors from HBO's *The Wire*, Season 5, episode 2

As the crow flies, it is 13 miles from San Marino to La Puente.

While San Marino, which was largely white in the 1980s, could boast its residents were the captains of industry, the titans of banking and publishing and the top professionals of the region in medicine and law, La Puente mostly supplied the workers, the tellers, the drivers, and the maids that keep those businesses running. It was likely someone who lived in La Puente was keeping the children of the executives fed and their gardens neatly trimmed.

It's a working-class town with working-class problems.

Historically, though, La Puente and San Marino are inexorably linked. The first Europeans to trek through California, Spaniards—led by explorer Gaspar Portola in 1769—gave the locale its name after building a foot bridge (or Puente) over the San Jose Creek.

After spending the night, the group traveled north to modern San Gabriel/San Marino and ultimately established the region's first mission in roughly the same spot (where 225 years later) Linda Sohus would hold her final art show.

As the mission expanded, the Franciscans who ran it established a rancho near La Puente that grew much of the region's grain and penned most of its livestock. As the population of Southern California grew and Los Angeles became its cultural, economic, and psychological center, towns closer to L.A. like Pasadena, San Marino, and San Gabriel urbanized and thrived.

Those Los Angeles County towns further east, like La Puente, remained mostly rural. In fact, right up until WWII, La Puente was the nation's leading grower of walnuts. Its neighbors, meanwhile, were hubs of the citrus growing and packing industry through the mid-1940s.

Back then, San Gabriel Valley supplied the bulk of the nation's oranges, lemons, and grapefruit. Street names like Sunkist, Orange, Walnut, and Fairgrove are remnants of the bygone era. The ancient orange, lemon, avocado, and walnut trees in front yards, back yards, and empty lots stand as living witnesses to the growth of Los Angeles County in the second half of the 20th Century.

Following WWII, developers plowed the strawberry fields south of Puente and tore out walnut, orange, and avocado groves that stretched from East Los Angeles out to San Bernardino with a few small towns in between. The north end of the Valley bordered the fabled Route 66 and provided a destination for road-weary travelers from the east. The Valley's south end ran along the Union Pacific tracks from the freight yards in Vernon east to Pomona.

As WWII servicemen mustered out of their government issues, in the San Gabriel Valley and Los Angeles County, huge factories dedicated to the aerospace industry were constructed. Towns like La Puente and its neighbors El Monte, Valinda, and Bassett boomed overnight with new homes and new residents—mostly those veterans and their young families looking to live the modern American dream at the start of the Cold War.

The area made up the heart of California's 12th Congressional District, which sent fervent red-baiter and Whittier native, Richard Nixon, to Washington in 1946. He promised to take care of the regions' vets and run special interests and Commies out of Washington.

"If elected to Congress, my one and only allegiance will be to all the people of the district," Nixon wrote in one campaign flier circulated door-to-door from San Marino to La Puente. "The size of a man's pocketbook or the political power of an organization to which he belongs should have no bearing on the kind of representation he gets from his congressman."

La Puente's history through the post-war era was like that of neighboring El Monte. The boom, which catered to hillbillies and white trash, was rapid; the decline began at once.

La Puente, population about 35,000, and El Monte, roughly 120,000 residents, share Valley Boulevard, a 20-mile-long path at the western end of the Santa Fe Trail. When first constructed in the 18th Century, Valley connected La Puente to the mission and later Don Benito's rancho. Over time the road devolved into a corridor of seedy hot-sheet motels and run-down trailer parks filled with heroin addicts, transvestite prostitutes, and diseased down-and-outers.

By the late 1980s, those families who gutted it out in the tougher towns of the San Gabriel Valley did so at their own peril.

Sheriff's detectives in Los Angeles County mostly deal with the seedy side of life. It's exceedingly rare for a case to begin and end in wealthy enclaves like San Marino. What happens in the San Gabriel Valley more often mirrors their day-to-day lives on the job.

Anytime Sheriff's vice deputies put together a stake-out/sting operation on Valley, it would typically result in 30 or more arrests. I remember one such occasion in the early 1990s when detectives invited me and photographer, Leo Jarzomb, along to get a firsthand glimpse of their tactics.

We met in a briefing room at the El Monte Police Department. A lieutenant said we'd be listening in on johns soliciting undercover officers from a motor home parked on a side street.

The female cops posing as hookers were to lure their johns into a designated motel room. Over a wire, we could hear the deals go down.

"Hey sugar, you looking for some of this?"

"Yeah. Can I get full-service?"

"Sure baby just follow me through the parking lot. I've got a room right here."

Once inside the hooker's "room," the men were arrested. Most were cited and released at the scene. After about an hour, the cops asked us if we wanted to get a closer look. Of course we said, "Sure."

Soon afterward, a couple of beefy vice detectives, Leo, and I walked across a classic 1940s motel courtyard and into a tiny room that consisted of a queen bed with a quarter-fed vibrator, a television straight out of 1965, a dresser, and a closet-sized bathroom—all beneath a mirrored ceiling that hadn't been Windexed in months.

Four of us squeezed into the tiny bathroom. It had those little octagonal shaped white tiles that one finds in old construction. It smelled of mildew and rot. I stood in the bathtub and looked out the open back window, wondering if anyone had seen us go in and if they had, what they would be thinking about all adult men crowded in a cheap motel room in the middle of a weekday.

"OK. Now be quiet," one of the vice dicks said. "What's going to happen is this: The door will open; the john and our officer will enter the room. Once we believe an overt act has been committed, we'll rush out and make the arrest."

It didn't take long before the door opened. We couldn't hear much, but in a matter of seconds, the bathroom door flew open and all four of us rushed out into the room. Leo's flash was popping. It illuminated a sad sack of about 65. His pants were around his ankles. For a second his eyes showed nothing but bewilderment. Then he cried and tried to straighten his toupee. A cop cuffed the old guy. Someone read him his rights. He was run for warrants and cut loose. In all, 28 guys and five girls got a scare, a misdemeanor charge, and an AIDS test out of the deal.

When the excitement was over, business returned to normal on the stretch of Valley between El Monte and La Puente by the next morning.

It had been going on for years. In his 1996 book, *My Dark Places*, James Ellroy described the region as a 1950s honky-tonk paradise turned upside-down by drugs and crime.

"El Monte was a shit town now. El Monte was a shit town in 1958. It was a genteel shit town indigenous to its era. Dope was clandestine. Guns were scarce. El Monte was running at 10% of its current population and 1/30 of its current crime rate."

Ellroy's mother got murdered in 1958 and her body dumped in an alleyway about a half-mile north of Valley. Bobbie Long, a woman Ellroy believes was slain by the same killer, would turn up dead six months later and a mile or two away just off Valley in La Puente.

The region continued its slow decline through the 60s and 70s. By the time Didi Sohus moved to La Puente in the mid-1980s, aerospace was on its way out, hillbilly whites were moving to suburbs—even further east of Los Angeles—and the crime rate was soaring. Unlike peaceful and virtually crime-free San Marino, drive-by shootings, carjackings, stabbings, and kidnappings were almost commonplace occurrences in La Puente, Valinda, and Bassett.

In 2007, federal authorities would argue that over the two decades since Didi lived there, La Puente had become a stronghold of the Mexican Mafia and the Puente 13 street gang.

Streetgangs.com described La Puente in 2008 as a relic of a different era.

"The local government has been relatively unsuccessful in its attempts to attract big-box retailers and restaurant chains. La Puente retains many aging 1950s-era strip malls. In recent years, the city has become one of the most dangerous and crime ridden cities in Los Angeles," the website notes on a page dedicated to the Puente-13 gang.

The gang also got its start in the 1950s. At first, members called themselves the "Bridgetown Gentlemen" or "Old Town Puente." Members of the gang sold dope and committed low-level street crimes. They saw themselves as La Puente's protectors.

Somewhere along the way, the Bridgetown Gentlemen became simply Puente. Then, Puente became Puente-13. The number 13 has special significance as the 13th letter of the alphabet—Eme—in Spanish. It is the designation used by Sureno street gangs that declare allegiance to the Mexican Mafia. As the region grew, so did Puente-13. Members claimed territory in the neighboring cities of Walnut, Industry, Hacienda Heights, and West Covina.

Ultimately, members would form subsets or "cliques." Puente 13 has 14 cliques. Among them are Happy Homes, Blackwood, Northam, Balista, and Dial. All named after nearby streets.

Rival gangs would form in nearby Baldwin Park, El Monte (Flores), and Bassett (Grande). Turf wars followed with deadly results.

In a 1992 article on a string of slayings in the San Gabriel Valley, *Los Angeles Times* reporter, Laurie Becklund, described the Puente, Baldwin Park, El Monte region as "the antithesis of the American Dream."

Unlike bucolic San Marino, the area around La Puente was "an incubator of social turmoil: poverty, crime, unemployment, gangs, shifting racial composition, and high dropout rates."

According to the FBI's Uniform Crime Report, between '85 and '95 El Monte had 157 slayings. La Puente in that same period reported 78 homicides. The neighboring communities of Valinda and Bassett reported similar numbers, but because they lie in unincorporated Los Angeles County, for statistical purposes those homicides get lumped in with killings that occur in far-off Malibu or bodies discovered dumped in the Angeles National Forest. It's a safe bet to assume that in those 10 years as many as 400—mostly gang related—slayings occurred in the 49-square mile east San Gabriel Valley.

But murder was breaking out all over California. Pasadena during those same years had 197 homicides. Even quiet San Marino had its share of trouble during the late 80s and early 90s crack epidemic.

On the eastside of Los Angeles County, things began to settle down in mid-1994 after the heads of the Mexican Mafia declared a moratorium on drive-by killings. Leaders of the prison-based gang told its associates on the streets to come to terms with rivals and stop pulling drive-bys and begin paying taxes on drug sales to higher-ups in the organization.

Anyone violating those rules would be "green-lighted"—targeted for death.

Coupled with the boom years of the early 2000s, for the most part the violence subsided in and around La Puente.

Now and then innocent bystanders got in the way. Sheriff's Homicide detective, Tim Miley, caught his share of the investigations along the way.

LOG 102

SHERIFF'S HOMICIDE DETECTIVES ARE
CONTINUING THEIR INVESTIGATION
INTO THE SHOOTING DEATH OF
A MAN THAT OCCURRED IN THE
13400 BLOCK OF MOCCASIN STREET,
WEST VALINDA, ON MARCH 9,
2006, AT APPROXIMATELY 9:15 P.M.
DEPUTIES FROM CITY OF INDUSTRY
SHERIFF'S STATION RESPONDED TO
THE LOCATION AFTER RECEIVING
A "SHOTS FIRED" CALL. WHEN
DEPUTIES ARRIVED, THEY
OBSERVED THE MALE, ROBERT
WHITEHEAD, MW/44, RESIDENT OF
THE UNICORPORATED AREA OF WEST
VALINDA, LYING ON THE GROUND,
HE SUSTAINED MULTIPLE GUNSHOT
WOUNDS TO HIS UPPER TORSO.
DETECTIVES HAVE LEARNED THAT
THE VICTIM, ARRIVED HOME FROM
WORK, AND CONFRONTED TWO
MALE HISPANIC GANGSTERS SPRAY
PAINTING A NEIGHBOR'S GARAGE.
ONE OF THE SUSPECTS FIRED
SEVERAL SHOTS AT THE VICTIM.
THE VICTIM WAS TRANSPORTED TO
A LOCAL HOSPITAL WHERE HE WAS
PRONOUNCED DEAD.

Despite the proliferation of palm and old citrus trees,
late winter can be wet and chilly in Southern California.

The season has its share of unpredictable weather. Rain
can instantly turn to grapefruit-sized hail. Thunder and
lightning strikes—rare during the rest of the year—often

cause power outages. When those late winter squalls hit, they leave a lasting impression. Usually when a late winter storm subsides, it leaves behind large volumes of water to drain from dusty parking lots, runoff into trash-filled gutters, and flow straight through miles and miles of concrete culverts out to the Pacific Ocean. There's no slowing or stopping it.

On March 6, 2006, the region got hit with a typical late winter storm and saw nearly an inch of rain and several inches of snow in the San Gabriel Mountains.

It began as the kind of day Raymond Chandler once described as the sort with "the sun not shining and a look of hard wet rain in the clearness of the foothills."

As it had since the days of the padres, the heaviest downpours, usually in the late afternoon, flooded the lowlands of La Puente and Valinda.

The winter sun set early, and the cloud-filled sky faded into the kind of moist, cold night that hurts your toes and fingertips. It was the kind of day where most decent folks found a way to get out of work early, avoid problems with other drivers on the freeways, and bundle up indoors with a hearty meal, a good movie, or a long sleep.

Paul "Malo" Salazar had a union meeting that night at the International Brotherhood of Electrical Workers Hall, local #47, in Diamond Bar. His buddies, cousins Robert "Pee Wee" Lopez and Anthony "Youngster" Castillo, had plans to hang out. All three belonged to the Balista clique of Puente-13.

Somehow the three hooked up. And instead of going directly to a boring union meeting, Salazar offered to drive the cousins around. Hanging out turned into tagging, tagging turned into a foray into enemy turf in Bassett.

Armed with cans of black and silver spray paint, "Pee Wee," "Youngster," and "Malo" tagged utility boxes, dumpsters, and fences in Bassett. They sprayed over their rivals' names on a white 2-ton panel truck before making it clear who had been there.

Elsewhere they painted over and over:

"BSTP13"
"<-BST c P13 ->"
"Ball1STa ST CHS PEE WEE MaLO"
"Ball1STA GANG"
"P.WEE MALO BST P13 R"

It was just after sundown when Robert Whitehead arrived at the home he grew up in and shared with his mother and stepfather on Moccasin Street. It's about a block from one of the Valley's last drive-in theaters and about a ½ mile from a stretch of Valley Boulevard that caters to auto body shops, light manufacturing plants, strip joints, and taco stands.

Monday was trash day. Robert always brought in the cans when he came home. He stopped to feed something to a neighbor's cat when he noticed a couple of gang bangers tagging up a neighbor's block wall.

Whitehead's brother was a cop. Robert had heard the stories about gang members and knew what they were up to after dark and it was always no good. He had had enough. His mother lived in this neighborhood for God's sake, these punks need to knock it off. Calling the cops would be fruitless. They'd show up 45 minutes later—if at all—on a vandalism call, there's no glory in those collars; Just a lot of paperwork and hanging around the station waiting for some wannabe gangster's gangbanger parents to pick the little bastard up from the jail.

So, Whitehead took the approach that would get instant results. He confronted "Pee Wee" and "Youngster" and told them to get the hell out of his neighborhood.

They laughed at him. He grabbed for the spray can. A fight broke out.

Whitehead never saw the third man in the tagging crew. Rather than allow "Pee Wee and Youngster" to get the shit kicked out of them by some pissed-off gringo, "Malo" went to his truck, grabbed a handgun, and popped caps into the back of Whitehead's skull.

Whitehead was dead by the time he hit the pavement. "Pee Wee," "Youngster," and "Malo" jumped into "Malo's" truck and split, leaving their signatures on a piece of graffiti that would first lead homicide detectives to "Pee Wee" then to "Malo."

When it comes to newspaper coverage, murders in Bassett and La Puente don't often rate the front page. And when they get coverage, the amount of information about the circumstances is usually spotty at best.

Despite the "If it bleeds it leads" cliché, L.A. television stations don't send much more than a producer and a camera to slayings in gang neighborhoods even during those weeks when ratings are determined.

Years and years of experience have taught program directors and assignment editors that eyeballs stray from TV sets when too much gang crime is reported; it's better to stick with car chases and celebrity DUIs.

But Whitehead wasn't some macho Neighborhood Watch guy on a Charles Bronson "Death Wish" kick. And he wasn't a gang banger getting shot for some bullshit in Men's Central. Whitehead was a nearly classic innocent bystander.

***

At 44-years-old, Robert Whitehead still lived with his parents. His brother said he never wanted to be a hero. When he died, it was alone. Robert Whitehead had no children and never married.

According to his cop brother, Richard Wagnon, Whitehead didn't even have steady work. He was employed at a variety of seasonal jobs and spent much of his time indoors watching public television or the Discovery Channel.

"Once, my family said that he needed to go out and go somewhere. So, he packed up a sack lunch. He went to the desert and sat atop a big rock, ate his lunch and came home," his brother recalled when interviewed for a newspaper article. "That was just Bob."

Sheriff's Sgt. Tim Miley, who would later take over the Sohus case, caught the Whitehead investigation. CSI techs immediately zeroed in on the nearby graffiti.

Miley and crew turned their attention to Puente 13.

"In homicide, our diet is 70 percent gang and drug related. That's the diet of an average detective," he said later. This killing had to be solved. We couldn't let it go unsolved."

Whitehead quickly became political. Within hours of the shooting, county crews cleaned up layers of graffiti from freeway overpasses, cinderblock walls, and street signs in the neighborhood.

Neighbors remained too timid to speak up for fear of retaliation, but one-by-one the politicians spoke out. At first, it was just local school board members who chimed in, calling on parents to rein in their teens and take a stand against graffiti. As the investigation dragged on, the Los Angeles County Board of Supervisors found a way to get involved.

Los Angeles County Supervisor Gloria Molina offered a $25,000 reward for information leading to the arrest and conviction of Whithead's killers.

"We want to thank him for being a responsible citizen and remember him as a hero. He was just trying to step up and be a good citizen in our community and that's what we're all proud of," Molina said as she re-upped the award in the Board of Supervisors chamber in August 2006.

Miley's boss, Lt. Gil Carrillo—the same Gil Carrillo who participated in the Night Stalker investigation—welcomed the reward and said his detectives would put in whatever it took to bring peace to the Whitehead family.

"We will burn the midnight oil to solve this case, but quite frankly, we need some help," Carrillo said. "These suspects can run, but they can't hide forever."

The case would bring the heat on La Eme and its associates in Puente-13 like never before.

Miley and his crew operated wiretaps, tracked down "Pee Wee and "Malo," and began to piece together the inner workings of the Balista Avenue clique and, more importantly, the Puente-13 gang.

But Malo wasn't a run-of-the-mill gangbanger pulling off street shootings in wars over drug turf. He was different. There were no outward signs that this guy was involved in a street gang. Detectives put a tail on him. All they found out was that he went to work—on time—every day.

Not unlike a *varrio* Chris Chichester, Malo "was leading a double life," Miley said. "He was a union electrician, clean-cut, with a wife and child. The first time we interviewed him at his house, I thought, 'There's no way this guy's involved.' But the more we checked we began to realize he was the only 'Malo' out there."

Checking into "Malo," detectives learned he was raised by a single father who insisted on education. They discovered that their suspect attended Bishop Amat, a Roman Catholic High School in the *varrio* renowned for its prowess in both athletics and academics.

"Malo" even had a nearly airtight alibi for the night of the Whitehead shooting—he signed into a union meeting, Miley said.

Ultimately the wiretaps, the stakeouts, and the tails led investigators to Maria Llantada, 44. She had nothing to do with the murder of Whitehead, but Maria Llantada was running Puente 13 in the absence of her boyfriend Jacques "Jacko" Padilla. As for Jacko? He was doing life in Corcoran State Prison, alongside Charles Manson and Sirhan Sirhan, and collecting taxes from drug sales in La Puente, Norwalk, and Azusa, according to law enforcement.

With "Jacko" in the joint, Raphael "Cisco" Gonzalez and Ralph "Perrico" Rocha, a couple of *Emeros* recently released from federal custody after doing time in a 1993 racketeering/conspiracy case, tried to claim the La Puente and Norwalk drug taxes for themselves.

The fight over turf soon filled county wiretaps. Meanwhile, Miley's crew was applying as much heat as possible to get someone to roll over on "Malo," "Pee Wee," and "Youngster."

The death of an innocent bystander—a civilian—like Whitehead demanded justice.

Despite the dodge—posing as an innocent electrician— Miley knew Malo was good for Whitehead. In mid-July, he put out a composite drawing of two suspects sought in connection with the case. The drawings were eerily similar in appearance to "Malo" and "Pee Wee."

Los Angeles Times Homicide Report. July 25, 2007, 2:54 p.m.

> Paul Salazar, 31, a Latino man, was shot in the 15838 block of Fairgrove
>
> Avenue in Valinda at about 4:18 a.m. People nearby heard the crack of a single gunshot, then saw men loading the wounded man into a car. It was the man's friends, apparently trying to get him to a hospital. West Covina police pulled over the car, and called an ambulance. The man died at Queen of the Valley hospital. He may have been shot in a backyard, said Sheriff's Lt. Larry Lincoln.

Malo's death had all the earmarks of a straight-up gang execution. Gang cops recognized that the reason La Eme put an end to drive-bys happened because gang leaders didn't want the political scrutiny and the heat that comes from knocking off innocent bystanders.

Killing a civilian over a can of spray paint put too much heat on the gang. Malo paid the price. At least that's what detectives pieced together.

Even so, his buddies told cops that "Malo" was partying in the backyard of his father's home. The party went late, and he started playing with a handgun that was lying around.

"They said accidentally it went off and shot 'Malo," Miley said. "Our speculation is it wasn't an accident. There was too much pressure on them. That's speculation and rumor, but that's what we believed."

Malo's shooter pleaded no contest to involuntary manslaughter and served a short sentence in connection with the slaying.

The key to solving Whitehead, "Malo" was dead. The investigation didn't wind down, it intensified. Miley began to focus on "Pee Wee" and "Youngster." Both had split town.

Hoping a wiretap would lead them to "Pee Wee's hideout, detectives found Llantada. And Llantada's words on tape led detectives to discover the plot to kill "Cisco" and "Perico" for their disrespect of "Jacko."

The deal fell apart around Halloween when 26-year-old David 'Bulldog' Sahagun of Taft, was arrested in Montebello with an AK-47 assault rifle in his pickup truck. He was on his way to kill Cisco, police said later.

Press Conference, 18th Floor Clara Shortridge Foltz Criminal Justice Center Dec. 6, 2007, 3 p.m.

FOR IMMEDIATE RELEASE

WEST COVINA—A 20-year-old man was charged today with murder in connection with last year's fatal shooting of a Valinda man who was trying to stop taggers in his neighborhood.

Anthony Alex Castillo appeared in court in West Covina this afternoon ... He is being held on $1 million bail.

It was the investigation into the Whitehead murder that led Sheriff's investigators to an unrelated conspiracy-to-commit-murder plot involving the Mexican Mafia. Six people, including three women, were charged in that case. Their case is being tried in downtown Los Angeles.

The newspaper articles followed:

From the *San Gabriel Valley Tribune*, Dec. 6, 2007:

In police raids Tuesday, investigators seized an assortment of handguns, shotguns and assault rifles and quantities of methamphetamine, marijuana and heroin, said Los Angeles County sheriff's Chief Richard Castro.

'(The Whitehead murder) case turned out to have deep roots leading to the criminal organization known as the Mexican Mafia," Los Angeles County District Attorney Steve Cooley said at a press conference announcing the arrests.

... Among the arrested were Maria Dolores "Lola" Llantada, 42; Yvonne Colleen Montes, 30; and Angelita Martinez, 37, all from La Puente and Valinda.

All but Martinez were being held in lieu of $10 million bail. Martinez's bail was set at $5 million.

Meanwhile, the *Los Angeles Times* gave some other details:

> The case, together with interviews with law enforcement and gang members, paints a picture of the Mexican Mafia as a snake pit. Though calling each other "brothers," members constantly conspire against one another and use young street gang members to do their dirtiest work.

> A deep division exists between members in state prison and those in federal custody, (Deputy District Attorney Gary) Hearnsberger said.

The split began in the mid-1990s, Hernsberger said, when federal prosecutors began attacking the Mexican Mafia's street operations with racketeering prosecutions that sent many leaders to federal prison.

When the men who joined the Mexican Mafia in federal prison returned to Southern California, they expected to exercise power on streets where state prison members and their buddies are in control.

Within days, "Pee Wee" would join "Youngster" in county jail. As 2008 began, Miley prepared the high-profile case for court. He gathered up witnesses, got evidence in order, and stayed in touch with criminalists and the DA's office. By August, prosecutors had finished their prelim. All that remained would be trial.

In a 2023 interview, Miley recalled he was getting ready to move out of homicide when he wrapped up the case.

"I just been moved from fresh cases to sergeant of the unsolved unit," Miley said. "I was supposed to take over the wiretap room but then it moved to this location that was too far to drive to, so there was a spot in the unsolved unit. I kind of wanted to be done with being called out in the middle of the night on business."

He took the job.

"I'm about in my second week, and I walk in there, and the phones are going crazy. And they're, 'hey there's this guy's been arrested and has to do with this 1994 murder and skeleton recovery.'"

Opening the thin case file, Miley learned his assignment involved John and Linda Sohus, a young couple who disappeared from their San Marino home in 1985 and a guy named Gerhartsreiter who hadn't been heard from in years. He reviewed what he had.

CHAPTER 15.

A NEW NAME

A name, or identity, is a powerful thing. It is a descriptor that allows people to make quick judgments and assumptions about us. While we can understand the harm of assumptions, for the human mind it is a fast way to categorize a lot of information in a short amount of time. Assumptions also give us social context for the "rules" we need to interact with new and different people.
—**Tonya Ladipo, LCSW,** *Identity: The Power of a Name*, **2013, goodtherapy.org**

At first, Chris and Mihoko's relationship was primarily a series of booty calls at her place. But, as their relationship grew more serious, he prepared to leave Greenwich and move into her apartment in Manhattan's Tudor City. The decision was made when he lost his job at Nikko.

Moving to the city meant Chris would have to sell some possessions. The white Nissan pickup, for example? He offered it to the reverend's son.

"Chris one day said he had a white pickup that he had used in a movie, and he no longer needed it," Chris Bishop said. "If you want it, just write to California for the registration."

Bishop couldn't believe his ears. The little Nissan was in pretty good shape. It had low mileage, a nice blue shag carpet interior, and a sweet camper shell.

"It looked in good shape. That's probably why I believed it was used in the production business," Bishop said.

Bishop paid $7 to register the truck and waited.

Even in 1988, the U.S. had a pretty well-connected database system of vehicle and driver information. Back in San Marino, when the police did their final missing persons report, they entered the Nissan in the system with a note that whoever was driving it might know something about the missing John and Linda Sohus.

Not only that, the company that loaned John and Linda for the initial purchase would no doubt want their money back. As if on cue, the first thing Bishop heard back came from California. The truck had a lien on it. He'd have to pay it off if he wanted the title.

Bishop loved the truck and didn't want to pay the lien, so he bought a beat-up version of the vehicle, took the plates and put them on the pickup he bought from Chris. He figured it would save some money.

"It was a bad idea. Not my finest hour," Bishop would say later.

Title in hand, Bishop drove the truck for a couple of weeks before speaking to a friend who said it was a stupid idea to drive a truck with fake plates. So, he called Chris and offered the truck back.

Chris told Bishop, "Nope. I don't care what you do with it, I don't want it."

Bishop took the truck to a train station parking lot somewhere between Greenwich and New York City, parked it, left it unlocked with the keys in the ignition, and walked away.

Within hours, a detective was knocking on the door at his parents' house. The detective had some questions and held out a photo of Chris.

"Do you know this person?" the detective asked.

"Yes, that's Chris Crowe."

The detective, veteran Sgt. Dan Allen, one of the first Black police officers in Greenwich, was known for his compassion but also his ability to cut through all the bullshit he'd heard over the years from hardened criminals and practiced, if wealthy, liars.

No, Allen replied. His name is Christian Gerhartsreiter. He's wanted in connection with a missing persons case back in California.

And that truck you tried to register? It belongs to the missing couple.

"I lied and said I knew nothing about a truck," Bishop recalled. "I said, 'Yes I know Chris, but know nothing about a truck.'"

Allen's appearance coincided with George Yankovich's promotion to detective at San Marino. In the fall of 1988, Yankovich began a search for the missing truck and reopened the missing persons investigation. When he heard there was a sighting, he called Greenwich and spoke to Allen, explaining he was looking for someone known as Chris Chichester or possibly Christian Gerhartsreiter.

Almost immediately after Allen left the front door, Bishop got a call from Chris. He asked what was going on.

"What's going on is a detective just showed up at my house and said you're wanted for a missing person investigation," Bishop exclaimed. "Who the fuck are you really?"

Chris replied, "I gotta go," and hung up the phone.

Bishop never again heard from him.

Although Allen's contact with Bishop was initially unsuccessful, the young minister's son began to have second thoughts about his actions related to the truck and lying to the police. He called Allen back and gave up Chris' Greenwich address.

By the time Allen arrived, Chris had already moved out.

Allen dug in. He discovered a post office box registered to Christopher Crowe and was able to identify Ralph Boynton as Chris' boss at Kidder Peabody. On a Sunday afternoon, just after he and Chris had returned from Los Angeles, Boynton got a call from Allen.

He gave Allen the three phone numbers he had for Chris. Allen, frustrated that he was unable to catch up with Chris, asked Boynton if he could arrange a meeting at his Wall Street office on Monday morning.

So, Boynton set up a meeting, telling Chris to show up at 6 a.m. He didn't mention that Allen would be there waiting. But Chris didn't show. Boynton arranged two other meetings and Chris dipped out of showing up for those as well.

"He offered the excuse that he had been busy working for his parents," Boynton recalled. "I suggested we have dinner someplace, maybe he agreed?"

The issue, as Chris explained it, was that "his parents were in harm's way. They had been possibly kidnapped by foreign entities, possibly Pakistani or Asian. I can't remember which," Boynton recalled.

Although he had the possibility of making hundreds of thousands of dollars in the lucrative Eurobond trading business, Chris never again showed up at Kidder Peabody.

He called Ralph one more time and asked to go on an extended leave. Boynton didn't allow it.

Even though he couldn't get a meeting, Allen was undeterred. One of the three numbers Boynton had given him belonged to Mihoko Manabe, a slight soft-spoken Japanese woman, who was living with Chris. So, Allen called and asked to speak to Chris.

Manabe took a message and gave it to her lover. He pleaded with her not to reveal that he was with her. Chris explained that Allen was not a real cop and their lives, and the lives of his parents were in extreme danger.

"Chris said I should disregard what (Allen) said and to tell him if he should ever call that Chris wasn't there. Detective Allen did call again, and I did say what Chris told me to say. What he said was that his parents were in grave danger and because of that he was in danger and that there were people coming to get him and his family."

There was only one way out. They would have to marry and escape to Europe where they could go into hiding. It sounded dangerous and a little crazy, but Manabe loved Chris and ultimately agreed to go along with the scheme.

Before setting off on their adventure, Chris called the Greenwich post office and closed his P.O. box. He never returned.

Then, the couple went to the German Consulate in New York. Chris had his passport stamped for a planned return.

"We went together, he had a passport with him, a German passport, I believe it was green it had the emblem of Germany on the front," Manabe said. "And I asked why it was a German passport? And Chris said it was a fake one."

Unable to reach Chris, Allen closed his investigation, and called Yankovich. There was no plan to follow up. The manhunt, such as it was, ended there.

Chris had no idea that Allen had ended his search, but when the calls ended, he told his fiancée that they didn't have to go to Europe after all.

"The first thing he did was grow a beard and a mustache and he started to wear contacts instead of glasses, changed his hair color. I helped color his hair and eyebrows as well to blonde," Manabe said.

There were other changes too, she said.

"We never went out together. We always walked down different sides of the street. We never came out of the building at the same time, and we never received mail at our address. We always had a post office box."

It was all Chris' idea to act this way, she said.

"He was always paranoid that someone would be rifling through our trash, so he always shredded all the mail. He shredded the garbage, and we threw them out in a public place."

Eventually they moved to an apartment in Manhattan.

Chris was deep into counter-surveillance.

"He told me that he had dumped his car off the side of the street at some point. After that he never had a car. He never drove after that. I was the one driving."

And Chris never worked again. He took care of household matters, he set up leases, bank accounts, utilities in "my name," Manabe said.

The couple also planned their wedding ceremony. In the summer of 1989, Chris had taken out an American Express card on Manabe's account with a new name.

Manabe learned the name as they scoped wedding locations. They decided to look for a place in Maine and stayed at a seashore inn that had a restaurant. One night, Chris called the restaurant seeking a reservation. The maître d' said the restaurant was taking no reservations that night.

A few minutes later, Chris called again. He changed his voice slightly and again asked for a reservation. This time he was Clark Rockefeller. And the reservation sailed through.

"That's the first time I heard that name," Manabe said.

Chris would now be Clark. Clark Rockefeller.

He liked the name and the doors it opened, Manabe said.

CHAPTER 16.

BACKYARD, 1994

"Precautionary acts are the 'behaviors that offenders
commit before, during, or after an offence (sic)
that are consciously intended to confuse, hamper,
or defeat investigative or forensic efforts for
the purposes of concealing their identity, their
connection to the crime, or the crime itself."
—**Turvey, Brent E.** *Criminal profiling: An introduction
to behavioral evidence analysis*, **Academic Press, 2011**

Didi, John, and Linda had been gone from 1920 Lorain Road
for several years.

The home's new owner had done a meticulous job of
erasing their presence. First, he transformed the little ranch
house into a two-story Tudor estate. Secondly, he refurbished
the guest house/garage so that he would have an office/man
cave.

Chris was just a distant memory too. After Det. Dan
Allen failed to catch up with him in Greenwich or New
York, details about him and the missing truck began to fade.

Parada now had a home that befitted the San Marino
lifestyle. There was just one thing missing: A swimming
pool. Everyone might have lived happily ever after, but it
wasn't to be.

The pool created complications no one could have
foreseen—especially after the discovery of those bones.

Pasadena Star-News, July 3, 1994

Man sought in case of San Marino bones

Police say missing renter's not a suspect, but he may have important information.

SAN MARINO—He surfaces in affluent towns, talks his way into high society by joining a good church, then suddenly disappears.

Police said Christopher Crowe Mount Batten Chichester doesn't take his wealthy new friends for much. Just a few nice dinners and perhaps a little of their innocence for buying into his fantastic stories.

But he took something of great value to police when he suddenly left San Marino nine years ago—an account of what were probably the last days of a murdered man's life.

Sheriff's Homicide Detective Bob Carr told reporters that Chris was "not a suspect. However, it is crucial that we talk to him."

Police also wanted reporters to know that the missing man had several aliases. They were: "Christopher Crowe; Chris Chichester; Christopher Crowe Mount Batten Chichester; Christian Gerhartsreiter."

The Star-News described Chris as a transient socialite who dressed well and told sometimes unbelievable tales.

Carr had spent at least three weeks on Gerhartsreiter's trail. It was cold. The detective was able to establish that after leaving San Marino in 1985, Gerhartsreiter had passed himself off as a computer expert, a film producer, and sometime stockbroker. He'd been in Connecticut and possibly New York City.

"He dressed well and was articulate and knowledgeable about whatever subject he happened to be talking about. He's a very interesting character."

But as every good homicide detective knows, there's only so much time to make a case. And in the mid-1990s, the crush of gang- and drug-related cases making their way through the doors of Sheriff's homicide threatened to distract the detective sooner rather than later.

"We're running against the clock," he concluded.

In another age, the reporting on Chris might have had resonance. The last local update on the case ran in newspapers about a week later. And, despite all the outreach, Carr was no closer to finding Chris even though detectives fielded calls from London and Brighton, England.

There were other problems. Like the San Marino School District in the mid-1980s, when Chris volunteered to paint the halls and take part in high school plays, the Los Angeles County Department of Coroner faced budgetary problems. Layoffs were threatened, and the quality of work would prove—especially in the investigation of the O.J. Simpson case—to be less than professional.

Take for example the autopsy of Nicole Brown done in June of 1994. Dr. Irwin Golden, the forensic pathologist performing the examination, didn't preserve her stomach contents, likely pasta. As a result, his entire work on the case was called into question. Golden's imperious and defensive manner on the witness stand in the preliminary hearing didn't help much either.

Unfortunately, the office didn't do much better with the remains found at 1920 Lorain Road. Most of John's body and his clothes had been cremated. Just a few pieces of skull remained in the lab a few years later. A lot of the forensic evidence from 1994 was mishandled.

I had seen those pieces during a tour of the lab in 2005. At the time, Steve Dowell, the coroner's tool mark expert, was using what remained of John for "educational purposes." Because John's skull was broken twice: once about the time he died, the other breakage from the pool-digging backhoe; the six pieces of skull presented a perfect opportunity to show students the difference in living bone—essentially an organ—and dried old bone. Bottom line? They break differently. Old bone is brittle. Living bone gives; it has what Dowell described as "plasticity."

If you follow Huntington Drive far enough west out of San Marino, eventually it will turn into Mission Road as it passes through the El Sereno and then Lincoln Heights neighborhoods of Los Angeles. Stay on it and the onetime trolley route designed by Henry Huntington will take you straight to the Los Angeles County Department of Coroner, at 1104 N. Mission Road.

The campus consists of two buildings: one that houses administration, the other bodies and body parts. There's a gift shop, called "Skeletons in the Closet."

Interested in a beach towel with the chalk outline of a body on it? How about an official coroner's coffee mug? Want to read a book about weird Hollywood deaths. Need a video detailing the coroner's investigation into the death of jockey, Chris Antley, a onetime popular favorite at Santa Anita? Chances are you'll find it at the gift shop.

Until his retirement in 2011, Dowell's lab in the basement of the laboratory building on North Mission Road contained the sanitized chronicle of weird passings, unconventional brutality, and sheer violence resulting in death in Los Angeles County.

On any given day, a visitor could examine a skull that had been pierced with a claw hammer, a thin slice of sternum nicked with a serrated knife, bone gnawed to the marrow by wild animals, a gold tooth that caused a woman's death when it was accidentally swallowed and lodged in her esophagus, and a whole host of other wounds fit for the TV show *1,000 Ways to Die*. Alongside the macabre display, Dowell maintained the collection of tools that resulted in most of those gruesome fatal injuries.

As Dowell would point out, not all deaths handled by his office involve guns or knives. Take the hammer-pierced skull. Two neatly rectangular and evenly spaced wounds are its only apparent damage. If you want to get an idea of how that might look, go to the garage, get a claw hammer, and bring the claw end down sharply on a piece of cardboard, Styrofoam, or wood. You will see the claw leaves two very distinct holes. If delivered with the same force to a living man or woman's skull, the claw would incise through tissue and bone causing massive trauma and death. In an instance like this, a medical examiner would classify the cause of death as sharp-force trauma, as opposed to blunt force trauma.

Blunt force trauma usually occurs in falls, traffic accidents, or beatings with blunt objects.

***

Study enough of these cases and, like Dowell, you begin to learn that it's not just the entirety of a wound that's important; it's the little things that matter most. For example, take individual tools. Like individual guns, they have specific signatures that could have only come from that tool. In a larger sense, the manufacturing process at any given tool plant will leave distinct markings as well.

Dowell's job was to match tools and wounds.

In Dowell's opinion, the person buried at 1920 Lorain Road was knocked in the head with a two-by-four. The weapon smashed his forehead. Two more blows were delivered to the temple. Any one of the blows would have been fatal.

That the skull was in pieces presented a problem. Dowell believed Joe Perez's Bobcat was probably the cause. And he explained that the original wounds exhibited an elasticity only seen in living bone and tissue. The other breaks and fragments didn't exhibit the same sort of pattern. In fact, the breaks looked like they came well after the victim died—as if the box he was buried in had been crushed when it was first unearthed.

The shattering presented a concern for investigators. Early on, the coroner's team fixed on the cause of death as blunt force trauma. They could see it in the way the skull had been smashed.

There was also a lingering question about identity. Did the bones buried in that San Marino backyard belong to John Sohus?

Another question, "Why one body and not two?"

There are a variety of methods used by the coroner to identify human remains. For example, a family member might view a picture of the decedent to establish identity. There might be a driver's license or other form of identification with the body to help make that determination. A coroner's employee might also make use of fingerprints, dental records, or historical X-Rays to put a name on a body.

Doing any of that proved difficult with the body found buried at 1920 Lorain Road. First, John Sohus' mother was dead and if his wife wasn't buried there in the backyard with him, then she was missing. So, there was no immediate next-of-kin to turn to for help. Secondly, there was no apparent identification buried with the body in the backyard crypt. Thirdly, because the remains had decomposed to just bone, there would be no way to extract fingerprints.

Also, frustrating investigators early on was their inability to track down accurate dental records or X-Rays that had been performed on John during his brief existence. Finally, because DNA science was in its infancy in 1994, and because John had been adopted (those records were sealed by court order), there was no sure way to do a complete scientific analysis of the bones when the body was finally unearthed.

Judith Daye reassembled the skeleton in a lab at the coroner's office on Mission Road. And immediately other problems presented themselves, For example, a few bones were never recovered—including a kneecap, a cheek bone, four fingers, and a few toes.

Conducting a standard analysis of the remains, which included measurements of the pelvis and the skull, Daye wrote up a report and concluded the body was that of a 5-foot-7-inch male, "possibly mongoloid." The unusual term could have referred to an Asian or Tongva native. Daye's initial conclusion didn't sit well with investigators who believed they knew better.

First of all—and perhaps most obvious—there was no way in hell that a member of the Tongva Indian tribe— present in the region during the establishment of the Spanish Missions in the 18th Century—would be found buried in a flannel shirt and blue jeans. Loin cloth and headdress maybe; jeans, socks, and boots—no fucking way. It was even much less likely that the head of such a native would be buried in a fiberglass box and wrapped in a plastic book bag from the University of Wisconsin, Milwaukee and USC or that a telephone cord would have been found among the skeletal remains.

Needless to say, native burial was ruled out early by those reading the clues at the crime scene.

Secondly, although no less obvious, John Sohus, who had gone missing back in 1985, was decidedly Caucasian— white. Daye's conclusions, if allowed to stand, would seriously screw up any chance to prosecute a case against the person or persons who buried the body. Knowing there was a problem, the investigative team, including Suchey, ultimately re-wrote substantial portions of Daye's report. The final copy wouldn't be ready until October.

Daye didn't like being overruled. She felt disrespected.

But "I acceded to their judgement," Daye said. Several years later, Daye, now a schoolteacher in Northern California, defended her initial findings. "I felt that was my best report at that point."

Daye's original examination also included some other curious details. She observed that the skeleton had cracked ribs, "as though some sort of pressure had been applied." Daye couldn't tell if the ribs had been cracked before or after death. The fact could be a minor, but important point, in determining the role of Joe Perez's Bobcat in the destruction of the skeleton.

Detectives and analysts processing the crime scene at 1920 Lorain Road cataloged what seemed to be volumes of evidence. For example, there were the plastic bags that held John's severed head.

One appeared to be red and gold—almost USC colors. In fact, it had the Trojan Stores logo that was only used from 1979 until 1982. The other, when examined closely under what crime scene analysts call an alternate light source, appeared to bear the logo of the University of Wisconsin, Milwaukee.

Los Angeles County criminologist, Lynn Herold, knew almost immediately she was looking at specialty bags; the distinctive kind that universities give out with bookstore purchases. The logos appeared to be stuck in time too. They were right out of the late '70s or early 1980s.

A Ph.D., Herold, who has been known to wear her strikingly long black hair tied into twin buns on either side of her head, described the Lorain Road crime scene as one she could never quite shake. "This case had some outstanding features," she said.

The reasons that made it so memorable had little to do with John and Linda or Chris or Didi or even the three-foot-deep makeshift grave in the backyard of a fancy San Marino estate. Nope.

The day John turned up was Lynne's 10th wedding anniversary. Earlier in that May 1994 day, she had been attending a funeral put on by a friend whose young son died suddenly.

"The funeral was that day," Herold said. "I was actually relieved to get the call."

There were other connections as well. Mr. Parada, the homeowner, was in business with Lynne's across-the-street neighbor. "It has, from day one, stuck in my head."

Herold is no stranger in L.A. courtrooms where she can be often found explaining cutting-edge forensics in high-profile cases. In the 2007 murder prosecution of music producer Phil Spector, it was Herold who provided some of the most graphic testimony in the prosecution's case laying out the difference between clotting and stringy blood, blood splatter, and bodily fluids as jurors reviewed gruesome crime scene photos.

County law enforcement officials believe few scientists are better at identifying trace evidence at a crime scene and using it to piece together a scenario that might explain how it got there. While criminologists like Herold have to be experts in histology—the study of the body's seven primary tissues—they also have to be proficient in a variety of subjects. In Herold's case, that includes understanding how underwater plants and sea life interact with dead bodies.

Herold once amazed other investigators when, after studying barnacles attached to a gunshot victim found floating in the L.A. harbor, she was able to determine that said victim had been dead for about 15 days.

In another instance, while working a 12-year-old cold case body dump in the Angeles National Forest, Herold was able to reconstruct a woman's murder by reexamining items that had been in storage all that time.

That examination was like one that Herold performed on some of the clothing found with John's bones. Under a microscope, it appeared that John's button-down shirt had been pierced with a "tool like an ice pick."

It also appeared that there were several areas of the shirt that were cut by a "sharp force," Herold said.

Under a microscope, Herold explained, crime scene investigators can learn a lot from something as simple as a shirt, and with the right lighting and magnification, "you can see threads and fibers that they're made out of and if they are disturbed in any way, it tells you something."

Dr. Frank Sheridan, the San Bernardino County Chief Medical Examiner, speaks with the lilting Irish brogue of a priest directly imported from the old sod. A receding salt-and-pepper hairline, he wears the goatee of a distinguished professor from some old movie.

An expert in neuropathology—the study of fatal brain injuries—Sheridan, as San Berdoo County's chief ghoul, estimates he's performed upwards of 8,000 autopsies. That's about the size of Siegsdorf, the town where Christian Gerhartsreiter was born in 1961.

L.A. County officials asked Sheridan to examine what was left of Sohus' skull in 2008. He determined the skull exhibited several fractures that occurred around the time of John's death and several others that occurred long after John's death.

***

Sheridan, a 1971 graduate of Dublin University, has a well-rounded and worldly resume. More than one attorney described him as being "straight out of central casting."

The pathologist interned at St. Vincent's in Dublin; then, in 1974 Sheridan became a medical officer for the government of Malawi, a central African nation and one of the poorest countries on Earth. From there, it was back to Ireland, where Sheridan was a graduate student in pharmacology for two years.

In 1978, Sheridan left Ireland for the U.S. and took a teaching post at the University of Oregon. In 1982, he took up residency at Loma Linda University Medical Center. To become a U.S. citizen, Sheridan worked as a family practitioner for a year in Yucca Valley. In 1988, Sheridan was appointed San Bernardino County's head M.E. He still teaches at Loma Linda, where Kelln, a Canadian immigrant, also taught.

As with anyone in his position, Sheridan has seen his share of human tragedy. Sheridan's resume includes piecing together evidence in the grim slaying of 5-year-old Arthur Jennings Jr., who was drugged, starved, tortured, and beaten to death by his parents in 1996.

The tale is so horrible and sick it's hard to imagine what homicide detectives—or Sheridan—felt as they conducted their investigation into the crime.

In February 1996, the Jennings family reported to the San Bernardino County Sheriff's Department that their son, Arthur Jr., had gone missing. The truth was far more disturbing.

"Defendant acknowledged that at various times he pushed, elbowed, kicked, shook, and hit Arthur. After initially blaming (others), defendant eventually admitted striking Arthur on the back of his head with the fireplace shovel on the day he died. Defendant did state, however, that he did not want Arthur to die. Nevertheless, when later asked whether he ever had attempted to suffocate Arthur, defendant responded, 'I don't know, maybe,'" according to California Supreme Court documents.

"During the interview, the detectives posed questions regarding incidents that had occurred prior to Arthur's death. Defendant acknowledged he and Michelle had discussed 'killing' and 'getting rid of' Arthur. Michelle said defendant wanted to shoot Arthur in the head, but she suggested returning him to Wilma or giving him to Art, Sr. Defendant admitted that two days prior to Arthur's death, he and Michelle drove around the desert looking for a place to 'dump the body,'" the documents added.

After they killed their little boy, the Jennings dumped his naked body down an abandoned mine shaft in the desert.

Recounting the sad tale for jurors, Sheridan went through the child's injuries one by one.

Ultimately, "Dr. Sheridan gave the cause of death as 'the entire problem'—the drugs, the physical injuries, and the malnutrition and emaciation—'together,' that brought about the resulting death. He described Arthur as in a 'downhill slide' and 'very near to the end of his life' because of malnutrition and 'the whole body not functioning properly,'" according to court records.

In 2005, Sheridan testified against two Kern County deputies accused of so severely beating a jail inmate that his brain stem was severed as a result. The case, People v. Lindini, is one of the few ever in California that found law enforcement officers responsible in the death of an inmate. Inmate Lance Moore was pepper sprayed, then pummeled by at least six deputies while his hands were shackled to his waist. He suffered four beatings while in custody. Deputies later beat the chained man with batons, boots, and other weapons.

Eventually, Moore's "eyes were swollen shut; his face was covered in blood," a witness testified in a criminal hearing. "His face actually was crushed. (As if) you took a doll and squeezed the face in, a rubber doll; his face looked like it was caved in. It was swollen ... actually crushed in. It was pretty nasty."

Moore also had a significant amount of blood coming from his ear when he was strapped to a medical gurney and beaten again—even being punched in the nuts by a female deputy taking part in the battle. The fatal blow was delivered by a deputy who twisted Moore's head to one side, pushed his forearm into Moore's throat and trachea while forcing the inmate's jaw closed.

As Moore lay suffocating to death, deputies took turns taking cell phone pictures, which they later shared with one another.

"[The] mechanism of death here is basically the brain gets this impact injury to the base of the brain and the breathing simply stops. Person stops breathing. And then, even though he was resuscitated, he can't breathe any more. And from the initial resuscitation from the initial event, his brain is now suffering from hypoxia [i.e., lack of oxygen] plus the trauma and it swells," Sheridan testified.

Sheridan also played a role in determining how Briele Johnson, an 18-year-old woman stuffed into a suitcase by her boyfriend after the pair got high on methamphetamine, died.

Inland Valley Daily Bulletin reporter Rod Leveque remembered dueling perspectives of forensic science in the courtroom as being "pretty cool." In court, Sheridan matched wits with Dr. Michael Baden, a one-time New York City Medical Examiner turned host of HBO's *Autopsy*. As Leveque recalled, Baden, hired by the defense in the case, argued that the young woman, "a tweeker," died because she had overdosed on speed.

Sheridan, on the other hand, concluded that "the tweeker" was strangled or suffocated by her boyfriend. Maybe it happened during an episode of rough sex; maybe he got tired of the young woman and offed her. It wasn't the kind of stuff that could be ruled out based on the autopsy findings. Sheridan said it could have been just as likely the young woman died as result of being stuffed into the suitcase alive.

No matter how you slice it, the death was a homicide, Sheridan opined.

Not a suicide, not an accident, but straight-up murder.

***

Enough Southern Californians have seen hopped-up, acne-scarred, and toothless speed freaks acting like stupid tweakers to know there's a possibility the victim could have climbed into the suitcase on her own to get away from the prying eyes, or the spiders or the Yakuza, or whatever paranoia she may have been afflicted with at the time.

Her boyfriend only admitted helping Briele into the suitcase. Here's the lede from one story on the case that appeared in the *San Bernardino Sun* shortly after Briele's body was discovered.

"Mark Edward Thomas denied killing his 18-year-old girlfriend to police but admitted to stuffing her body in a suitcase and hauling it from one Ontario motel to another," according to police reports.

Although detectives found pictures suggesting Thomas may have severely choked 18-year-old Briele Johnson in the past, he steadfastly denied ever harming her ... according to the documents.

Testifying for the defense, Baden said the teen prostitute OD'd on speed.

Sheridan said the overall condition of Briele's body told a somewhat different story.

"Sheridan said a normal person can die of strangulation in as little as three minutes," Leveque wrote in a story on the trial. "Methamphetamine, however, can speed up the process because it excites the body and can accelerate heart failure."

At trial, Sheridan said a wound on the dead girl's neck told him that a "cord or strap" had been wrapped around it. She also showed signs of

petechial hemorrhaging—burst blood vessels—around her face. It's a classic sign of strangulation. The other is a broken hyoid bone.

Despite the petechiae, Sheridan didn't completely rule out the chance Johnson was choked into unconsciousness and stuffed into the suitcase.

"There was the possibility she was strangled unconscious and dying when she was put in the suitcase," Leveque reported. "That would have finished her off."

Ultimately, a superior court jury chose the testimony of the understated Irishman over that of the celebrity pathologist. In the end, Mark Edward Thomas received a life sentence for committing second degree murder.

Prosecutors and detectives knew Sheridan's track record when they asked him to give a second opinion on the death of John Sohus.

It was only after he examined the remaining pieces of John Sohus' skull, that Sheridan concluded the young man was alive when the fatal blows were struck by his killer in 1985. He examined the "reconstructed" remains in the crime lab at Cal State Los Angeles, less than 10 miles from where John's body was originally buried.

After examining the fractured bone, and determining which puzzle piece might fit where, Sheridan said a break on the right side of John's head—one of seven such fractures—was the result of a blow that was delivered about the time he died.

"The individual was alive when these fractures occurred and died very shortly afterward," he testified during a preliminary hearing in the case.

Careful not to refer to the skull as belonging to an actual living, breathing human being who dreamed big dreams but never really left the confines of his mother's home in San Marino, Sheridan, his Irish brogue only slightly softening the gruesome detail continued his testimony about John's skull. He needed to explain that these fatal injuries were delivered by another human being—not the result of an errant pool contractor's wayward Bobcat.

"This individual would have died shortly after receiving these injuries in the absence of medical care," he continued.

While John's body rotted away in a shallow grave, the decomposition process left investigators clues they could interpret 23 years later.

Over time, blood, brain tissue, nerve, and muscle all become liquid. That "fluid gets into the crack of the bone," Sheridan calmly explained. "Look for it at the edge to see if they are discolored or not."

Newer, fresher breaks—like those caused by a pool contractor's tractor—would be pale.

The seven pieces of skull yielded other clues about the violent nature of John's death. Sheridan called them signs of "plastic deformation." Living bone has an elasticity. When it's broken, it deforms in much the same way as a piece of plastic might slightly change its shape if it were torn in half. When treated in a living patient, plastic deformations of bone can be repaired. Not so for the dead. The breaks Sheridan used to come to his conclusions showed no signs of healing.

The heavily damaged side of John's skull also exhibited a sort of "eggshell fracturing" that suggested to Sheridan the dead man was struck twice by his killer.

Using an exhibit, Sheridan explained how the eggshell fracture also told experts what sort of weapon might have been used in the slaying.

"Two blows in this area are very strongly suggestive of an object," he said. "The impact surface is curved."

What sort of weapon might that be?

"Like a baseball bat with a rounded top," Sheridan said, differing slightly with Dowell, the tool mark expert who believed John was struck in the side of the head with a flat 2 X 4.

Whatever hit him, it's very likely John's scalp was shredded by the blow, blood probably poured profusely from the wounds.

The human skull itself is about ¼ inch thick. It is, however, an incredibly strong bone and cracking it is like cracking a coconut—it requires a lot of force. The blows that killed John were delivered with anywhere from 200 pounds per square foot to a 1000 pounds per square foot of force, Sheridan said.

For comparison purposes, 200 pounds per square foot is about the outside limit of force that the wing of a commercial Boeing 737 airliner can withstand. On the other hand, 1000 pounds per square foot of pressure is about what a small tractor like a Bobcat exerts on the ground beneath it.

Experts say the jaws of a Great White Shark exert a pressure of 400 pounds per square inch when clamping down.

"It's an area with a lot of room for fudging," Sheridan admitted. Nonetheless "These are significant. There's a lot of force involved with these blows."

Sometimes weathered, torn, abraded, or cut.

In this case, Herold "clearly saw tearing and sharp force cuts." They appeared to be the type of cuts that could have been made with a box cutter, a razor blade, or scissors—although it didn't seem likely from the shape of the cuts that scissors were involved.

Herold counted six cuts—four in the back of John's shirt and two on the left sleeve, all of which she said were inflicted by a sharp instrument. At least two—on the left sleeve—might have even been defensive wounds. All of the cuts occurred before John's body began to decompose.

At some point early in the investigation, detectives decided that even though the new homeowner had turned it into a makeshift office, they needed to tear up the guest house where Chris lived to see if there was any trace evidence of bloodshed.

Herold took part in the examination, which required the use of Luminol, a very sensitive liquid that when mixed with dried blood will glow in the dark under a black light.

Someone decided to perform the test on the same night as the summer solstice, six weeks after the body was discovered.

"We needed complete dark to do it and we were out there for a very long time," Herold recalled.

The test determined that dried blood was present in four spots on the guest house's slab foundation. The spots varied in size and were identified as 1, 2, 3, and 4.

Stain #1 Herold described as about 55 centimeters by 59 centimeters or about two feet by two feet; stain #2 was slightly longer, 60 centimeters, and 30 centimeters wide; stain #3 was circular. It had a 14-centimeter diameter. As for stain #4, it measured 32 centimeters by 8 centimeters, Herold said.

These weren't the sort of blood stains a shaving cut might cause; they were much too big.

All four of the stains exhibited some distinct qualities in that they appeared to have been wiped. Standing there in the midnight darkness, Herold saw what she later described as a "wiping pattern."

"Either the blood was wet or the object wiping through it was wet, like a wet rag," she continued. If anything, it was consistent with someone attempting to wipe up a blood stain.

A body could have been dragged across the floor. Blood may have soaked through a carpet. Herold wrote up her notes and forwarded them to the detectives in charge of the case.

Sometime in 1995, the file went into storage waiting for Miley to reopen it.

PART II

CHAPTER 17.

PERSON OF INTEREST

"History is moving pretty quickly these days, and
the heroes and villains keep on changing parts."
—Ian Fleming, *Casino Royale*

An unshaven man in a blue polo shirt sits in a vinyl chair.
He's beginning to go bald, and his large forehead stops at
the top of a pair of oversized horn-rimmed glasses. There's
a rail fastened to the wall on the man's left. Other than that,
the whitewashed walls are bare.

A booking log will list his height as 5' 6". Weight 140.
A little guy.

The room is sparsely furnished and harshly lit by cheap
fluorescent bulbs. Catty-corner—across the table from
the man in the blue polo shirt—sits a woman with dark,
shoulder-length curly hair. She's wearing a rose-colored
blouse and black polyester pants. She's got a notebook in
front of her and a bottle of water at her left. The table is large
enough to seat four.

A video recorder flips to life.

Grey screen. Fizzzzzt.

"The date is August 2. It is 2008. It is 7:04 p.m. And
I'm here at the Baltimore office of the FBI, um with Clark
Rockefeller..."

A second man pulls up a chair next to the woman. He's
wearing a blue work shirt and dark tie. He's big and mostly
bald. The mustache gives him away. He's a cop.

The woman continues to speak: "...And sergeant Detective Ray Mosher of the Boston Police Department. I'm Special Agent Tamara Harty with the FBI out of Boston."

Rockefeller, the man in the blue polo, fidgets in his chair. An elaborate charade is taking place.

Detectives already know his real name is Christian Karl Gerhartsreiter, a German national who came to the United States on a student visa in the late 1970s and never left. For now, they will allow the man in the blue polo shirt to play dress up as Rockefeller. When a fingerprint analysis comes back it will prove their suspicions. Meanwhile, in California, Tim Miley, the homicide detective booked a flight to the East Coast.

As for the man in the polo shirt, his left wrist is cuffed to the rail on the wall. It stays in place. In a soothing voice, Harty reads the man the standard Miranda warning. He'd been arrested on suspicion of abducting his daughter, Reigh "Snooks" Boss, a week earlier in Boston. The man is not ready to talk or explain.

Harty passes the man some paperwork. He signs, "Clark Rockefeller."

***

The abduction of Reigh took planning—lots of it. As investigators would later learn, the dazed and defeated man sitting across from them put together the kidnapping over a period of months—then executed his plan with precision.

Assigned to the FBI's Child Abduction Rapid Deployment Team in Boston, Harty and Mosher, a Boston PD detective, had been on the case since the call first came in from Reigh's mother. Both the special agent and street cop were expert interviewers.

Harty was good at being a cop. A few years before hitting the national spotlight, Harty spent several weeks convincing an underaged prostitute to become the FBI's first juvenile witness in a case against a group of East Coast pimps. The pimps ran a call girl ring that stretched along the East Coast from Maine to Miami, the *Globe* reported. Harty put her case together by "accumulating a trove of evidence including phone and hotel records."

The investigation resulted in the federal indictment of six men associated with the prostitution ring, which pimped hundreds of underaged girls between 2001 and 2005. Ultimately, Darryl "Young Stallion" Tavares and Eddie "Young Indian" Jones were convicted and sent to federal prison—largely as the result of Harty's work with the underaged hooker.

Tavares and Jones, along with other members of their gang, "used force and intimidation to keep the girls in line," according to authors Larry J. Siegel and Brandon Welsh in their 2007 book, *Juvenile Delinquency: Theory, Practice, and Law.*

"A 17-year-old girl who wanted to get out of the life went back to work for 'Young Stallion' after he covered her head with a garbage bag and secured it with duct tape; another 17-year-old girl was allegedly raped by Tavares with a hair brush in April 2005 because he suspected she turned over some of the money she made from prostitution to 'Young Indian' Jones. The following month the same victim was allegedly kicked in the face by Jones while he was wearing Timberland boots for using a cellphone, he gave her to call a man who wasn't a customer. After disfiguring the girl's mouth and kicking out her teeth in the attack, Jones 'gave' her back to Tavares because he didn't want her working for him anymore," Siegel and Welsh wrote of Harty's case.

As for Mosher, he'd been working child cases since at least 1984 when he was assigned to Boston PD's Youth Assistance Unit. A June 1985 report by then-Boston Police

Commissioner Francis Roache commended Mosher and other members of the unit for their training in child abuse and sexual exploitation cases and noted the unit cleared dozens of missing children cases, including 22 which involved parental kidnappings.

Although he was preparing for retirement, for now Mosher had been assigned to stay with the man in the Lacoste polo shirt and bring him back to Massachusetts.

But before that could happen, Mosher and Harty needed to interview their suspect; they wanted to know what happened. Bit by bit it would spill out. Some would come from the man himself; some would come via the media, the rest would be told over the next several years by friends and acquaintances.

"Are you willing to speak with us tonight, Mr. Rockefeller?" Harty wants to know.

"Yeah, within a limited extent, you understand," he answers. "Call me Clark."

Harty takes notes. She offers Clark a drink. He declines.

"I guess I just want to start off by getting to know you a little bit," Harty began. "And I just thought that was kind of important. And I want to say you've kind of given us a run for our money this week. You've put some of the best of us to the test. You really have."

Clark responds. He's feeling proud but doesn't want to show it yet. A slight trace of a German accent peeks through the words.

"I could say thank you, but ..."

An interview was now underway. Clark, in handcuffs, is offered an opportunity to say a few more words. He turned to Mosher, somewhat ignoring Harty.

As he began to speak, the slight German accent disappeared.

"Well, my sincere apologies for the problems I caused to you," he says to Mosher.

"Accepted," Mosher responds.

"I don't like to cause problems. I am not a violent person. I just want to be a father. That's all I want to be," Clark explained. Then he blamed Sandy for the fact that the three of them were locked up in this interview room.

"I have a beautiful, amazing little girl," he continued. "I just want to be with her. I want to get her up in the morning, send her off to school, walk her to the bus, wait for her when she comes back, give her something to eat at night, and put her back to bed... She was taken from me four days before Christmas, which was evil."

The back and forth continued for several hours. Harty, Mosher, and the man in the polo shirt covered a lot of ground.

He talked about his wife and their relationship. He explained he earned money writing college term papers. He talked about his educational background and his upbringing.

After explaining he was born in New York; he backtracks and becomes "not totally clear. It could have actually been Boston. Yeah, I forgot a lot of things. There's a lot of things I just could never really quite recall."

They knew he wasn't who he said he was. And he admitted that taking on the Rockefeller name gave him standing. As Mihoko Manabe once told him, the name worked "like a charm" on everyone who heard it. "It was easy to get into clubs by just saying you are a Rockefeller."

Eventually, Clark asks for something to eat—turkey on white bread, if possible. Harty continues to hammer on the question of the man's identity. The man continues to stall.

More than four hours in, the man in the blue polo gave up. He slumped his back into his chair. Defeated.

Why?

It didn't make sense that he would lie about places he never visited, jobs he never held, and names that were not his.

Names like Clark Rockefeller, Christopher Mountbatten Crowe, Chip Smith? Christopher Chichester?

"Nobody notices a short man," he replied. "If you are born short, you want to be bigger."

Just like that the interview comes to an end, Mosher prepared to fly his man back to Boston. Full circle. He is now Christian Karl Gerhartsreiter and will be charged as such.

On the flight back to Boston with Mosher, Clark was now Chris again. He threw out another story. He told the detective he had worked as a secret agent on a project he said was called "Operation Hat Trick."

The operation—a conspiracy really—resulted in the deaths of two U.S. senators and a political operative, Gerhartsreiter explained. He told Mosher that the man who hired him to take part in the plot later assaulted him when he asked questions about it. The next day Gerhartsreiter went to work, and the entire operation was "gone and shut down."

Tim Miley, a Los Angeles County Sheriff's homicide detective, who had been working on the gang case in La Puente was assigned to the Sohus case now. He hoped to talk to Gerhartsreiter about John and Linda Sohus and the bones at 1920 Lorain Road and never got the chance.

Miley, as well-dressed as a stylish homicide detective should be, is a stocky guy. He wears his graying hair close-cropped. His glasses might make one believe he's soft. Anyone who knows the tradition of the "bulldogs" in the Los Angeles County Sheriff's Homicide Bureau knows Miley is persistent and will do all the investigative work it takes to put a case down.

On the off chance he could get Rockefeller/Gerhartsreiter/Chichester to talk, his bosses sent him to Baltimore. Lili Hadsell, the San Marino Police Officer who had taken one of the original missing persons reports from Didi Sohus nearly got on a plane herself. By 2013, Hadsell had become the police chief in the small L.A. suburb of Baldwin Park, Hadsell's plan was to fly to Boston to be closer to the media covering the story. After all, she had something to offer.

Someone at County homicide told a dismayed Hadsell she was grounded. If she wanted to talk to the media, they could call her and she could refer the calls to the sheriff's public information officer, Steve Whitmore, son of the late actor James Whitmore. Otherwise, Hadsell was told, "keep quiet."

In Los Angeles, officials with the coroner's office were scrambling. Lakshmanan Sathyavagiswaran, the Los Angeles County Medical Examiner locked himself behind closed doors in meetings with his public relations staff and the office's Chief Operating Officer, Anthony Hernandez.

Sathyavagiswaran known as Dr. Lakshmanan or "Dr. Laks", was much more cautious around the media than his predecessor, Dr. Thomas Noguchi. Where Noguchi would talk to reporters about cases his office was investigating, Dr. Laks was more calculating.

For good reason. Noguchi's big mouth got him in trouble with the five-member Board of Supervisors. Back in 1981, his bosses—the powerful supes—told Noguchi to shut up. He declined to listen and was asked to leave.

Almost no one knew Dr. Laks. If a statement had to be made, he delegated the task to investigators. For the most part it worked. Until Dr. Irwin Golden testified in a preliminary hearing for O.J. Simpson. The onetime NFL great had been charged in the 1994 murder of his estranged wife Nicole Brown and her friend Ronald Goldman.

Golden's botched autopsies of the victims became a subject of a heated cross-examination that resulted in the veteran forensic pathologist being characterized as a hostile bungler. He sealed the perception days later when he showed up to work at the coroner's office on North Mission Road in Los Angeles waving a gun and threatening to kill all defense lawyers.

Ever hoping to stay out of the limelight, Dr. Laks relied on his spokesmen.

First came Bob Dambacher, a holdover from the Noguchi era. When Dambacher retired, ace investigator Scott Carrier stepped up to the plate. When Carrier left in 2003, the task of speaking for Dr. Laks fell to Chief Craig Harvey and his deputy Ed Winter, a one-time cop turned coroner investigator.

Dr. Laks would avoid the spotlight in this Sohus case, too, but there was going to be hell to pay in the office. Most of the bones, which had been dug up in 1994, had been cremated. What remained had been crudely reconstructed and sat in the lab of the department's tool mark expert Steve Dowell.

None of the men in the room wanted to tell the detectives on the case what had happened in the years between 1994 and 2008.

After a quick inventory, officials determined that among the missing remains were two pieces of jawbone. The items might have been used to make a dental records identification of John Sohus once and for all. Additionally, no one in the office could find a complete case file. Large chunks of the written reports were missing. Others had been rewritten weeks or months after they were originally filed.

Internally, Hernandez argued it would be best to blame Sheriff's Homicide for any missing material. After all, he argued, detectives maintained much of the remaining evidence in the case including items of clothing and plastic book bags recovered at the scene in 1994.

There was another problem. The identification. In the early '90s, the technology didn't exist to extract DNA from bone and, even if it did, John Sohus—the presumed victim—was adopted. It would be a bitch getting those records unsealed.

Fortunately, there was time. With a kidnapping beef hanging over his head, Gerhartsreiter wasn't going any further from Baltimore than Boston. Meanwhile, the story of a phony Rockefeller—dubbed by the New York tabloids

"Crockefeller"—had become national news. The story played out on CNN, Fox, and MSNBC.

**

By the time Miley arrived in Boston, the police and FBI would have a lot of details he could add to his thin case file. "So, we get to Boston, and they know more about it than we do," Miley said.

The details filled in the blanks between Chris' disappearance in November 1988 and his resurrection in custody of the FBI.

Rockefeller met his wife, Sandra Boss, in New York in 1994. For a while, they leased from Manabe. Eventually the couple married in 1995 at the Quaker Meeting House on Nantucket Island. Built in the 1830s, the meeting house originally served as a school. Now owned by the Nantucket Historical Association, the site provides a quaint locale for intimate wedding parties.

Their daughter, Reigh "Snooks" Boss, was born in May 2001. In 2006, the family moved to Boston. In 2007, Sandra and Clark separated. They battled in court over custody.

Clark was an unpleasant asshole.

"The immediate agreed upon custody order was that (Clark Rockefeller) would have child custody five days a week and the mother two," John P. Zanini, an assistant Suffolk County District Attorney, noted. "Over that year, the custody shifted so that by December the child was spending almost all of her time with her mother."

The charade was quickly coming to an end. The advent of Google, Wikipedia, and the Wayback Machine played no small role in Clark's change of fortune.

As part of the divorce, Boss hired a private investigator, then filed documents in the divorce raising the question of (Rockefeller's) identity...

"Within days his attorneys approached her attorneys and agreed that she could have full custody of the child ... the ultimate financial settlement that the defendant received was $800,000, two cars, her engagement ring, and a dress.

Detective Frank Rudewicz, the detective hired by Boss, described the difficulty he faced doing a background check on Clark during the divorce.

"When we were first retained, it was during the divorce proceedings to look into his background and particularly some assets," Rudewicz said. "There were some suspicions on her part that had accumulated through the years of their marriage. There were just some questions that were never answered. As we started looking into him it was more telling what we were not finding as opposed to what we found.

"Here was an individual that was basically born as a 37-year-old man in 1993," he continued. "No history, no addresses, no credit, no driver's license—nothing of the typical things you would find."

In court, Rudewicz would testify that in his 30 years as a PI he'd never seen anything like it.

Rudewicz's work laid the groundwork for the divorce settlement.

Given that Clark had been formed from nothing, child psychologist, Liza Brooks, suggested that Rockefeller could have three supervised visits per year and spend eight hours a day with his daughter during those visits.

"She acknowledged that he was weird and quirky, but he was an interested, caring, loving, doting father and she thought it was concerning that he gave up lots, including contact with his daughter, for money," Zanini wrote.

As always, there was a story.

"He told me that his parents were deceased," Brooks said. "That he had been raised by an older gentleman, sort of an uncle-type of person."

On another occasion, Rockefeller told Brooks he had another family and would soon be the father of twins.

Whatever the stories, the truth was far harsher. As the reality of losing Snooks for good loomed large in his life, Clark stewed over his misfortune. He began to cook up a kidnapping plot.

In November, using the alias Charles "Chip" Smith, he contacted Baltimore realtor, Julie Gochar. Via email, "Chip" Smith told Gochar he was in Chile and would be arriving in town by boat with his daughter, Muffy.

Smith explained his daughter was homeschooled. He said the little girl's mother was a surrogate from Sweden. He said Muffy's identity papers had been destroyed. In any event, Smith would be coming to Baltimore to supervise the construction of catamarans. He needed a place to stay. Chip and Gochar exchanged emails and chat messages for months.

Meanwhile, Boss took Reigh to London just days before Christmas.

At a Christmas get-together, Clark told Mason Peltz, an investment banker, he had a daughter out of wedlock with a woman he met in England. He told Peltz that he had sole custody of the little girl but lost a brutal court battle. Rockefeller was angry, distraught, distressed, and believed the outcome was unjust, Peltz recalled.

If he had to do something, Rockefeller would go to England and bring the little girl back. Peltz read between the lines. Clark—a guy who worked "in some capacity in the financial industry"—might do something crazy.

Of course, he was distraught, as Rockefeller later told reporters, little Snooks was everything to him.

"For me taking care of Snooks was a vacation," he said. "At two years old, I taught her how to read. At first, I taught her how to read for purely selfish reasons. I thought that if she knows how to read, I can put her in front of a book, and she will leave me alone."

Snooks was a quick learner and Clark loved showing off just how smart—and well-read—she was. Several of his friends believed it validated his efforts as a father.

According to his friend Aileen Ang, Rockefeller probably had the framework of an abduction scheme in place by February 2008.

Ang met him in August 2007 at the Boston Sailing Center. She was an out-of-work investment banker and struggling artist. Clark said he was a businessman and graduate student of astronomy at Harvard. He told Ang he had a daughter, Snooks.

Founded in 1977 on a Louisiana riverboat docked at Lewis Wharf on the Boston Harbor, the Sailing Center's "floating classroom and clubhouse is an excellent venue for parties and other functions," the center's website notes. It's "also close to a wide variety of historical sites, restaurants, and nighttime entertainment spots."

Ang and Rockefeller first connected at a Sailing Center "member's night." The evening was an informal get-together advertised as a meet and greet with dinner and drinks. Ang got to meet Snooks the next night. Between August and November, Ang and Rockefeller attended two boat shows and two parties.

When Ang asked about Snooks' mother, Clark explained she was out of the picture and only came around when she needed money.

In November, Ang took off for Europe. When she came back to Boston in February 2008, Rockefeller told her he had a plan to take her on a sailing trip around the world. She expressed interest, probably expecting it would never happen. Clark didn't really seem like much of a sailor.

The getaway plan continued to unfold.

Clark's first supervised visitation with Snooks was to take place in March. He cancelled at the last minute, explaining to Sandra he was too busy to make it.

Less than a month later, Clark, now using the name Charles "Chip" Smith, met with Gochar, the realtor, in hopes of finding a house. He entered her office wearing a hat pulled all the way down over his glasses. His hair was dyed bright red. Gochar heard Smith say he was a sailor, but his skin was pale—not the sort of color one gets out at sea. He explained that the past two months had been extremely rainy on his boat, and he spent a lot of time below deck.

He entered into a two-month lease for a pad on Wolfe Street, just a couple of blocks away from Obsidian. The lease cost $2,000.

For several weeks, buyer and realtor were in daily contact. Smith confided to Gochar he hated the name Charles and preferred his nickname "Chip." Gochar allowed Smith to use the internet when he visited her office at Obsidian Realty. Gochar said he spent most of that time researching real estate prices and the gold trading index.

Gold prices began a slight fall in late May that continued until September. He would need gold to pay for a getaway.

The first gold purchase came in June. A man identifying himself as Clark Rock contacted Kenneth Murphy of Boston Bullion in Arlington, Massachusetts seeking to convert $2 million cash into gold coins.

The first buy occurred on June 10. Mr. Rock wired $465,000 to Murphy. Ten days later, Murphy delivered 527 Krugerrands to Mr. Rock. On June 24, Mr. Rock decided he'd rather have his loot in $50 U.S. gold pieces.

The transactions were unusual but not suspicious, Murphy said. As for Clark Rock? He picked up gold on July 7. One week later he wired another $300,000 to Murphy and picked up more tubes stuffed with American Gold Eagles on July 21.

Although there was little exchange of pleasantries, to Murphy's eye, dressed in "business casual" attire and wearing a sport coat, Clark Rock appeared to be a professor.

"He seemed like an Ivy League, ivory-tower kind of academic," Murphy recalled. "(I) did not talk to him long (and the) transaction was unique but not suspicious."

About the same time, Rockefeller introduced himself to Bruce Boswell as "Chip McLaughlin." He bought a barely seaworthy catamaran from the North Baltimore resident for $10,000. Boswell was only too happy to unload the dirty, broken-down craft moored at Anchorage marina just off Baltimore's Boston Street. He said his new friend Chip, who identified himself as President of Obsidian Realty, took him up to the Obsidian office in Fells Point and wrote up a bill of sale.

Chip entered the building by punching in a security code. If Boswell thought his new buddy was a little odd, he must have really been scratching his head when Chip McLaughlin wanted to make out a bill of sale on the catamaran to Chip Smith. Weirder yet, Chip couldn't explain why—as president of the realty—he didn't have an office.

"He said he didn't like the name MacLaughlin," Boswell said.

The deal was done in cash. Chip paid $500 down and made up the balance a few days later when he handed Boswell a stack of $20 and $50 bills. Boswell said his brother, Harry, leased the catamaran's slip to Chip for $2,200 a year. Marina manager, James Ruscoe, would later describe the catamaran as "chainsaw food." He estimated its worth at $5,000.

Chip didn't know jack about boats or yachts or sailing. His broken-down catamaran, with the dirty hull and visibly frayed lines, would never make it out of the Chesapeake Bay—or out of Boswell's name for that matter. Paperwork wasn't Chip's thing either.

But "he talked a big story," Boswell said. "He's a very engaging guy with big ideas. I trusted him completely."

From time to time, Chip would disappear from his Baltimore haunts. He told Gochar he traveled to Europe. Another time he said he visited his sisters and his daughter in Wisconsin.

On July 18, Chip Smith showed up at Obsidian with a cashier's check for $450,000 and bought a home on Ploy Street in Baltimore's Mt. Vernon neighborhood. The home was walking distance from an art gallery and the University of Maryland at Baltimore.

A week later, he was back in Boston preparing Clark Rockefeller's disappearance from the face of the earth.

CHAPTER 18.

BOSTON

And this is good old Boston,
The home of the bean and the cod,
Where the Lowells talk only to Cabots,
And the Cabots talk only to God.
—*Boston Toast,* John Collins Bossidy

Clark Rockefeller was ready-made for Boston. His patrician manner was suited for Boston society and its inhabitants. After all, here was the home of Harvard, MIT, and many more institutions of higher learning.

Wikipedia, relying on descriptions of Boston's elite, known as Brahmins, explains exactly what it means to be a wealthy Bostonite.

"Cultivated, urbane, and dignified, a Boston Brahmin was supposed to be the very essence of enlightened aristocracy. The ideal Brahmin was not only wealthy, but displayed what was considered suitable personal virtues and character traits.

Clark did his best to be just that, a modern version of Thurston Howell III. It was obvious by the way he carried himself that he had money—lots of it. Not everyone in Boston in 2007 was so lucky. The economic crisis roiling the country that year hit Boston limo driver, Darryl Hopkins, damn hard.

He'd made his living chauffeuring well-heeled, big spenders through Boston's maze of monuments, museums, and historical landmarks. And by his account, he was the best Boston had to offer.

As the bomb dropped on the economy, Hopkins watched his business dry up. Struggling for a break in summer 2007, he came across a wealthy looking guy standing alone in the rain. Hopkins picked him up. It wasn't for charitable reasons. Seeing an angle, the chauffeur figured a rich guy would give good word of mouth to other rich guys. Guerrilla advertising is what Hopkins called it.

When he learned the dorky little guy with the imperious manner sitting in the back seat of his Suburban SUV was American royalty—one James Frederick Mills Clark Rockefeller to be exact—Hopkins breathlessly called his daughter to brag.

During his conversations with the faux Rockefeller, Hopkins learned that Clark, who had a "1930s very eloquent way of speaking," went to Yale and sold construction materials to the Pentagon.

The whole act impressed Hopkins, who was reminded of millionaire Thurston Howell III from *Gilligan's Island.* When Clark opened his mouth, he had a "very elegant, educated way of speaking." He would call on Hopkins a couple of times to drive him and Reigh home from her school. In Hopkins' eyes, Rockefeller was living a happy family life. Clark and Reigh came off as "happy dad, happy daughter."

Their relationship continued into the next year.

On July 23, 2008, Clark called Hopkins and asked for a ride to Manhattan from Boston for a routine board meeting. It was, Clark explained, a meeting he attended on the last Friday of every month. He would need Hopkins to pick him up on the 25th at 7 a.m. sharp. Hopkins said the fare would be $600.

On the ride to Manhattan, Hopkins said he needed to pee. Clark told him to quit complaining. "Hurry up," he insisted. They arrived and Clark disappeared into a building to be present for his board meeting and to attend to some business on behalf of the defense department.

After the meeting, Hopkins and his wealthy fare hit a sandwich shop before heading back to Boston. Ever the patrician, Rockefeller ordered steak tartare. Hopkins ordered a turkey club and paid his own way, which annoyed him.

"I was upset. I was his driver," he said. "He could have at least bought me a sandwich."

Back in the Suburban limousine, Clark explained to Hopkins he had an issue. He planned to take Snooks sailing with the son of U.S. Sen. Lincoln Chaffee in Newport, Rhode Island. The problem was a clingy, crazy, and very gay family friend named "Harold." Clark arranged a ride to the sailing adventure, but needed Hopkins' help getting rid of Harold, who was a pain in the neck.

For Hopkins, getting rid of a freak wasn't an unusual request. His job was to serve his wealthy clients, no matter how strange or weird they—or their friends—might seem. Clark had problems that were neither too weird nor even out-of-the-ordinary for men and women of his station.

Hopkins had got clients out of jams with women, with drunks, and maybe even a bill collector or two. Clark's problem with a crazy, clingy friend was par for the course with these people. Hopkins explained to Clark he could lose "Harold" with the limo.

To be on the safe side, he also suggested standard techniques for dumping a social drag. Perhaps Mr. Rockefeller should get a restraining order. How about just telling this guy not to get in the car when it's time to leave?

None of that would work, Rockefeller insisted. Crazy "Harold" needed to be left behind in a cloud of dust. Only then would he get the message he wasn't wanted.

The conversation turned to Hopkins' financial situation. Clark offered him "two grand" to get rid of the "cling-on."

A dry run was in order.

Hopkins picked out a quiet spot on Marlborough Street that seemed perfect for a getaway. Clark practiced tossing his backpack through the open rear door of Hopkins' black

Suburban. In the same fluid move, he jumped in and shut the door.

The visitation drew closer. Clark should have picked up Snooks on Friday. He passed, asking if it would be OK to take his little girl to see the Red Sox and Yankees at Fenway on Saturday instead.

Clark's crazy, clingy friend was Howard Yaffe, a social worker hired to supervise visitations. On Saturday morning, he met up with Sandra and took Reigh to meet Clark at the Algonquin Club where he'd been staying off and on since the divorce.

The Algonquin Club might be the real-life version of "The Heritage Club" in the 1983 Dan Akroyd, Eddie Murphy movie *Trading Places*. It's a place where society's elite—both men and women—meet to dine, discuss literature, and do business.

The clubhouse itself was built in 1888 and has hosted "presidents, heads of state, foreign dignitaries, and preeminent local and national leaders in virtually every field of human activity," according to its website.

Since it was built as a club—and not purchased from a homeowner—Algonquin fashions itself as unique among Boston's many social clubs. It has several works of art, an extensive library, and seven plush guest rooms—each complete with a fridge, telephone, cable TV, and internet access.

In 2007, "Mr. Clark Rockefeller" was named to a three-year term on the club's board of directors. Others on the board at that time included attorneys, doctors, bank presidents, corporate leaders, and philanthropists. Take Rockefeller's fellow director, Frank E. Ferguson, for example. His biography on the website of Social Venture Partners, a Boston-based group that funds various nonprofits, points out he's been a soldier, a journalism student, and more.

A onetime president of Bose, Ferguson's "interests include Japanese Netsuke, string figure construction, hiking (and formerly climbing), cooking, angel investing, drama and theatre, Scottish and English Country Dancing, and the application of Dr. William Glasser's concepts of Choice Theory and Reality Therapy to corporate management, to quality schools, and to the reduction of recidivism," according to a biography on the website Social Venture Partners—Boston.

Ferguson thought Clark's demeanor was aloof.

"He came across as very bright, reserved, diffident," Ferguson recalled. "Although friendly, (he was) a bit distant. And I was respectful and reluctant to probe. None of the members had reservations about him, so far as I know."

Others saw a different, engaging side. Thomas McCann, on Algonquin's Membership Committee in 2005, remembered his first conversation with Rockefeller took place one afternoon that fall. Clark was headed to Boston from his home in Cornish, New Hampshire.

"He and I met for breakfast the next morning," McCann recalled. "He knew quite a bit about the club, and he knew something about my background—the stuff one might find on Google."

McCann, author of the 1976 bestseller *An American Company: The Tragedy of United Fruit* chronicled his rise from office boy to vice president of the banana growing and land development corporation that virtually controlled several Central American countries in the mid-20th Century.

The book details the dark side of American politics including the CIA's overthrow of a Guatemalan president in 1954 and a bribery scam that led company CEO Eli Black to jump to his death from his office window on the 44th floor of the Pan Am building in New York City in February 1975.

Following the success of the book, McCann went on to become a documentary producer and put together several PBS specials on Watergate.

Rockefeller and McCann's breakfast meeting took place at the club, McCann recalled.

Eventually the conversation turned to Clark, his family, and his interests. Rockefeller, dressed casually as always, said he was a scientist and a businessman. He collected vintage Cadillacs and had an interest in fine art and writing.

"At that first breakfast, he said he had in excess of 30 Cadillacs. I commented that he must have a very big garage and he said he had a fairly large garage but by far the majority of them were kept in leased garages, barns, sheds … all over the state," McCann said. "He said he kept them in storage zippered car bags and that inside he placed buckets of desiccants to keep them dry and the mold off. "

McCann had no reason to doubt the fantastic story. Any questions about his collection were answered with a sort of smooth precision.

"The man was very careful and most convincing," McCann said. "He fooled God knows how many thousands of intelligent people."

"Clearly he anticipated that question someday by someone and he was ready for it when I asked."

Clark and Sandy would be looking to buy a place on Beacon Hill. Obviously, they would need to find a good private school for little Snooks.

One thing that stood out to McCann was Rockefeller's detailed knowledge of the Algonquin's admission process. "He met all of our requirements."

Rockefeller explained that he needed to feel the club out. He wanted to see if the members and atmosphere fit *his* requirements. He asked that the Rockefellers be invited to the Algonquin's annual Christmas party. The wish was granted. Clark, Sandy, and Snooks celebrated the holidays among peers at the club.

In January, he accepted a membership offer.

And "He was a good member," McCann said. "He used the club frequently. He brought people to the club. He made good suggestions. He enjoyed the club and those members who got to know him enjoyed him. He participated in as many member events as he could."

Besides his Cadillacs, his work, and art collection, Clark also found time for small talk. When he mentioned Snooks or Sandy, it was with love. He was proud of his family too, McCann said.

"Snooks was a regular at the Algonquin," McCann said. "Sandy less so; I assumed because of her demanding work. Snooks, too, was brilliant. My guess is her IQ was off the charts."

Within months, the divorce would take its ugly toll. Clark would be elected to the board about the same time he was forced out of the $2 million mansion he and Sandra shared on Beacon Hill. When that happened, Clark took up as a boarder at the club.

Now, six months since Sandy moved to England, he was staying there Friday night and planned to meet his daughter and Yaffe, her chaperone, there on Saturday morning.

Meanwhile at The Four Seasons, Sandra Boss worried about 7-year-old Reigh's first visit with her father in several months. Sure, Yaffe would be there to keep an eye on things, but she needed more assurance and called on Rudewicz, the detective, for remote surveillance.

Before the divorce, Reigh Storrow Mills Boss had been the center of her father's universe. Clark taught her to read, appreciate good cuisine, and to know the difference between modern artists like Cubist Piet Mondrian and the American abstract expressionist Mark Rothko.

Snooks and her father, Clark, were regulars at the Southfield School in Brookline, Massachusetts. He arranged her play dates and was a "great dad" according to one friend. When he had custody of Snooks, Clark even promised to pay for and build a planetarium at the school.

But now that she'd been gone for several months, Clark was devastated. Friends and family could see it. He was changed. He became less charming and more secretive.

Perhaps a weekend visit with Reigh would bring out the old Clark.

On Saturday morning, Boss planned "to meet Howard about a block from the Algonquin Club and Howard was to take Reigh to meet her father," Sandra Boss recalled.

Clark intimated he had an informal day planned. Father, daughter, and social worker would go play at Clarendon Park, a tidy green space filled with children's playthings in the middle of the rather quiet residential neighborhood. They would do lunch and take in the baseball game. Snooks loved the Sox.

Boston that Saturday was downright muggy; 81 degrees, humid, and partly cloudy. The Yanks and Sox were locked in a duel for second place in the American League East. Boston held a one-game advantage, but it was New York's day as the Yanks posted a 10-3 rout.

Clark and Snooks never made it to the game. Despite a promise he could score tickets, even a Rockefeller needs connections when the Yankees come to Beantown.

Not knowing Clark and Reigh couldn't get into Fenway, Boss, in her room at the Four Seasons, sweated the afternoon out, worried about what might happen.

"I had my concerns," Boss said. My concern was that it was a difficult environment to ensure Reigh was OK."

When Yaffe returned with the little girl, her mother reflected on the events and thought everything turned out as well as could be expected.

"It went smoothly from a logistical perspective," Boss said later.

Just one more day of this and she and Reigh could leave Boston and return to London. Sunday morning promised to be as sunny and muggy as Saturday.

Across town, Hopkins made arrangements to arrive on time for his 11 a.m. appointment to pick up Clark and little Snooks. Even though he was still smarting from the sandwich slight on Friday, Hopkins needed Rockefeller greenbacks. He "got dressed, left the house and drove into Boston."

After stopping for coffee and a pack of smokes, Hopkins made his way to Marlborough Street. He double-parked facing west toward Berkeley and waited. It was shaping up to be a hot day in Boston. Hopkins sipped his coffee, puffed on a cigarette, and flipped on NPR.

Morning Edition had a story about the war crimes trial of Osama bin Laden's driver.

Reporter John McChesney in Guantanamo Bay interviewed Army Colonel Lawrence Morris, who was prosecuting the driver, Salim Hamdam. From the NPR transcript:

> "**MCCHESNEY**: Another point of contention about this trial is why the government chose a lowly driver as the first detainee to be tried. Here's chief prosecutor Lawrence Morris.
>
> **Army Col. MORRIS**: I don't accept the characterization that he's just a driver. In the government case, as you've seen now through several days, is that he's an al-Qaeda warrior who, among other trusted functions, drove the highest-ranking terrorist in the world …

Hopkins, who drove a black SUV with a Red Sox license plate frame and bumper sticker paying homage to his favorite team, paid nominal attention to what he was hearing.

"I sat there on Marlborough Street listening to the radio …on a Sunday morning," he said. "Had a cigarette, had my coffee."

Eleven o'clock came and went. Hopkins had been promised a payday. Now he was wondering if Rockefeller had stood him up. After the steak tartare deal, Hopkins thought for sure Clark stiffed him again.

"I texted him, 'What's going on?'" Hopkins said. "You never knew. You never know if people are going to show up."

Clark, who told Hopkins he would be brunching at the Paramount on Beacon Hill, fired off a message of his own.

It read, "Are you at the location? On the way," Hopkins recalled.

The driver waited some more. His phone buzzed. It was another text message from Clark. This one was a lot like the last: "On the way."

A guy who makes his living navigating one-way streets in an urban environment, Hopkins knew all the approaches to his spot from The Paramount. By his reckoning, he would see Clark, Snooks, and Crazy Harold approaching from behind his SUV. When Hopkins first caught sight of the trio, they were coming from the opposite direction. It made no sense.

Walking briskly on the brick sidewalk underneath the shade trees, past the gas lamps and row homes, the three were about 75 feet from the limo and Hopkins.

Clark, wearing a blue polo shirt, had Snooks on his shoulders. Wearing her glasses, Reigh was dressed in a pink and white sundress and wore a brand-new pair of red shoes. Yaffe thought the little girl seemed "happy and energetic." He had the impression Clark was taking them to breakfast at that moment.

It was shaping up to be a smooth weekend from Yaffe's perspective, even though Rockefeller had some revelations. He wondered, for example, if it would be okay to introduce Reigh to his new wife and children. Yaffe said such a move would be inappropriate.

At the limo, Hopkins tensed and readied for what would happen next.

"I saw it was Clark. Finally. I'd been waiting there all this time. I didn't want to sit there and run my air conditioning," he said. "When they got closer, I sort of looked away. I was trying to help out. They were going to jump in the car, and we were going to drive off and just leave him standing there."

As they walked, Clark pointed out a construction project to Yaffe. The visitation monitor turned to look and the next thing he knew, he was being shoved to the ground.

Within seconds, the limo's back door swung open. Hopkins heard a clunk. Clark yelled. Yaffe fell to a knee.

"There's a crying girl in my back seat and he's saying, 'Go! Go! Go!' Snooks was cryin'. I didn't turn around to look. I dropped it into drive and started to accelerate. I didn't stomp on it. I thought, "Oh we're leaving the guy behind. I'm looking straight ahead. I knew he was trying to pull on the door, you can feel that as a driver."

When Hopkins did glance out, he saw Yaffe holding on to the rear passenger door and running alongside as fast as he could.

"I ran over and tried to climb into the (car)," Yaffe said. "(I wanted) to try to stop Reigh from being taken by her dad. Inside the SUV, Clark pulled hard on the door in an effort to shut Yaffe out for good.

Hopkins stepped harder on the accelerator. Yaffe finally let go and tumbled into Marlborough Street. By now he had bruises to his knees, hip, chin, and likely suffered a concussion. Eventually, Yaffe would be taken to Massachusetts General Hospital.

As Yaffe picked himself up off the ground, Hopkins checked the limo's rearview mirror. Within seconds, Yaffe had a cell phone to his ear. He was pointing and from what Hopkins could tell as he turned right onto Berkeley, Yaffe appeared to be shouting.

A wave of relief swept through the car even as Snooks continued to whimper.

"This guy was as crazy as Clark mentioned he might be," Hopkins thought. He checked the back seat. "She's crying. I'm saying 'Snooks, it's okay. At least we got rid of Harold.'"

A P.I., assigned by Rudewicz's firm, arrived at the scene seconds too late. Yaffe called 9-1-1.

"A daughter was just kidnapped by her father," Yaffe told the emergency operator. "I was walking down the street. He knocked me over and ran off in the car."

Back at The Four Seasons, two hours had passed since Sandy last saw Reigh and Yaffe. The phone in her suite came to life, shattering the quiet of a Sunday morning. It was Yaffe. He was hysterical and screaming.

Boss processed what he was saying. Her mind raced as she headed out to Marlborough Street where the Boston cops were waiting.

"Terror. Horror. Consternation," Boss recalled. "I was freaked. I spoke to Howard first, then I spoke to one of the police."

As he sped away from Yaffe, Hopkins raced up Berkeley toward Storrow Drive and left onto the expressway. He believed he was headed to Rhode Island. In the back seat, Clark began to give directions. He demanded Hopkins turn right. Hopkins assumed they were heading back to the scene. When the car got several blocks further north, Rockefeller told Hopkins to turn right onto Revere. The SUV picked up speed as they passed Charles Street.

Reigh continued to whimper. Her head really hurt from bumping into the limo's steel frame as she was shoved into the car.

A few blocks further—at the bottom of Garden Street—Clark told Hopkins to pull over. He was going to grab a hack from the cab stand outside the White Hen, a convenience store, and take Reigh to the emergency room at Massachusetts General a few blocks north.

"He told me to wait over at the Charles Street Whole Foods parking lot," Hopkins said.

Back at the scene, Boston police officers set up a temporary command post at Marlborough and Arlington—up from Clarendon Park and around the corner from Cheers, the Boston bar made famous in the 1980s NBC sitcom.

Several minutes later, Boston Police Detective Joe Leeman escorted the distraught mom back to her hotel room. He would need pictures of Reigh and Clark. Leeman instantly realized this was not some welfare mom in a dispute with her druggie ex-con boyfriend over who was the better parent. Boss was a high-powered Stanford-educated Harvard M.B.A.

A senior partner in the London Office of McKinsey & Company, and head of the group's "Global Corporate and Institutional Banking Practice," Sandy didn't fit the mold of the typical ex involved in an ugly custody dispute—unless the typical ex involved in an ugly custody dispute was a keynote speaker a few weeks earlier at the Global Financial Services Conference in Dublin.

About the time Sandy was getting Leeman caught up, Clark and Reigh caught a cab.

Next stop was Lewis Wharf and the Boston Sailing Center, where Aileen Ang awaited. Earlier that morning, Clark asked his sailing buddy for a lift to New York. There he planned to check out a recently purchased yacht. He promised to pay for gas and throw in an extra $500 for the trouble.

Aileen couldn't believe her fortune. Clark was loaded. He even let her in on a family secret; he had the master key to the Rockefeller Center in New York Center.

On her way to the Sailing Center, Aileen passed the good news onto her mother.

"She said, 'I'm on the highway getting ready to pick up somebody. He wants to pay me $500 to bring him to New York City," Ang's mother told the *Boston Herald*. "I said, 'How come? That's a lot of money.' She said, 'Well, he's rich and he wants to rent a private car.'"

Ang had been in the parking lot for about 10 minutes when she caught sight of Clark and Reigh. It was now about 1:30 p.m.

"They were walking up from the Sailing Center building," she said. "His daughter was with him. I was surprised his daughter was with him. (They were) walking rather quickly. Clark was carrying a box and a backpack. The box was about the size of a ream of paper."

Father and daughter hopped in the back seat. Clark explained Reigh was tired and needed a nap.

"I love you, Daddy," Reigh said.

"I love you more," Clark replied.

Then he ducked down as Ang made her way south onto the expressway and out of Boston.

"Which way? 93 or 95?" she asked her passenger which Interstate road he preferred, one that cut right through town or the one on the outskirts.

Interstate 95 would be the most direct route between Beantown and the Big Apple. Clark opted for the backroads that branched south and west from Interstate 93, Ang said. Somewhere near Connecticut in a maze of interstates, Ang got lost. Reigh fell asleep. Clark climbed into the front seat. Boston PD issued an Amber Alert. The story went national. It was the first and only time in anyone's memory that a Rockefeller was involved in an Amber Alert.

"At approximately 12:44PM this afternoon, officers from District D-4 responded to the intersection of Arlington and Marlborough Streets for a custodial kidnapping.

The victim was last seen wearing a pink and white sundress and red shoes. The victim also wears prescription glasses.

The suspect, when last seen, was wearing a blue Lacoste shirt, and khaki pants."

As they sped away from Boston, Ang drove with the radio off. Clark gave directions. He played with Ang's cellphone and turned it off. When she went to call a friend, Rockefeller told her to put the phone down. He said distracted drivers made him nervous.

Ang had to pee. Clark insisted they press on. Ang noticed her fuel gauge. The light came on. She needed gas. Again, Clark insisted they press on. Closer to New York City, traffic was a mess. Ang checked her phone again. Again, it had been turned off.

Sometime around 7 p.m., Clark, Ang, and Snooks rolled into New York on fumes. Ang finally convinced her friend that she needed gasoline. They stopped at a place in the high numbers on FDR Drive and filled up. It was close to where Clark once lived with Sandy and, before that, Mihoko Manabe.

Despite the stop, Clark remained controlling. Ang still needed to use the restroom. He told her no. Under no circumstances would he miss his boat launch. Two or three minutes later, they were back on the road. Ang made her way down FDR, crossed into midtown, and pulled up in front of Grand Central Station.

Clark grabbed Snooks, his box, and the backpack.

"I don't think he said much," Ang recalled. "I said, 'Have a nice trip.'"

Clark dropped an envelope stuffed with cash on the front seat, slammed the car door, and took off toward the train station. As Ang drove away, she turned her phone back on. Immediately it began to ring. It was Tom Kennedy, a friend from pottery class. Odd that he would be calling, she thought.

He told her Boston police were looking for Clark. She called 9-1-1 and drove to a city police station. Ang had the idea Clark was headed to Long Island for a sailing excursion.

Back in Boston, sitting around the parking lot of Whole Foods wasn't going to cut it for Hopkins. He split and headed north on 93 toward home when a business acquaintance called with the offer of another fare. Hopkins turned around and headed back into town.

"After I got through the tunnel by the fortress museum where the old HoJos was there was one of those Amber Alert things," he recalled. "They were looking for a black Tahoe with Red Sox stickers and Red Sox plates." Hopkins knew his black Suburban fit the description. He flipped on WBZ, CBS' Boston affiliate running an "all news, all the time" format.

"All I had to hear was 'Clark Rockefeller' and my world collapsed," Hopkins said. "He had kidnapped his daughter, and I was the getaway driver, thank you very much."

Hopkins cursed his bad luck. He cried a little, then pulled the Red Sox stickers off his SUV and continued down to New Bedford to collect his customer. Sometime around 9:30 or 10 p.m. Hopkins got home. He still hadn't checked in with the police.

CHAPTER 19.

WHO IS THIS GUY?

"Clark has absolutely no self … He's like a spore
who blew in on a cosmic wind from Jupiter."
—Walter Kirn, "Writer recalls friendship with
'Clark Rockefeller,' *USA Today*, March 7, 2014

Down in Baltimore and using a cold phone, Clark had
become Chip Smith. Chip was arranging by text message to
have the keys to his Ploy Street pad delivered by an Obsidian
employee.

Back at the Four Seasons in Boston, Sandy admitted she
didn't know anything about her estranged husband. He had
no credit cards, no driver's license. She knew some of his
history. He told her a fall down some stairs left him mute
until he was about seven. A dog brought him out of his funk.
Clark once told Sandy his first word was "woofness."

As Leeman listened and took notes, Sandy spilled her
guts.

Clark once told her he was a member of the Trilateral
Commission. He said he owned a multi-million-dollar
art collection. He explained that he traveled to Texas on a
weekly basis because he was involved in the oil business.

He told Sandy he handled debt negotiations for small
countries that couldn't afford to pay back the lenders. He
identified his dad as "George Rockefeller" and his mother
as "Mary Roberts." Clark said he was born in New York. He
said his parents were killed in a car accident when he was
18.

He said he was raised in Sutton Place—one of Manhattan's most affluent neighborhoods. He said he went to Yale at 14.

As for money?

Clark told Sandy the family fortune was tied up in a lawsuit.

Sandy said when they first met in 1993, she thought Clark was intelligent, thoughtful, and courteous. He was charming, fit, and handsome. After their wedding, Sandy said Clark became controlling. He distanced her from her friends and took over her bank account.

They split up. Then she got pregnant. They got back together. He had more stories. Now Clark was working as a physicist with a start-up that specialized in jet propulsion. He told her he applied for and received a patent. He hoped to sell his design.

Reigh was born in May 2001. Sandy went back to work three months later. Clark took care of the baby.

Through it all, she made $2 million a year and he spent it. If Sandy pissed him off, he'd stop allowing her to eat. He said he owned a billion-dollar art collection. She never saw it. She told Leeman, the Boston detective handling the missing persons investigation, that when she and Clark split up for good her biggest fear was that Clark would get custody of Reigh and disappear.

Now it appeared as if he had done just that—perhaps forever. The cops scratched their heads trying their level best to piece it all together. Meanwhile reporters began to circle. Sure, it was an election year. But the summer lull after the primaries—and before the conventions—had set in. Cable News viewers needed a break from stories about Barack Obama, Hilary Clinton, and John McCain.

An Amber Alert for a kidnapper with the last name Rockefeller fitted the bill.

The *New York Times* pushed an update around 7:30 p.m. that summer Sunday evening.

The New York City police are searching the city's streets and area harbors for a man, Clark Rockefeller, who is believed to have snatched his 7-year-old daughter, Reigh Rockefeller, from a Boston street and brought her to New York...

Law enforcement authorities in New York said they believed that Mr. Rockefeller arrived in Manhattan on Sunday night with his daughter, with the intent of ferrying her to Bermuda by boat. Harbor patrols were searching marinas in an effort to find the father and daughter, the authorities said...

In telephone interviews with reporters on Monday, Amy Fitch and Michele Hiltzik, senior archivists at the Rockefeller Archive Center in Sleepy Hollow, N.Y., which maintains the records of the Rockefeller family associated with Standard Oil, philanthropy, and politics, said there was no indication that Clark Rockefeller was a descendant of William Avery Rockefeller, the father of John D. Rockefeller Sr. and William Rockefeller....

For reporters, it was hard getting a fix on this guy. An archivist somewhere pulled up a 2004 article from *The Valley News*, in Lebanon, N.H. The paper reported that Clark Rockefeller refused to confirm whether he was related, directly or otherwise, to the famed Rockefeller family of Standard Oil fame.

"Maybe I am, maybe I'm not; it's not something that I would either confirm or deny," he said. "I just don't want anything to do with the whole question."

Normally, no one might have cared. New Hampshire was precisely the place where a Rockefeller (related or not) might want some anonymity. But this was no normal Rockefeller. The newspaper was trying to determine Clark

Rockefeller's lineage after he reportedly wrote a $110,000 check to the town of Cornish, N.H., in exchange for a deed to a historic church in the town's center.

All this was pieced together in about 24 hours as the search for Rockefeller coalesced.

Later that morning, Ang also met with the FBI. Agents took her cell phone and dusted her car for prints. They pulled some and ran them through the Bureau's Integrated Automated Fingerprint Identification System. Thirty minutes later, they had a hit.

Hours, and then days, passed. By the time Friday came around, the media was in a frenzy and Sandra Boss was in a state of panic and distress.

They wanted a statement. And she was willing to give one.

Dressed in a worn lime-green blouse, someone had clipped a mic to it. The mic pulled her collar down slightly. Sitting at the sort of banquet table one might find at a Knights of Columbus dinner or its weekly bingo game. The backdrop was a hastily hung black curtain. She clasped her hands together atop a manila folder and began to speak.

> Clark, although many things have changed, you will always be Reigh's father and I will always be Reigh's mother. We both love her dearly and have only her best interests and well-being in our hearts. I ask you now please, please bring 'Snooks' back. There has to be a better way for us to solve our differences than this way.
>
> I also want to thank everyone for your help.
>
> And Reigh, honey, I love you and miss you so much. Remember you're always a princess.

By now, every news story carried a link to contact the police for those who had information. Twitter, now X, in its infancy as a social media outlet, had thousands of sightings, theories, and developing news stories.

Detectives weren't necessarily stumped. But it would take some work to unravel it all. Knowing who they were looking for was one thing. Catching this guy would be something else. The investigation would be helped by hubris.

When he took on the name Rockefeller, Gerhartsreiter knew it would buy him entrée. What he didn't plan on was the notoriety that a "Rockefeller" involved in a parental kidnapping would bring.

On the East Coast, the story instantly rocketed to the lead on television, the front pages of the newspapers, and generated tons of traction for true crime blogs. In the United States, parents on the wrong end of custody disputes abduct their kids every day. Most of the time, parental abductions don't qualify for national media attention. When they do, it's usually because there's a high-profile connection.

A Rockefeller is about as high profile as it gets. Boston PD was hammered with media requests for information. At the end of each day, officials put out a press release summarizing what they knew. It was a lot.

BPD was working overtime. All the media attention meant following up on tons of tips. Clark and Reigh had been sighted in Port Jefferson, NY; Smyrna, Delaware; and the Turks and Caicos Islands. None of the sightings panned out. BPD began working closely with the FBI.

Investigators had some standard requests. They sought witnesses from any of the places where they knew Clark and Reigh had been after the abduction. They had an unusual request too and sought "anyone with past or current information about Clark Rockefeller prior to 1993."

Agents believed there were lots of people who knew Clark Rockefeller before 1993. This guy was too memorable.

No way could he go unnoticed for the first 40 years of his life.

The joint statement from the Boston PD and FBI didn't give much away.

The suspect, when last seen, was wearing a blue Lacoste shirt, and khaki pants, which is typical attire for him. He dyes his hair a shade of orange/red, however, he has a permanent white patch of hair on the back of his head that is difficult to conceal. He is reported to speak with an accent that has been described by various individuals as Boston Brahmin, European and Scottish sounding. He also reportedly speaks some Russian. His interests are in sailing, physics and art. He frequents libraries. He reports that he was home schooled and may tell others that Reigh is home-schooled. He also may have cut and dye her hair and be dressing her in boy's clothing.

That afternoon, the cops left out a critical couple pieces of information. First off, they knew "Clark Rockefeller" was "Christian Karl Gerhartsreiter," a 47-year-old German national, wanted in connection with a decades-old missing persons case and possible homicide in San Marino, California.

Now the employees of Obsidian were clued in. They were convinced that the pesky and temperamental Chip Smith was in fact Clark Rockefeller.

Julie Gochar and her husband were watching television early on Aug. 1 when they "saw a bulletin on [the] morning news with several photos of a 'Mr. Clark Rockefeller'—the man we knew as Chip," she said in a statement released several days later. "We contacted law enforcement and told them we believe we know his whereabouts."

618 Ploy Street in Baltimore is a home built of brown brick with lots of windows. In the summer of 2012, hometryst.com, a real estate website, described it as a three-bed, three bath, 3400-square-foot "carriage house" built in 1900. The two-story walk-up has French doors and a rather large kitchen with stainless steel appliances.

One week after Clark's abduction of Reigh, officers attached to the task force set up shop in Baltimore and developed a plan to grab their bad guy and get the girl out safe. Their stakeout on Ploy Street began about 1 a.m. that Saturday. Cops took up positions in Baltimore's Mt. Vernon neighborhood and waited. Initially, there was no sign of father or daughter. The wait began. Someone had an idea.

Maybe the manager of the marina where their suspect kept his rundown catamaran could lure him out with a phone call. They had the manager call "Chip Smith" on his cell phone.

Twenty minutes later, their man was on the move.

"Hey, Clark!" FBI agent Frank Watt called.

He heard his name and spun around.

"Where are you going, Clark?" Watt asked.

"To get a turkey sandwich," he replied.

A group of five agents and cops swarmed the little German. They cuffed him.

Watt asked for the house keys. Gerhartsreiter turned them over. Agents entered the house. Inside, they found Reigh watching TV. She seemed happy. Immediately, Sandy got the good news. She collapsed and wept tears of joy.

Someone put Reigh on the phone. She wanted to be home with her mom. Inside 618 Ploy Street, the FBI sorted through Clark's boxes, bagged and tagged evidence. Included in the haul were 321 gold coins and $12,960 in cash.

News spread fast.

In Berlin, Connecticut, Ed Savio saw an image of Rockefeller on a cable news channel and was reminded of Chris Gerhartsreiter, the German teen who lived with his family for several months in the late 1970s.

"The first pictures I saw of him when he didn't have any glasses on, didn't look anything like him," Savio told the Associated Press. "But the pictures after he was apprehended, with the glasses, those look just like him."

On a cruise ship sailing south from Alaska to Vancouver, the kidnapper's image flashed on a television in the state room of Elmer and Jean Kelln, celebrating their wedding anniversary.

"Elmer, look, it's Chris," Jean said pointing to the picture of a man they knew as Christian Gerhartsreiter, a man they met in Germany in 1978.

Miley, ready to begin adding to his case file, dispatched a San Marino detective to Riverside, California where Linda Wetherbee gave a statement of sorts.

Watching television at home in San Marino, Daniel Banks sat up straight in his chair when he saw a mug shot of Boston's Clark Rockefeller.

Many years had passed since Banks had last seen Rockefeller. Only then he wasn't a Rockefeller, he was young Christopher Chichester, XIII baronet of Chichester, and a fellow parishioner at the Church of Our Savior in San Gabriel. Banks called up former pastor, Warren Raasch, in Milwaukee.

"Dan," Raasch deadpanned, "Chichester has risen."

Miley reviewed these details on the five-hour flight from LAX to BOS and slowly his file began to grow, By the time the L.A. Sheriff's homicide detective arrived in Beantown, Chris wasn't talking.

"In California, a lawyer cannot invoke someone's right to remain silent, they have to be approached personally by the person doing the interview," Miley said.

"In Massachusetts, that's not the case."

Stephen Hrones, Chris' lawyer, tried to intervene. Miley explained that because they were going to try a murder case in California, Massachusetts laws didn't apply, and Chris could be interviewed by police.

Within minutes Hrones was on the scene blocking Miley's attempt to talk to Chris.

Hrones didn't stop NBC or the *Boston Globe* from interviewing him though.

Several weeks after Miley's attempt, Gerhartsreiter, in custody and awaiting trial, was asked by NBC correspondent, Natalie Morales, to recall that week on the run with Reigh.

> "July 26, 27th was the first visitation that I actually had had. I had not seen my little girl in almost eight months," he told Morales. "Well, seeing her, of course, was a moment of intense joy. And I had not seen her in so, so, so long. And I missed her so much. She came back to me—slightly changed. Speaking in a British accent. Being much more grownup. Having teeth. Real teeth. It was quite different."

Like his ex-wife, Gerhartsreiter, clearly emotional, had a message for little Reigh.

"I would just say that there is, she should wish that we'd be reunited. And that there is hope for the two of us to be together again."

When asked by Morales if he thought there was a possibility he'd ever see his daughter again, he replied, "Natalie, I cannot predict the future. I don't know. I only hope so. And I wish for it."

When asked if he was involved with the San Marino murder of John Sohus or the disappearance of Linda, Chris explained to Morales that he was a Quaker and "I believe in non-violence. I can certainly say that I've never hurt anyone."

To Miley, the statement alone was as good as a confession.

Miley, now the lead detective on the homicide case, was on his way back to Los Angeles fretting about lack of straight answers from the coroner, dealing with leaks from law enforcement in Boston, and behind in the work he had to do to get a case filed. He needed to interview Linda Wetherbee.

CHAPTER 20.

CUSTODY

"One word of truth outweighs the world."
—Russian Proverb

In late May 2009, Suffolk County prosecutors tried Gerhartsreiter on four counts related to Reigh's kidnapping and the assault of Howard Yaffee. In June, a jury found Gerhartsreiter guilty of parental kidnapping and assault. He was not guilty on two other counts.

Nearly two years after the kidnapping, Gerhartsreiter was firmly in position as a person of interest in the California homicide case. A story that appeared in the Boston newspapers just hours before the jury delivered its verdict stood as a stark reminder of that fact.

In Massachusetts, there is no delay between verdict and sentencing. After taking the verdicts, Judge Frank Gaziano opened up the court for victim impact statements from Sandy and Yaffe.

A former prosecutor appointed to the bench in 2004 by then-Gov. Mitt Romney, Gaziano led the federal prosecution of Gary Lee Sampson, a career bank robber and drifter who carjacked and murdered three men: Phillip McCloskey, 69, of Taunton; Jonathan Rizzo, 19, from Kingston; and Robert Whitney, 58, of Concord, New Hampshire. All three victims were Good Samaritans who offered Sampson a ride after he said he needed help. Before he worked for the feds, Gaziano cut his teeth going after drug dealers and killers in state court.

Before Gaziano imposed sentence that afternoon, Sandy addressed the court via a written statement read by prosecutor David Deakin.

This statement will be brief. It is very difficult for me to think and write about the abduction of Reigh because the experience was so profoundly traumatic, and the memories are so painful.

While Reigh was gone, I faced a mother's worst nightmare—the possibility of losing a child without a trace. The emerging horrors about her abductor's nefarious past only heightened my concerns that she might come to harm.

Since Reigh's recovery and return, I have struggled to distance us both from the events of that terrifying week, to regain the normalcy of our lives, and to restore a sense of trust and well-being in Reigh. Restoration—emotional, physical, financial, and professional—is a slow process at best after any trauma. The media attention to this case, and the resultant sustained loss of privacy, has made our situation unusually complicated.

The long-term effects of the abduction are yet to be known, but anxiety about Reigh's safety and protection, which neither court orders nor my every precaution were able to provide in July 2008, will certainly be the most lasting. Inevitably, this crime will force us to expend substantial effort and resources for many years to come as we balance concerns over Reigh's safety with her growing need for independence.

All that was left was the open murder case. Miley and the DA's office wanted Chris returned to California. That day, Ellen Sohus in Arizona asked about her brother's disappearance.

"That was my father's worst nightmare," Sohus said. "My father went through that very agony and pain when John disappeared without a trace. I watched my father go through that as the result of the same man's actions."

* * *

As they pieced together their next steps, Miley and others would review an interview Chris had done with NBC reporter Natalie Morales. In the interview, Chris continued to identify as Clark Rockefeller. He claimed he had a normal childhood, growing up in the United States and traveling to places like Mt. Rushmore and Oregon.

"I remember clearly going to Mount Rushmore in the back of a woody wagon and being an aficionado of station wagons, I believe it was a '68 Ford, with the flip-up headlights. I have a clear memory of once picking strawberries in Oregon. And this, I believe, it would've been, perhaps, the 1960s, when I was together with a lot of other children. And we were picking strawberries in Oregon."

As he had previously told investigators, Chris/Clark had no recollection of his family. He did remember the "garbage strike in New York. I remember that very clearly. I remember the taxi strikes. I remember going to the zoo in Central Park. I have those distinct memories. I don't know where I got them. I'm quite sure I grew up in New York City."

Morales had one last question. "Your brother in Germany says you are Christian Gerhartstreiter. And the family hasn't seen you in 20 years."

Chris/Clark pretended he didn't know what she was talking about.

Miley continued to gather string.

He reviewed autopsy reports that declared a cause of death to be "blunt force trauma" ("BFT" for short). That's as opposed to "sharp force trauma," or "SFT," the sort of injuries O.J. delivered when he killed Nicole Brown Simpson and Ronald Goldman.

The substitute coroner, Sheridan, said John died as the result of BFT.

But how?

By themselves, either of the two blows would have rendered John unconscious. Which came first? Sheridan said he couldn't be certain. Doubtless, after he was hit the first time, John would have been "less able to defend himself." At the very least, either blow would have resulted in a concussion.

"The injuries we are talking about here would have been fatal," Sheridan concluded. John "might well have been lying on the floor when the second blow was delivered."

But was the little guy, who never lifted a finger in real work, capable of killing in such a brutal way? Sheridan said the blunt force trauma suffered by John in his last moments alive could have been delivered by anyone "given the right instrument."

A "plank of wood, hammer, something you have at your fireplace," he said, perhaps referring to the shovel that helped kill little Arthur Jennings. "As long as it's heavy enough and blunt."

Reading the reports that began to stuff Miley's investigative blue book was like getting into a time machine and traveling back to 1985 before finding his way to 1994 and the early 2000s.

CHAPTER 21.

THE ROCKEFELLER FILES

"The most important thing for a young man is to
establish a credit—a reputation, character."
—**John D. Rockefeller**

That Chris soon discovered there's mystique and power
in the Rockefeller brand shouldn't come as too much of a
surprise. It's been done before. It will be done again.

There is no name in America that carries as much weight.
Hell, the Rockefellers practically built modern New York
City. They financed the great oil boom that put the engine
on the American Industrial Revolution and the American
Century. If conmen know anything, it's that names like
Rockefeller or Vanderbilt carry the kind of weight that can
make a mark drop her drawers or write a check without ever
thinking twice about it.

The rich, the wealthy, always make the best marks for
small cons who assume they won't miss the money. Of
course, that relies on the mostly false assumption that the
rich never paid attention to how they became millionaires or
billionaires in the first place.

Take the case of Mike Rockefeller, aka Harry Gerguson,
aka Prince Michael Alexandrovitch Dmitri Obolensky
Romanoff. Mike owned a Hollywood restaurant frequented
by the film industry's top stars in the '40s, '50s, and '60s.
They knew he was a fraud and a fake, but he—and his
customers—had so much fun at the joint no one seemed to
mind.

In truth, Mike Rockefeller—or Mike Romanoff as he would be known later in life—was a Lithuanian immigrant who came to U.S. alone at 10 and bounced from New York orphanage to New York orphanage until he hit on a way to make some dough by pretending to be someone he wasn't. Along the way, he attended Harvard on a scam. There in 1923, for a semester of grad school, he conned fellow students and Cambridge merchants borrowing money and running up outrageous bills. Mike stayed one step ahead of authorities by hightailing it out to Chicago and Wichita before returning to New York.

In New York, Mike, a short man with a fabulous accent who always dressed impeccably, briefly became Mike Rockefeller and made a decent living selling phony works of art. His resume contained no reference to that incident, nor did it include Mike's habit of writing bad checks. It had tons of other interesting details, though.

> (Mike) had been schooled at Eton, at Harrow and at Winchester, and had attended not only Oxford and Harvard, but also the Royal Military College at Sandhurst, Cambridge, Yale, Princeton, the Sorbonne and Heidelberg. It might have been only a little remarkable for a man who—at least according to his own account—had driven a taxi for the French army during the defense of Paris and then fought on the Western Front as a British lieutenant, and on the Eastern Front as a Cossack colonel; who 'knew the Sudan like the back of my hand', who had won the Legion d'Honneur for some act of unspecified gallantry, and had gone on to defend the Winter Palace against rampaging Bolsheviks; had served six years in solitary

confinement for killing a German nobleman in a duel...

—mikedashhistory.com, "A Russian Prince on a Wichita Road Gang"

Along the way Mike got busted a few times, was the subject of a magazine article exposing the fact he wasn't a Rockefeller and ended up in Hollywood where he became friends with the real Rockefellers, the Vanderbilts, and a whole host of celebrities, including Humphrey Bogart, Lauren Bacall, and David Niven.

Maybe it worked because Mike was only trying to outrun bum checks and bad debts. Those who knew him said he had a soft heart; he meant no harm. His marks appreciated it and ultimately loved him for it.

No one ever said Clark Rockefeller had a soft heart—at least until his daughter Reigh was born. He was an insulting, condescending, imperious, pretentious fake who always rubbed people the wrong way, even when he didn't necessarily intend to. It wasn't the name that did it for him. He was that way already. The name just amplified all those bad qualities.

By the end of 1989, Chris had become someone else. He stopped speaking to his family in Germany. He lost touch with the Gerhartsreiters, the Kellns, the Eldnors, the Browns, the Bishops, the Boyntons, and anyone else who knew Chris.

A new man emerged from thin air—complete with a platinum AmEx and a line of credit supplied by Mihoko Manabe but fit for a Rockefeller. With the new identity came new responsibilities. A Rockefeller needed a personality quirk; Clark's became his Gordon Setter, Yates. As the American Kennel Club notes: "The Gordon Setter, the black avenger of the Highlands, is a substantial bird dog named for a Scottish aristocrat."

Clues as to Chris' awareness that he had done something wrong were everywhere in the files Miley reviewed. For example, after Detective Allen's visit, Clark quit driving. He abandoned his car.

For several months, Clark refused to see anybody. As Mihoko would later recall, he basically cut himself off from the rest of the world; rarely emerging from their apartment on 57th Street in Manhattan.

The routine broke down briefly in 1991 when the couple flew out to Hawaii and spent two weeks at a bed and breakfast on Kauai.

In the early '90s, Clark and Mihoko Manabe subscribed to a New York City newsletter devoted to dogs and their owners. The publisher of the newsletter noted the subscriber—an M. MacNabe—listed a P.O. Box in Blue Bell, Pennsylvania, which (as it turns out) is not too far from a property owned by Mihoko's family.

Clark loved the newsletter and when he learned in 1992 it was about to shut down, he arranged to meet with the publisher in New York City to see what could be done to keep the enterprise afloat.

"We took a walk, and he told me he had the means to open up a publishing office for my newsletter because (and he whispered), his real name is Clark Rockefeller," the publisher recalled. "He didn't use the name because of the 'death threats."

The deal never went down, but the publisher remembered being struck by her good fortune in meeting a Rockefeller. Clark became so fixated on the dog that he once got physical with Mihoko, when she accidentally locked Yates in a car with the windows up on a warm summer day.

"I had locked (the) dog in the car in the parking lot and he got furious," she said, recalling Clark launched into a tirade of derogatory terms. "You could tell by looking at his face."

Clark's words in that moment were "cutting, angry. It wasn't the loudness; it was the tone and the content. I'm not sure if there were any profanities," she continued. It was usually the way he displayed his temper—with words.

Clark would often berate Mihoko's driving and her choice in clothes.

"He had a temper but not in a physical physically violent way," she said. "He was just very caustic and derogatory. He could be very mean. In the matter of my driving, he was always getting mad."

Clothes shopping was also sometimes dicey.

"When we went shopping at Laura Ashley and he asked how much something was," Mihoko recalled, adding that when she repeated the price, "He was furious about that. So, there were those kinds of incidences."

By 1994, Mihoko had enough of the imperious Clark. He did no housework, no yard work. She made the money, and he paid the bills from her checking account. The couple grew apart. Mihoko met a man she would marry.

Eventually Mihoko moved, Clark stuck around in Tudor City until the lease ended and he latched onto Sandra Boss, a Harvard Business graduate. The couple met cute over a game of Clue in his apartment. He played Professor Plum. She was Miss Scarlett.

The last time Mihoko saw him was sometime in 1994.

"He came to bring a painting," she recalled. "It was a painting that he had done. It was a gift."

Boss and Rockefeller soon became a couple.

"My daughter was in love with the guy," said Sandy's dad, Bill Boss, who lives in Seattle. "He can be likeable and charming. But he's very deceptive. I should have hired a private detective before they got married."

As he reviewed the files, Miley learned Clark told everyone he was going to marry Sandy because she would be successful in her own right and therefore didn't need "Rockefeller" money.

"We were all very gullible," William said. "And we were so willing to accommodate him and his whims."

One day on a walk-through New York City with Clark and Sandy, Bill said the trio passed the U.N. building. Clark pointed to it and casually remarked "that's the property my grandfather gave up." When Clark was pressed for details, he would offer a pat response, usually suggesting it was rude to invade the Rockefeller family privacy.

"I like to keep secrets," Clark would often respond.

He told Sandy he never got together with his family because all they ever talked about was money and that was just too boring. On other occasions, Clark explained that his family did not understand why he would want to work. But he explained how his work was necessary.

The couple often visited Bill in Seattle. There, Clark bragged about a private contract he was working on with JPL and Caltech in Pasadena to create a "miraculous" propulsion system that would revolutionize space travel.

To Bill, Clark looked as he if could have been a Rockefeller. His facial features and receding hairline bore all the traits of American royalty, "no question about it." Clark also told Sandy and her family he was the son of a child actress, Ann Carter.

Carter had several roles in what would be considered film noir, a genre Clark admired and often discussed with friends like author Walter Kirn, who said Clark enjoyed discussing the plot twists of several films of the genre.

Some of those films hit pretty close to home. Take Orson Welles' 1946 flick, *The Stranger*. The plot of the movie involves a German war criminal named Franz Kindler who is hiding out in a small New England town and posing as a professor named Charles Rankin. When Rankin, who has married the daughter of a U.S. Supreme Court justice, is discovered by a fellow war criminal, he strangles the man and buries the body in a shallow grave.

RKO, the studio which produced *The Stranger*, also produced *The Curse of the Cat People*, in which Ann Carter, the child actress, had her most extensive role.

When Bill Boss Googled Ann Carter, he was struck by how much young Reigh resembled the onetime child actress.

"Well, there it is," Boss thought. "The guy is probably telling the truth."

Now more comfortable as a Rockefeller, Clark dressed the part of an aristocrat from the open-collared polo shirts to the Topsiders sans socks. With a powerful new last name, Clark became more extravagant and eccentric. Clark told friends like author Walter Kirn that he "worked as a freelance central banker for third world countries who couldn't afford their own."

When Kirn pressed him on it, asking which countries hired him, Clark said, "Thailand."

In other conversations with Kirn, Clark explained how China was employing a modern version of *Lebensraum,* "Living Room." It's the idea in the 1930s that Hitler pursued as he expanded Germany's reach into Poland and France. As China expands its influence in Asia and employs its wealth to expand overseas markets. It seemed perfectly reasonable that a man so immersed the world banking industry would understand China and the country's place on the world stage.

Kirn, who would eventually write *Blood Will Out* detailing his 10-year relationship with the wealthy oddball who lived just off Central Park, bought into Clark's intelligence and hoped that perhaps one day he might benefit from knowing a Rockefeller.

"I spent a lot of time with him in New York in the highest echelons of Blue Blood society," Kirn said.

Kirn also recalled Clark's pad in rural New Hampshire. It was within spitting distance of J.D. Salinger's place, nestled in the heart of the Cornish art colony.

Cornish got its first whiff of Clark in 1998. He was bidding on Doveridge, the onetime home of Judge Learned

Hand. Alma and Peter Gilbert were interested in the home too, primarily as a potential location for a planned museum. His move to town came as he and Sandy left New York and took up residence in Boston.

The Gilberts had no idea who was interested in the estate, but soon began hearing rumors that "a famous person" was moving to the tiny New England town of about 1,600 residents. Alma, a writer, was in the midst of putting together a very lovely coffee table book and hoped to include historic and contemporary photos of the Doveridge grounds.

Although she had permission from the previous owner to send a photographer over to Doveridge, Mr. Rockefeller wasn't having any of it, Alma said. He refused to allow any access to the home or its grounds.

"I called Mr. Rockefeller to congratulate him and welcome him to the town," said Gilbert, a tiny dynamo who spent many years in Cornish chronicling the art of Augustus Saint-Gaudens and others like Maxfield Parrish who turned the town into a premiere center of American art at the turn of the 19th and 20th centuries.

"I'm getting ready to write my 13th or 14th book on The Cornish Colony, and I truly would appreciate if you would give me permission to send my photographer over for outside photographs of your garden."

"He said, 'Definitely not. I'm a very famous man.'"

"I said, 'Mr. Rockefeller there's a lot of very famous people here too. You are not the only one."

"He said, 'Yes, but people don't know where I live."

"Very well, if you don't want me to do it then I won't do it," Alma said. "However, I will just use the vintage photographs given to me by the historical society."

"He says, 'I'm not going to let you do that either."

"He got my Latin up," Gilbert, a native of Mexico City, said. "So I said, 'Well I'm awfully sorry, but I am going to use those photographs."

"He said, 'Well if you do, I will put an injunction on your little book."

Gilbert paused for a second or two reflecting on Clark's tone and added, "You know, underlined like that."

"I said, 'If you do that sir, how long do you think you are going to stay unknown in Cornish? If you are going to fight me, you should realize that when I get into a fight, I go all the way. I will contact my publisher in California immediately."

At that, Clark backed off, changed his course, and set aside his opposition to Gilbert's use of the historic photos. Gilbert said she didn't think much of his change of heart at the time, but upon reflection later thought Clark's manner was odd and that something was not right in the way he reacted to the mention of California and a possible California court battle.

After about a year in Cornish, Clark became embroiled in a battle with the Saint-Gaudens National Historic site, which abutted the rear of the Doveridge property. Clark didn't want the site expanded. Alma hoped she and her husband Peter could soothe things and invited Clark to visit the museum they set up at Mastlands, just up 12A from Platt Road.

"I'm not interested in unknowns," Clark responded.

"I said, 'You say you know a little about art history and these artists are unknown? Saint-Gaudens is considered the foremost American sculptor and Maxfield Parrish was quite successful. During the 1920s, one out of every five persons in this country had a painting of Parrish's in their home. These are not unknowns.'

"He wasn't interested."

Sometime after that, Clark contacted Alma again to tell her he had discovered some paintings that might be of significance to the museum. He was willing to donate them but had some conditions.

"If the museum accepted them, they would have to make a binding promise that they would never have anything to do with the Saint-Gaudens historic site," Peter Gilbert explained.

They and the museum board of directors turned Clark down. He responded with an email that explained his position.

To: Alma Gilbert
From Clark Rockefeller
Date: 12/2/02 2:05 p.m.
Dear Ms. Gilbert,
I finally received and read your letter from
last month. Thank you very much!
I love writing more than anything else. My day-job
deals with numbers and scientific concepts six days
a week and I always reserve Sundays for my writing.
None of my novels, which I submit under a pseudonym,
have had any success. No agents want to take me on.
Perhaps your cartoon will indeed bring me luck.
Sorry that your museum had to turn down the invitation
for the lot of paintings. Of 105 invitations, four institutions
declined and two never responded, which leaves us with
a vast choice. We already have one in mind—not an
New England museum, but one that will take good care
of the works. I have not yet made up my mind about the
two remaining works who owned the lot of twenty-two
works, but if I take the,, I will give them away in the same
fashion as the last lot and I will inform your museum.
I shall not have any extended stays in Cornish in 2003
except for occasional overnight visits during my monthly
trips to Montreal. We just cannot find adequate childcare for
our young daughter in the Upper Valley. Also new Dept. of
Defense regulations require me to do my work in a "secure
environment." (whatever that means ...). I can no longer
remove papers from my office. Similar new regulations
in other industries will certainly give city living a boost
to the detriment of home offices and telecommuting.

Lastly, my anti-Saint-Gaudens lobbying effort has had greater than expected success this year. Any politicians who supported the site in the past will think very carefully before they vote for any more money for the site and no future bill in support of the site shall escape my sentinel's notice. I would like to say now that the site's expansion no longer presents a serious threat to our neighborhood, but I will wait one more election cycle before I can say it with complete certainty.
You now have my e-mail address and I invite you to write whenever you like. Please keep in mind that I usually receive about one hundred e-mail messages per day and that I may not respond immediately.
Clark Rockefeller
Non-business-related e-mail
—dictated but not read
E.H.

Clark cast an odd shadow in Cornish, a town not too unlike his German home in Bavaria: remote, tiny, conservative, and private. He could often be seen riding his Segway scooter along New Hampshire 12A, Cornish's main road. Before Clark and Sandy split for good, he would bring Reigh up and appeared to celebrate life away from the crush of Boston.

He often dressed the little girl in clothes like his own. Polos, deck shoes over sockless feet, patterned belts, and yacht caps.

"I think he wanted a rural, quiet area where he could strut his stuff and be believed," Alma said. "He had to go to a place where he would be a believable entity. The artists that came to Cornish were not artists who were trying to make it, they had already made it. There's a lot of money in the area. He must have thought the name Rockefeller is going to fit right in and no way would anyone think to bother him."

Like the Kellns, the Gilberts often finished one another's sentences, Peter rounded out Alma's thoughts with some insight of his own.

"You have to understand the nature of New Englanders. They are people who mind their own business. They don't care what you are. You are allowed to be what you want to be. The New Hampshire motto is, 'Live free or die' and that's what they allow you to do."

A 2004 Cornish newspaper article delved into Rockefeller's claims and concluded he was not related to the oil baron Rockefellers.

Reports published in 2008 indicated that neither he nor Sandy reacted well to the pieces. Nonetheless, it set the stage for a showdown at City Hall between Clark and Peter Burling, a New Hampshire state senator.

During his time at Doveridge, Clark put together a strange collection of items. For example, he bought three retired police cars, had them re-painted and lettered in gold script, "Doveridge Security." He parked the cars at the street entrance to the property to discourage visitors. Despite the fact he never drove, Clark also bought an antique fire truck he kept on the grounds.

At the gateway to Cornish on Route 12A lies the oldest church in New Hampshire—Trinity. Built in the early 19th Century, the building with its white siding, even windows, and black shutters looks a lot like you might imagine an old New England house of worship or meeting house to appear. It could be either comforting or scary, depending on which story is being told. The building sits in the middle of a large clearing and is surrounded by a white picket fence.

In 1980, the church building was added to the National Register of Historic Places. Burling, whom Alma described as a "tall patrician looking guy from one of New Hampshire's oldest families" took over the church. Over the course of several years, he rebuilt it piece by piece and intended to donate it to Cornish.

"Rockefeller offered to buy the church and Burling wouldn't sell it," Peter said.

On the night Burling completed the paperwork for the deed transfer to the town, a discussion arose at a town hall meeting about the need for $110,000 to renovate the Cornish police station.

"You have to realize New Hampshireites are so tight," Peter said. "In Vermont, they say New Hampshireites are tighter than bark on a tree. For a town of less than 2,000 people, $110,000—that's a lot of money. Town hall meetings are where you go to hear them argue until five in the morning about a five-cent increase on the tax rate. These people are something else."

The town elders were nonetheless about to receive Burling's loving gift as they turned to the discussion of the police station.

In the middle of the debate, a door flew open and "Rockefeller came out and waved something that seemed to be a check," Peter recalled.

"I will build the station and give it to the town in exchange for the church," Peter remembered the moment with a chuckle.

Clark continued: "I have a check right here. The town needs $110,000 to build that police station. I've got a check made out to the town for $110,000 provided you accept Burling gift of the Trinity Church and then you sell it to me for one dollar."

At this point in his retelling of the story, Peter's chuckle becomes the closest thing to a hearty laugh a stoic and serious New Englander can reasonably get away with.

Burling was trapped by Clark's ploy.

"You could hear a pin drop and all the collective teeth of the locals fell to the floor," Peter said.

Realizing he'd been had. Burling got a sort of last laugh when he explained to the Town Council that they would get the building, but he would retain the contents, which he planned on donating to the Cornish Historical Society.

Clark was none too pleased.

"It (was like) Peyton Place," Alma concluded. "Peyton Place, with some aristocracy thrown in."

You could almost hear the air quotes when the word "aristocracy" passed her lips.

Despite his small victory, Clark's visits to Cornish became fewer and fewer. By the time he and Sandy divorced, and Sandy had sole custody of Reigh, Clark had pretty much abandoned Doveridge. His final months of freedom were spent mostly bouncing between Boston, Baltimore, and New York.

CHAPTER 22.

INMATE 2800458

"If you want total security, go to prison. There
you're fed, clothed, given medical care and so
on. The only thing lacking... is freedom."
—**Dwight D. Eisenhower**

Sgt. Tim Miley, the L.A. County Sheriff's detective leading
the inquiry into John's death and Linda's disappearance
wanted a handwriting sample from Chris, whom he refers to
as Gerhartsreiter. The exemplar might help prove who wrote
the postcards.

In all, there were four of them. Three had not been
booked into evidence until after Miley took the case.

"Luckily they had been saved," he said.

The fourth was in Sheriff's custody in 1994, but had
since disappeared, in what Miley called "another example of
investigative malpractice in the case."

About the same time "Clark Rockefeller" sat for his
interviews with Natalie Morales and the *Boston Globe*, Los
Angeles County investigators paid another visit to 1920
Lorain Road, where Christopher Chichester once lived. In
the heat of a summer afternoon, they closed off the road to
through traffic and set up camp.

Across the street, TV trucks, radio and newspaper
reporters, and curious neighbors gathered under shade trees
and swapped stories about Chris. Walt Mancini, the great
and widely respected *Pasadena Star-News* photographer,
convinced a neighbor to allow him into their backyard. He
peered over the fence and caught a photo of investigators

lugging various pieces of high-tech equipment around the swimming pool in the backyard that was once John Sohus' grave.

We "wanted to go to the Lorain Road location to see if a second person could be buried in the back yard," Lynne Herold recalled. "We looked in the pool house for the presence of blood using new techniques."

Among the new techniques was an alternative light source and what Herold described as a "crime light"—a flashlight that's well-suited for searching crime scenes. A photographer re-imaged the backyard; a special 3-D camera was used to hunt for any clues.

Miley had hoped to conduct the search without reporters and photographers looking over their shoulders but is convinced someone from the coroner's office wanted to get on camera that day.

Regardless, nothing turned up.

In 2023, Miley finally acknowledged he and his partner also interviewed Linda Wetherbee, to get an understanding of Didi's will and her state of mind. They hoped to learn more about Chris' actions in the weeks before he left San Marino in 1985. The Wetherbees were not loving caregivers.

"Basically, they were just crooks," Miley said. "Con people.

The conversation was "really labored," Miley said. Although she was lucid, Linda Wetherbee didn't want to say too much of anything.

Realizing Wetherbee was in her final days, and it could be months or even years before the murder case would go to trial, Miley wanted to conduct a conditional exam of Linda Wetherbee at her bedside. He hoped the interview would yield usable testimony. He got a judge to agree.

"So I get everything set up. I call the nurse … And when I get her on the phone, she says, 'Oh, no, she died last Friday.' Our motive? It's gone."

Back in San Marino, Peggy Ebright, star of Gypsy Moth Production's *Inside San Marino*, which Chris produced back in 1984, dusted off her files and relived the several weeks she worked alongside the young man she called a "remittance man."

"There was no reason for all the lies he told," Ebright said. "It wasn't like anyone would check."

Bill Boss, meanwhile, wondered how he had been taken in by Clark's con.

"I guess I was a gullible dad," he said. "I just hope what happened to my daughter and granddaughter will serve as a warning to other dads out there."

Convicted in the kidnapping case, Christian Karl Gerhartsreiter, was brought to California on July 6, 2011, and booked into Los Angeles County Men's Central Jail the next day on suspicion of murder. California investigators and Massachusetts prison officials reached an agreement that allowed Christian to serve out the remainder of his kidnapping sentence while awaiting trial in the Sohus case.

If Chris had looked around during his first appearance in Alhambra Superior Court, he would have seen some old San Marino friends. Dan Banks, who knew him at Church of Our Savior, was there. So was Jann Eldnor, Jann of Sweden, the barber who said goodbye to Chris back in '85.

"Oh my, he looks so much older," Jann, clad in full cowboy attire, said outside the tiny courthouse. "I wonder what will happen to him." Jann did plenty of TV interviews that morning.

Christian arrived at court in the early morning on a bus loaded with other inmates.

In court, he was very quiet. He didn't say much and seemed slightly disoriented. He wore rimless glasses and appeared to have not washed his hair or shaved.

Back in Boston, one of the suspect's acquaintances, whose daughter was friends with Reigh, hoped his former neighbor was OK.

In a July 8, 2011, email, the acquaintance explained his interest and concerns.

"I've known Clark for five or six years and visited him most recently on Saturday at the prison ... He also writes and calls me frequently," the man noted. "His daughter Snooks was a friend and classmate of my daughter's before Clark got divorced and Snooks moved to London with her mom Sandy Boss. We used to get together frequently for play dates, dinners... He proved to be a great Dad to Snooks and a good friend to my wife and family."

When asked why Chris didn't want to acknowledge his former acquaintances from San Marino, the Boston friend, who like many others who knew Gerhartsreiter only as Clark, was thoughtful.

"As to Clark's demeanor, I'd guess he is a bit jet lagged and probably dismayed at his current predicament. That being said, he is not an overly boisterous person; he's more soft-spoken, I'd say."

As for the glasses?

"Generally speaking, he is pictured with the black-rimmed Chichester glasses or the thick black Wayfarer glasses."

Throughout the day, the Boston man did his best to process the predicament his friend faced in California.

"With respect to John Sohus, I can't picture Clark actually killing someone. However, Sandy often stated that he had quite a temper, and the people in Cornish, NH made the same claims," the acquaintance wrote.

Things were little different when Christian's preliminary hearing rolled around in January 2012. Dan Banks and Jann Eldnor came to court every day. But, while Dan was allowed in, Jann was kept out. He'd been subpoenaed as a witness but was never called to testify. I got the impression his feelings were hurt. Walter Kirn flew out from Montana.

Many San Marino residents who knew Gerhartsreiter when he was Chichester refused to answer detective's questions about him and refused to testify about what they did know.

The suspect never turned to gaze into the audience. Kirn was disappointed, but left California at the end of the week with enough good material for a book on the case and a whole bunch of theories as to what happened to John and Linda Sohus and how this slight German immigrant managed to evade law enforcement even though he was a wanted man.

For the most part, Chris got through the five-day preliminary hearing without doing or saying much. He had a pencil and paper to take notes and had to be calmed after a brief outburst. Ultimately, Alhambra Superior Court Judge Jared Moses ordered Christian bound over for trial in Los Angeles.

After his return to Southern California, Chris had been held in at least three separate county jails—Men's Central, the North County Correctional Facility, and Twin Towers. Just before his trial commenced, Chris was moved from NCCF to the Twin Towers, but his celebrity caused some difficulties, according to court documents.

"Defense Counsel indicated to the court that he has a real concern about the safety of the defendant at the Twin Tower Facility," according to a minute order from a Nov. 7, 2012 hearing in the case. "Counsel states that the defendant's status has gotten out amongst the population and the defendant has become a target for autographs and requests to be a voice greeter for the telephones at Twin Towers as well as a variety of things."

"Counsel also indicates that the defendant has become frightened because of recent threats and the situation is getting worse."

The case file may have been thin, and the motive dead with Wetherbee, but Miley and prosecutors began to make connections that would circumstantially link Gerhartsreiter to the killing.

Kristie Macrakis, a University of Georgia history professor who spent time and swapped stories with Clark and a group of friends in a Beacon Hill coffee shop in 2007 and 2008, remembered how he used to "hoard the hardy plastic bags the Athenaeum Library in Boston provided to members." She wondered if it implicated him given the book bags discovered with John's body in 1994.

"It was good to hear that Didi Sohus actually named the mystery man who told her the far-fetched stories about secret missions," Macrakis wrote in a 2012 e-mail after the preliminary hearing.

She listed the questions about the case Miley believed would be answered.

"It sounds like Linda told people they were going away. I wonder if John was still around when she said that," Macrakis wrote. "I also wonder if John's death was an accident. Whatever happened, I wish Clark would just confess. He'd feel a lot better."

Macrakis died in 2022. Clark/Chris never confessed and in 2012, he went on trial for the murder of John Sohus. Miley sat at the prosecutor's table throughout.

CHAPTER 23.

MURDER TRIAL

"A bad day in L.A. is better than a
good day anywhere else."
—**Elnaz Golrokh, Instagram influencer**

The final day of trial for Christian Karl Gerhartsreiter began as one of those unforgettable Los Angeles mornings.

The winds had blown hard through the Los Angeles Basin overnight. The weather system cut the power for thousands and knocked down more than a few trees. But when dawn came, what had been hazy, smoggy, foggy skies became crystal clear for the first time in weeks.

Under those magnificent skies, Wednesday seemed like the morning Los Angeles finally gave up all her secrets. To be certain, there are plenty. I parked at the same lot on North Hill Street in Chinatown where I had deposited my car since jury selection began a month earlier. The smell of incense burning in the Thien Hau Temple a block over on Yale Street added its perfume to the stiff morning breeze.

Circumstances had presented themselves in a forthright and clear manner to the six-man, six-woman jury as well. After getting instructions and hearing closing arguments, it took just about five hours to render Christian Karl Gerhartsreiter guilty of murder and guilty of having used a blunt object to kill John Sohus all those years ago.

***

Considering how quickly it came together, prosecutor Habib Balian admitted he had some worries that Chris might just pull off his final con.

"Sometimes you're afraid that this guy has conned so many people for so many years that this would be the one last time he pulls off his last con," he said to a group of reporters crammed together outside the elevators on the 12th floor of the Criminal Courts Building following the verdict. "But that didn't happen. The system worked and the jurors looked at what was reasonable and rejected what was unreasonable." In answer to question after question, Balian repeated a couple of scripted phrases again and again:

"Fair and just." "The system worked."

He went off script just once.

"The defendant wanted John Sohus dead, and he accomplished his goal," Balian concluded.

Standing away from the crowd, Chris' attorneys, Jeff Denner and Brad Bailey, said if an acquittal wasn't in the cards, they did hold out hope for a hung jury.

"There was a lot of emotion," Denner said. "People feel (Chris) is a bad person."

Denner read the jury he had previously described as "incredibly urban," and he instinctively knew this was not a group that would like Chris one bit.

"This did not feel like a jury that could relate to this defendant or the complexity of this case," he said. "They viewed it differently than us. In the end, jurors weren't persuaded that an evil Linda Sohus killed her husband and left the hapless German renter holding the incriminating book bag. No. They said that all the circumstantial evidence—the University of Wisconsin book bag, the Sohus' pickup truck's presence in Connecticut, the name changes, and the odd behavior—pointed to one reasonable conclusion."

There wasn't much for the jury to deliberate.

Juror Vincent Garcia, a truck driver from Baldwin Park, recalled a vote taken early in the process showed there was a 10-2 split in favor of conviction before there had been any discussion. I couldn't help but appreciate the bluntness of Gemma Vasquez, a nurse from Lincoln Heights, who explained that Chris, the man who had conned high society on both coasts, was "really stupid" to put a dead man's head in plastic bags bearing the logos of universities Chris had attended.

And of course, there was the truck. "I'm like, if you haven't killed him why do you have the keys to the truck?" Vasquez said in the straightforward manner of someone familiar with the concept of street smarts. "Why are you giving it away and taking it back and giving it away to somebody else and telling everybody that it was from a film, and it wasn't from a film?"

But while it was easy to figure who killed John, Gemma admitted she would always have questions about the case.

"How can a person kill another person? In a lot of our minds, we were thinking why did he do it?" she asked. "What did John do to him or Linda do to him that he wanted to kill them? It was really stupid to get rid of them if you wanted to stay in the house."

Salvador Ruiz, a juror reporters knew as "Hat Man" for the straw hats he wore to court each day, thought it would be nice if Chris would tell the police what happened to Linda. Among trial watchers, Ruiz could have been known as "shirt man" for the unique guayaberas he wore too, or "sunglasses man" for that matter. To us watching the case, Ruiz seemed to hold the key to Chris' future—probably because we couldn't see his eyes behind the pair of dark Ray-Ban™ sunglasses.

Judge George Lomeli agreed to the unusual court attire as Ruiz had some sort of medical condition.

Miley watched the hallway interviews from a safe distance. He hadn't said much to reporters and didn't plan to say more than that, even though a verdict had been rendered.

"He was fortunate that over the course of years things broke his way," Miley said, claiming that there would have been an arrest eventually. "I don't know if he would be free today. Somebody, other than myself, was already digging into the case. We would have eventually gotten to him."

Miley gave testimony at the trial that was brief and to the point. Clearly sheriff's detectives back in 1994 fucked up. They didn't keep a solid murder book, they lost key pieces of evidence, including Linda's postcard to her mother, and made no effort to follow up on the leads that had been in the file since John's body was uncovered. "(The detective) did not file a report. All we had to go by was his notes. I can't tell what was documented or not," Miley said. "I don't know that everything was (documented). (The lackadaisical approach) is not how I did it."

There's little doubt that if detectives in 1994 had made a couple of phone calls and physically tracked down Mihoko Manabe, she would have led them to Christian Gerhartsreiter, who was posing as Clark Rockefeller and living under her roof.

Instead, they turned to *Unsolved Mysteries* for leads, probably thinking they had a self-solver on their hands. Like who wouldn't turn this little freak in, right?

No one except Chris counted on Mihoko Manabe keeping his secrets.

Regardless, catching up with Chris would have to wait until 2008. And then it wasn't until 2012 that Miley got a glimpse into Chris/Clark/Chip's private life. It came from the inside of a storage locker just off Orleans Street in Baltimore. The detective noted furniture, books, credit cards, business cards, letters, and a blank check signed by Sandy Boss. There was also a collection of antique postcards, some from England and France. The implication was clear—even without being able to travel outside the country, Chris could get his hands on foreign postcards and incorporate them into a con.

He also cataloged a wedding photograph of Clark and Sandy, a photo of Ann Carter—the woman whom Clark once claimed was his mother—and a Christmas card with the greeting "Merry Christmas and a Happy New Year" inscribed Peggy and David Rockefeller. Among all the stuff was a document identifying the defendant by the name he would toss around every now and then: James Frederick Clark Rockefeller. More than one item bore the name associated with the unusual birthdate of Feb. 29, 1960. There also appeared to be several cardboard tubes of the sort usually associated with blueprints. Miley said they contained "what looked like modern art."

"I want to say there were 12 to 13, large, about six inches in diameter and eight to 10 feet in length with caps on the end," Miley recalled, describing what were likely the remnants of the fabulous modern art collection author Walter Kin recalled seeing in Clark's Manhattan apartment in 1998 for an article he wrote in *The New Yorker* shortly after the jury reached its verdict.

The collection, as Kirn recalled, included what appeared to be Motherwells, Rothkos, and Mondrians. Forged works by all three artists became the subject of several lawsuits and a federal tax investigation in 2013. And here's where the story gets slightly weird—or could take an even weirder turn with a real investigation.

Federal court documents indicated the forgeries were sold by the Knoedler Gallery in New York. Chris (as Clark) had a relationship with the gallery. At the time his murder trial wrapped up, no one knew—or would say—if he was connected to the scandal that ultimately led to the closure of the Knoedler Gallery in 2011 and roiled high society in 2013 with the arrest of art dealer, Glafira Rosales, and the search for a mysterious Chinese painter living in Queens.

The *New York Times* linked Rosales to Pei-Shen Qian who allegedly sold fakes to Rosales' boyfriend. Before the FBI could talk to him, Qian skipped town.

Ultimately, Rosales fingered an abusive boyfriend for cooking up the scheme. She was sentenced to probation.

The boyfriend, identified as José Carlos Bergantiños Diaz, remains in Spain.

None of that was Balian's concern, nor Miley's for that matter. Under cross examination, Miley admitted he got into the garage-sized storage room with the help of a Baltimore cop who picked the lock.

The modern art didn't rate much of a second look. Miley said he took pictures of the tubes and tried to make note of the signatures.

"Is that part of the billion-dollar collection Mr. Rockefeller had?" Denner asked Miley.

"I'm not an expert," came the reply.

***

As the lawyers, jurors, cops, and survivors talked to reporters in the hallway that brilliant L.A. morning, sheriff's deputies brought the newly convicted Christian Gerhartsreiter back to his cell at Men's Central Jail. His eyes were red, and it appeared to some in Men's Central that Chris had been crying.

He certainly didn't agree with the decision. A couple of hours before his return to jail, as the verdict was read, Chris stared wide-eyed at the panel. Behind the pair of wire-framed glasses that are standard issue in L.A. County, the enormity immediately took hold of him. Chris briefly slumped in his chair, then in the lock-up he shed the suit he'd been wearing for four weeks and shuffled back to the business of being an inmate no one cared too much about.

A month later, I made one of two visits with Chris and spent an intense half-hour conversing about the verdict, Linda, and his run as America's last great imposter.

A visit to the Los Angeles County Jail is a rigorous and unsettling experience. Visits are parsimoniously doled out via a website that leaves little room for experimentation or planning. Inmates get exactly two visitors a week for exactly a half-hour each. If the slots are taken, tough luck.

Walter Kirn and a producer for *48 Hours* got there before I did. Walter, who was once friends with Chris, also went twice. He had a pair of interesting conversations with the convicted murderer, which he detailed in the *New Yorker* article.

The TV producer debriefed Chris after all his other visitors had come and gone. She sought an exclusive interview and nearly got one by promising there would be no hard questions. Men's Central Jail—known in bureaucratese as MCJ—is a central planning monstrosity east of downtown at the intersection of Vignes and Bauchet streets. It lies across Bauchet from the more modern Twin Towers, where some of the more violent and mentally unstable L.A. County inmates are held.

MCJ's architecture resembles the coroner's office on nearby North Mission Road and is essentially a group of windowless concrete slabs fitted together by a low bid contractor in the '60s or '70s. The lone public entryway is at the southeast corner of a high-walled courtyard surrounded by coin-operated lockers and the lower level of a five-story cement parking lot in which the county charges too much to park.

Across Vignes there is a collection of bail bondsmen offering 24-hour service to families in need. A girl in a low-cut blouse, short skirt, and high heels often stands at the traffic light handing out cards to Bad Girls Bail Bonds, which is at the end of a narrow, trash-filled, and graffiti-enhanced alleyway. Family members and visitors are required to line up in the courtyard an hour before their scheduled appointments.

More than once, rioting in the jail has resulted in a lockdown that ends in a postponed visit. It's a worry family members have as they stand waiting in the hot sun for a deputy to decide whether or not there will be visitation today. In my first interview, Chris maintained his innocence, professed love for his daughter, and expressed angst that his subscription to *The Economist* had run out. Chris admitted reading newspaper articles I had written about him and scolded me for reporting that Tim Miley believed he worked a scam on Didi with the Wetherbees. "I took care of her," he told me. "No one else did. The idea that I would harm someone for $40,000 is too dramatic."

He also didn't like that I had described John's body as having been "trisected." He told me about his collection of 14 1941 Cadillacs and noted that it was Sandy who got him started.

"She bought the first one," he said. "It's not a highly collectible car, but it's one I enjoy." There is no such collection. Never was, as far as I could tell.

Chris said he's writing a novel—"a trilogy really with six parts; each third will have an A and a B." The first 600,000 words deal with a six-month period of European history between December 1918 and May 1919. "That's really the beginning of our modern era," he said.

According to Chris, the novel has three primary characters. Among them is a rogue diplomat. I asked him if he had read William Shirer's *Rise and Fall of the Third Reich*. His answer contained a touch of indignity, and I was informed that most of the action took place in France and England.

In between that and our next visit, Chris had fired his attorneys and declared he would represent himself in the sentencing phase of trial. He announced the move on June 26, the same day John's sister and Linda's friends held a memorial service for their lost loved ones at a beautiful, very informal ceremony in La Cañada.

Chris then sent me a neatly hand-written, single-spaced, two-page letter dated July 1, 2013.

Dear Frank,

Thank you for your recent visit. After you left I had a thought: my motion for retrial, once finished, will read far less like a legal brief, far less like the very trite and confusing retrial motions I have read so far.

It will read much the way I write: clear, concise, devoid of all too much jargon; in short, in a way the average reader might expect. Would you have any interest in publishing it? If so, I would ask that it be published in its entirety, unedited, unchanged even for style that you might find peculiar on occasion.

Please note that it might run quite long, though an exact word count I do not have in mind. Please also note that besides your paper, I might also extend this offer to the Boston Globe - a co-exclusive.

So far I have not asked anyone else, but I intend to ask persons in-the-know whether this idea might mortally offend the judge. If such authorities think it might, then I must withdraw the offer.

Also do you have interest in requesting my court transcripts once I finish with them? They will have all my margin notes. If no one wants them, I must throw them away. So please let me know your thoughts about my offer.

Here goes another hypothetical question for you, the reason for the question will turn obvious soon: Say you, Frank, will interview with The New York Times, and you have dinner with a friend who works there now. What would you ask your friend? Would you ask about inside information, about benefits? Would you ask about the kind of salary you might expect? Would you ask about meeting Salzberger?

Could you tell me your top ten questions please? Again the reason for this inquiry will become obvious soon.

The letter was signed, "Best, C."

I regret not taking up the offer of transcripts.

Chris called collect soon after the letter arrived. I turned down his offer.

During our second visit, he bragged about his exploits in the United States, at one point proclaiming he had penetrated deeper in American society than any European ever had. I asked about his mother, his brother, and his childhood. After teaching me the proper pronunciation of Chiemgau (Kimgow), Chris went on to describe how the residents of his hometown were too stupid to notice a prank he pulled on them.

"One night I went around and changed all the street signs, so that no street had its real name," he recalled. "In the morning I thought there would be great confusion. No one noticed. Even a week later people went on about their business. I finally had to point out what I had done. I think I had a good laugh about it."

A few weeks after that conversation, Chris would speak to a Los Angeles County Probation Department officer. The two talked about Siegsdorf and the circumstances of the crime for which Chris was about to be committed to state prison. The report—done in all caps—detailed Didi's first interaction with the police in July 1985.

"She believed John and Linda were working for the government. She believed this in part because the defendant, a renter who had until recently been living in the rear house on her property, told her he was forwarding John and Linda's mail to an unknown address in North Carolina.

The defendant now disappeared, and she had still not heard from her son, causing her to fear for his safety. Victim John Sohus' mother also informed the detective the couple's vehicle was missing and she received a postcard for John and Linda dated 4/28/1985, postmarked from Paris, France."

That postcard was never introduced at trial. Didi also told the cops back in '85 that when Chris left, he took a custom sofa cover and an oriental throw rug.

Didi thought it was strange because "the sofa cover was custom made and would only fit on that couch."

The report shows Chris donated DNA to the national database. As for the face-to-face interview with probation, it took place via video conference. Although Chris told me his mother was alive and probably suffered from Alzheimer's, he had another story for the state.

"He and his brother were raised by their parents in Germany. He had an 'OK' childhood because he did not get along with his father. His father is deceased, and he believes his mother may be deceased or residing in Germany. He has no contact with his brother. He migrated to the United States in 1978. He came to this country for a better life because Germany was a divided country at the time. It was not an easy life and there was a real threat of war.

Since arriving in the United States, he has lived in Connecticut, Wisconsin, Los Angeles, New Hampshire, New York, Boston, and Baltimore."

As for work?

The truth—such as it was—was a far cry from developing a new method of jet propulsion for spacecraft, the story he told his friends who might be interested. Nonetheless a whiff of grandiosity shone through.

"The defendant stated prior to his arrest he worked as a self-employed writer and researcher. His income varied. Prior to this employment he worked on Wall Street from 1986 to 1989 in corporate bonds, earning $500,000 per year."

At the end of the report, Frank Corrales, the officer who conducted the interview, made a formal evaluation of Chris and his crime.

"The circumstances of the offense indicate the victim's death was particularly violent. The body exhibiting severe trauma," he began. "The victim's surviving family members were cruelly subjected to the emotional pain of not knowing the fate of their loved one. The defendant utilized sophisticated means to not only cover up his crime, but to also elude law enforcement through the use of multiple identities for over twenty years."

Couldn't have said it better myself.

"Additionally, the victim's wife is still unaccounted for, and it is suspected that she too is the victim of foul play. The defendant's actions in the present offense indicate he presents a serious threat to public safety. "

The report was presented to Judge Lomeli in time for Chris' sentencing on Aug. 15. Chris came to court with some paperwork of his own: a hefty stack of single-spaced, handwritten notes that represented what would be his motion for retrial and a smaller two-page sentencing memorandum.

The larger piece was the thing he wanted published in the newspaper.

Yeah, right.

He wanted Lomeli to allow a full reading of the motion in open court. Lomeli denied it. Chris withdrew the motion and asked for it to be sealed. Lomeli gave him 27 years to life for killing John.

As the hearing was about to close, Lomeli asked Chris if he wanted to take part in an "exclusive interview" for the television program *48 Hours.*

Veteran Associated Press court reporter, Linda Deutch, asked me if I was OK with that. I said "Sure. Why not? I'm done talking with this guy."

At about the same time, Chris told Lomeli he wanted to be interviewed in the courtroom by me also. It caused some problems for *48 Hours.* They brought out one of their top reporters and paid for a crew to get the interview in full HD video and Dolby stereo surround-sound. The TV people tried to talk me out of it. I stood my ground. See, you can't take pictures or tape or take notes in a county jail interview. This would be the opportunity to get it all for posterity. We sat in separate chairs beyond the bar, while the crew set up their lights and sound equipment.

The only difference between us? Chris was handcuffed to his chair. The interview lasted 23 minutes and could have gone on longer. So what did Chris say? Not much. He denied killing John, said he believed Linda had gone off to North Carolina, and insisted she was there in 1987.

He took shots at the Sheriff's Department and insisted that if detectives really thought he was a killer they should have tracked down Mihoko Manabe. After all, he said, she knew all his identities and even knew how to find him right up until 2006.

From the beginning, I believed Chris' possession of John's truck in Connecticut after John and Linda disappeared pointed to his guilt. When I asked him about it, he gave me his version of a straight answer.

"What would you like to know? You've got to stop calling it trisected, OK? I've reinterpreted the entire testimony and found that it completely favors me; either through logical refutation or through the concept or—or the application of the concept of—reasonable doubt that I am, in fact, innocent.

"Take the secret mission. The secret mission was not kept secret from anyone, except from the victim. The victim's wife told her family, to whom one would reasonably disclose that. She told her employer, to whom one might also disclose that. I mean she also told Sue Coffman, to whom such a disclosure is unnecessary, and she also told (the art collector) who testified by stipulation."

Hardly anyone even realized he testified.

"She told all these persons about the secret mission. So, a week before they disappear on Feb. 8, they have a dinner with Patrick Rayermann, Col. Patrick Rayermann, a retired colonel Patrick Rayermann, then a second lieutenant at the time. And not a word. Not a word about the secret mission. Nothing whatsoever.

"Wouldn't you ask the person who works for the very organization for who she said she was working with—the U.S. government—wouldn't you ask a second lieutenant in the army, whom the victim has known since 1969, with whom the victim grew up? Wouldn't you ask him about interview advice? Wouldn't you ask him?

"A week before they disappear, she says nothing about the secret mission to Patrick Rayermann. Instead during a dinner somewhere in Altadena, they talk about the drudgery of living with the mother, with the victim's mother.

"They talk about not having enough cash, not being able to rent out—not being able to live somewhere other than the back bedroom. Come on. They didn't even know; they couldn't even afford to rent my guest house."

Chris, in his best Thurston Howell III voice, then said he couldn't remember how much he paid in rent, something like $500 or $600 a month, he recalled. How did he make that every month?

"Mostly I did term papers. And I also was a tea salesman. I sold Chichester's tea or the baronet's tea in 13 flavors. But hold on.

"Why wouldn't you ask Patrick Rayermann, the one person who could clear up a lot of these questions?"

I changed the subject. Probably too soon, but I had to. "Where's Linda? Do you know where she is?"

"No I don't. I wish I did. I had a hint of someone who, how do I explain this? Write out the word S-O-H-U-S, and change the O into a C. "We found someone who trains horses by the name of Beth-linda Schus, and we just thought it looked so much like Linda Sohus. And, but unfortunately since then the lead has gone nowhere. There was a Bethlinda Schus in North Carolina in 1987 who trained horses. I'm not sure where the lead is going."

Talk of 1987 opened the door for me to ask about the truck.

"I can't really say anything about that unfortunately," Chris said. "I can't say anything about it; it's not part of the testimony. I'll tell you everything I know in terms of the testimony.

"I can only tell you what's in the testimony. Look at it this way, why would I keep it parked in my driveway for three and a half years and not have it moved? And why was it not used at all during those three and a half years?

Look at (Chris) Bishop. Bishop said that the truck was in relatively new condition. Bishop also said that he had, that I had given him the vehicle with the plates attached. Well, he had the plates. He had the license plate to put on the check to the California DMV."

And the most salient thing about this particular part of the testimony is there was a condition involved.

"You can have the vehicle if you write to California to register." It was not suggested; it was a condition. It was a condition. It was a condition of possession.

"Doesn't that point to my innocence?"

The interview turned to his multiple identities. "We can address that too. Look at witness Manabe, 'Midge' as I used to call her, which she doesn't like, you might want to note that. She always knew where I was."

"In 2000, whenever it was that I moved to Boston, she said testifying that I sent her an email. That she replied to that email, and she found it a valid address.

"She knew every single one of my names, even the real name. She knew Gerhartsreiter, she knew Chichester, she knew Crowe, she knew those names being professional names. Chichester for film production. Crowe for writing. Crowe was used if you'll recall as early as the Los Angeles Olympics in 1984. Witness Savio said that."

We talked about life in San Marino during that time and his sudden decision to leave town.

"It wasn't exactly the ladder of success. I don't think anyone ever watched that TV show. I tried my best.

"The reason for leaving this area had to do with the complete and abject failure of my film career. It just never panned out. First, I tried producing under the name Chichester. That was the name I used for my producing career. And back then, if they still exist, there are lots of lawyers who would know of me in this area, with whom I tried to put together limited partnerships for films. There must have been at least 10 lawyers, 10 law firms with whom I tried to do that. They may all have died by now. They were all pretty old. There was an accountant at Price Waterhouse who tried to help me out on the accounting end.

"He may still be around. I don't remember his name. They were from my producing career. Producing career never worked. I had an investor for a while and once she backed out that was sort of the end of the producing career. Then I started to concentrate on writing—writing, writing, writing.

"And the writing just flopped. The worst thing was, I showed it to the one person I truly, truly admired ... and he was nice enough to focus on everything I had done. At one point I gave him the scripts and at one point they all came back to me. They all arrive in those self-addressed, stamped envelopes one provides for this sort of thing. It was every single script I had written. They had all been read by him. There are writers' tricks like gluing pages together to make sure that someone has read the pages and such. And um, they all were rejected unanimously by everyone. (One reader) called back and said, 'You have industry, but you have no talent. You should be writing novels. You should not be writing screenplays. You have no vision.... It was terrible."

I turned again to John.

"Chris, if you didn't kill him who did?"

"It was the victim's wife," he answered. "I'm absolutely convinced of that after reading the testimony. That there is simply no other possibility. Why would she not tell? Why would she not tell the victim about this secret mission? Why would she not tell Rayermann about this secret mission? Why was it secret? Only to the victim? Why did everyone else know about it?"

I asked Chris if he saw the connection between Linda's claims of a secret mission and his own use of secret government projects in several tall tales.

"What are you saying when you tell someone you are doing top secret work? You are really saying don't ask me any questions about what I do. That's what that means.

"But if you don't want to address something directly, the easiest way is to say it's top secret. It's classified. She may have used the same tactic. I don't know. Aren't we all products of the same movies and televisions and books that we read? I'm sure it's not isolated to two people in the United States out of a population of 310 million. I think it's actually a common movie plot.

"I've never done anything with malice. I've never done anything to hide myself. Talk about the name change for a moment. Just stay on the name change. Midge, Mihoko Manabe, always knew my name.

"She knew Chichester, she knew Crowe. All the way through '94. She knew every single one of my names including Rockefeller. She knew the Crowe writing name, the Chichester producing name, she knew the Rockefeller name, which according to her really only came about to get a restaurant reservation, and I stayed in touch with her until after 2006.

"So why did the Los Angeles Sheriff's Department just never call her? They could have called her. She was the last person who police were in touch with. They could have just called her. They could have just called her and asked her, 'hey where is whatever name?' And, considering her forthcomingness, she would have told them, say in 2006, oh yeah, well he lives in Boston. I just got an email from him. Here's his email address. I didn't hide myself. I didn't hide ever."

As for any future appeal, Chris said he would hire another lawyer, but paying for it might be a problem.

"I'm completely broke," he said. "It will have to be a publicly appointed appeals lawyer, unless something comes about. Who knows?"

Since his arrest and convictions, Chris has had little contact with the outside world, and none with his family.

"You know I write to my daughter a letter every day, every single day and I have since all this. I have since she left me in 2007. So right now, there are a good 2,000 pages of letters to her approximately. If I could say something to her I would say I love her."

As I sat there with the TV crew surreptitiously shooting video of my interview with Chris for *48 Hours*, without ever acknowledging it, I couldn't help but think about what John's sister Ellen told the court about how her father dealt with the loss of his son, John. It stayed with me.

When Ellen spoke, it was heartfelt and powerful.

"My father was irrevocably separated from his son," she said. And I can't be the only person in court who wiped a tear from his eye as she continued: "This destroyed him. He told me he thought of John every day. He would periodically call me, deep in his grief, and ask, Why John? He was the kindest person I have ever known. He would never hurt anyone. I don't understand."

"There was nothing I could do in those moments to ease my father's pain. I once suggested to him that we have a memorial service for John. Through tears of grief and anger, he responded, 'No! Not until his killer has been found and brought to justice."

CHAPTER 24.

2023

Every year is getting shorter
Never seem to find the time
Plans that either come to naught
Or half a page of scribbled lines
—*Time*, **Pink Floyd's *Dark Side of the Moon***

Christian Gerhartsreiter has been in state prison for more than a decade. By all accounts, he is a model prisoner.

He appealed his conviction, claiming there was no evidence that he committed a premeditated first-degree murder. Let that sink in. He didn't deny committing murder in his appeal, he only denied that he planned it.

Miley says otherwise.

The theory is simple. Linda didn't want to live with Didi, John thought they could take possession of the guest house.

"That's where I think everything started, that's where he formulated it," Miley said.

The appeals panel, who heard Rockefeller's motion, mentioned Dana Farrar in the opening lines of their opinion.

Dana, a journalist who once worked at the *LA Times*, and someone I once played poker with, knew Chris in San Marino. She sat in Didi's backyard one afternoon and saw the spot where the ground had been dug up. When she asked Chris about it, he said there was a plumbing problem. At one point, he went into the house without asking permission; when Dana asked him why, he said the owners were away and wouldn't mind.

Dana's interactions with Chris were a template for most of those who met him, the court noted.

"Dana Farrar met defendant in 1984. Ms. Farrar studied journalism at USC. Her aunt, a San Marino resident, introduced her to defendant, thinking that defendant could help Ms. Farrar's boyfriend get into film school at USC. Defendant introduced himself as 'Christopher Chichester, the 13th Baronet.' He told Ms. Farrar he was from South Africa and gave her a business card with that false name and a crest on it. He portrayed himself as wealthy. During this same period of time, defendant told others he was British, and that he ran the Chichester family trust."

Then, they delivered the death blow to Chris' appeal.

"We find substantial evidence supports the jury's determination that defendant acted with premeditation and deliberation. The prosecution's theory of the case was that defendant convinced John and Linda Sohus that they were going on a top-secret government mission, but after creating the illusion that they were leaving San Marino to start new lives elsewhere, he killed them. Just before their disappearance, John and Linda Sohus spoke to close friends about taking on secret government work in satellites. Neither of them had discussed such work before, but the defendant, over the years, told many people he was involved in secret government work involving satellites. Mrs. Sohus's postcards also provided evidence of planning. The prosecution conceded the postcards may have been written by Mrs. Sohus but argued that defendant convinced Mrs. Sohus to write the postcards in preparation for her "top secret interview" with the government, and that he arranged for someone else to mail the postcards from abroad. Mrs. Sohus never traveled abroad. She did not have a passport, and customs had no record of her ever leaving the country. DNA on the postcards came from an unidentified male. The plan to use postcards written by Mrs. Sohus, falsely telling family and friends she was in Paris, is similar to defendant's past act of causing a postcard to be sent to a former college girlfriend from whom he wished to conceal his current residence, by telling her first that he was going to California to work with George Lucas, and then sending a postcard from Great Britain telling her he lived in England. In fact, defendant was not in England but had rented Ruth Sohus's guesthouse. Defendant kept a number of postcards, from various destinations, in a storage facility only he had access to."

There's more, but suffice to say, none of it supported a whit of Chris' argument. And it destroyed the notion that somehow Linda Sohus must have been a confederate or involved somehow in the death of her husband.

To do that, they quoted prosecutor, Habib Balian. He delivered his rationale in closing arguments of the murder trial.

"And it struck me, as I was thinking about this case, is it's kind of sad, not necessarily—I mean, yes, what happened to them is sad, but what struck me as being particularly sad is that not only did the defendant kill John Sohus, not only does all the evidence indicate that he killed Linda Sohus, not only does all of the evidence indicate that both of these people are dead . . . Not only did he end these two people's lives, it's sad that they're going to have the gall to come in here and blame the very woman they killed. ... Not only did he repeatedly bludgeon John Sohus over the head, they're going to come in here—they did so throughout this trial—and with their words assault Linda over and over and over again. They're going to repeatedly batter her. ... They're going to tell you . . . she must be the killer. Just wait and see... They're going to tell you that Linda is a mastermind. She kills her husband, plans it out, mails these postcards, then disappears herself for 28 years. She's a mastermind. Just wait and see. This is what you've heard. This is what you're going to hear. When all evidence in this case points you to the fact that there's only one person who's a mastermind. Not Linda."

The court did do one thing for Chris, they tossed out one of the enhancements a jury found true and shortened his sentence by a few months.

Miley had a footnote regarding Dana Farrar. She saw him in San Marino in 1988 driving Ralph Boynton's rental car. She was a key witness on two circumstantial points tying Chris to the murder of John.

As for Linda?

Early on, San Marino detectives theorized that she was somehow romantically involved with Gerhartsreiter and plotted with him to kill her husband. Miley said there was no way it happened like that. Chris plotted to kill John and had to kill Linda to cover it up.

She's not buried in the backyard because Chris realized it was hard work to kill someone and bury them. Linda's body was likely dumped somewhere on the road between San Marino and Greenwich.

"I think there's someplace between here and Connecticut, you know, someplace off the beaten path and he dumped her in a cave or an abandoned mine or any number of places," Miley said.

Gerhartsreiter's prison time has been eventful.

In San Quentin, he's taken on the moniker of "The Artist Formerly Known As Clark Rockefeller." He's among several inmates participating in an art program.

His one public work—a 16-inch, by 20-inch piece—is titled "Make Skeletons Dance." It's a series of diamonds with signal flags arranged in patterns. A catalog description of it contains an "about the artist" that notes TAFKA Clark Rockefeller "believes all art should deliberately and meaningfully break at least one rule."

The description goes on to note that TAFKA's style is known as "Neo Constructivism" and says, "The artist works as a grammarian at Mount Tamalpias College and lives in Marin County in the San Francisco Bay Area. In other words—San Quentin."

A guy I know who did time with Chris/Clark interacted with him quite often. He described his fellow inmate as a guy with "shifty eyes."

"One of the stories he told me was that he and his friends went camping and they found some kind of a shipwreck. And he found a bunch of stuff that he stashed away for when he got out."

Chris had several other stories for the inmate including explaining that he was descended from German royalty, and that his parents were Holocaust survivors.

"I just saw him as a tiny little guy with very thick glasses and a bald spot that is habitually unable to tell the truth."

In his last letter to me, Chris said he was reading Dickens and working on his tan in the yard.

"Pretty soon you'll see me recalled to life too."

ACKNOWLEDGEMENTS

First of all, thank you to Steve Hunt and Luanne Gambone for encouraging me to write this in 2011 and 2012 before there was a murder trial and a conviction. Steve passed away in 2019.

Thank you also to *Breaking Bad* star, my friend, fellow guitarist, and bandmate Dean Norris for reading the very first draft of this book and providing commentary.

My co-worker at the *Pasadena Star-News*, Janette Williams, also an early reader of the first draft, provided me with insight and encouragement. May she rest in peace.

Thank you to retired Los Angeles County Sheriff's Sgt. Timothy Miley who made himself and files available in 2023 and played a huge role providing deeper insight into the crime and criminal.

Thank you to my friends Walt Mancini and Walter Kirn and to sources including Alma Gilbert, Jean Kelln, Peggy Ebright, Jann Eldnor, and others living and dead who shared their stories, photos, and Gerhartsreiter memorabilia with me.

Also thank you to Burl Barer for encouraging me to keep on writing "true crime" and to WildBlue Press for taking me on as a writer among so many great writers in their catalog.

Thanks to my wife, Sarah, for being by my side, reliving the case with me, and providing endless amounts of valuable insight into reporting, re-writing, and structure as this came together.

Final thanks to my mom, Mary Lou Girardot, who bought one of the first copies of the original version and let me borrow it back when I needed it for reference. May she also rest in peace.

*For More News About Frank C. Girardot,
Jr, Signup For Our Newsletter:*
https://wbp.bz/newsletter

*Word-of-mouth is critical to an author's long-
term success. If you appreciated this book please
leave a review on the Amazon sales page:*
https://wbp.bz/bcr

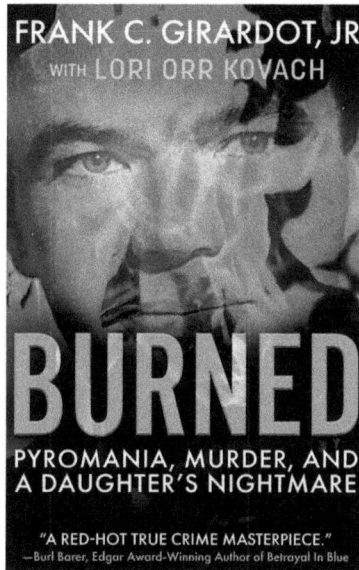

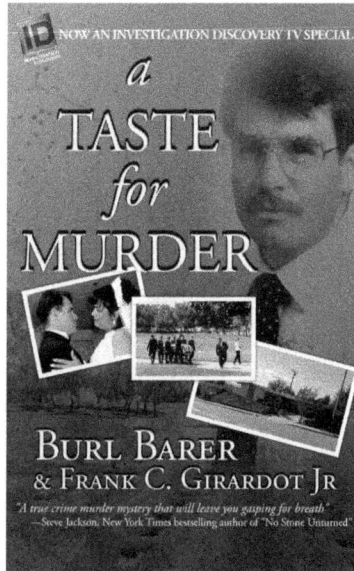
Frank Rodriguez, a much-loved counselor of troubled teens, lies dead on the bedroom floor. His wife and stepdaughter are in shock, and so is the medical examiner when he performs the autopsy. Aside from being dead, Frank is in perfect health. His wife, Angie, badgers the police, insisting that Frank was murdered. When the police enlist their #1 suspect to help in the investigation, things spiral out of control.

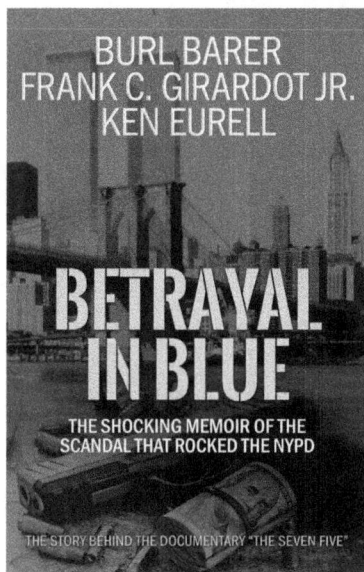

BETRAYAL IN BLUE by FRANK C. GIRARDOT, JR.

http://wbp.bz/bib

They had no fear of the cops because they were the cops. NYPD officers Mike Dowd and Kenny Eurell knew there were two ways to get rich quick in Brooklyn's Lower East Side. You either became drug dealers, or you robbed drug dealers. These "Cocaine Cops" decided to do both and ended up running the most powerful gang in New York's 75th Precinct in the 1980s.

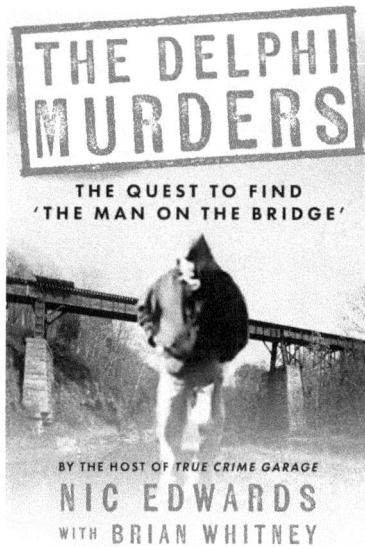

THE QUEST TO FIND
'THE MAN ON THE BRIDGE'

BY THE HOST OF *TRUE CRIME GARAGE*
NIC EDWARDS
WITH BRIAN WHITNEY

THE DELPHI MURDERS by Nic Edwards

http://wbp.bz/delphi

In February 2017, teenagers Abigail Williams and Liberty German vanished near Monon High Bridge. Nic Edwards, host of True Crime Garage, delved into the case, culminating in Richard Allen's 2022 arrest. The book offers detailed insights into the investigation and the efforts to capture the killer.

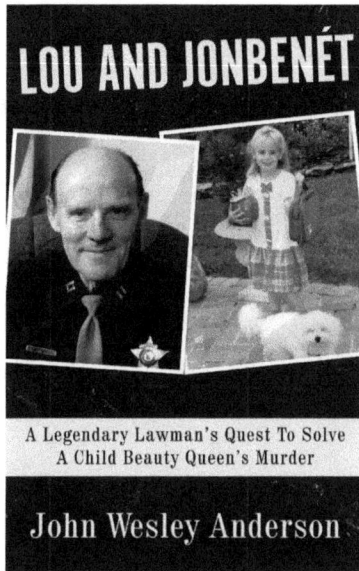

www.ingramcontent.com/pod-product-compliance
Lightning Source LLC
Chambersburg PA
CBHW070057030426
42335CB00016B/1915